1979

EXPERIMENTAL PSYCHOLINGUISTICS

An Introduction

LET US MAKE US A NAME LEST WE BE SCATTERED ABROAD UPON THE FACE OF THE WHOLE EARTH

THEREFORE IS THE NAME OF IT CALLED BABEL; BECAUSE THE LORD DID THERE CONFOUND THE LANGUAGE OF ALL THE EARTH. GENESIS

EXPERIMENTAL PSYCHOLINGUISTICS
An Introduction

SAM GLUCKSBERG
Princeton University

JOSEPH H. DANKS
Kent State University

 LAWRENCE ERLBAUM ASSOCIATES, PUBLISHERS
1975   Hillsdale, New Jersey

DISTRIBUTED BY THE HALSTED PRESS DIVISION OF

JOHN WILEY & SONS
New York   Toronto   London   Sydney

FRONTISPIECE: *Tower of Babel.* An original graphic by Trudy Glucksberg

Lawrence Erlbaum Associates, Inc., Publishers
62 Maria Drive
Hillsdale, New Jersey 07642

Distributed Solely by Halsted Press Division
John Wiley & Sons, Inc., New York

Library of Congress Cataloging in Publication Data

Glucksberg, Sam.
    Experimental psycholinguistics.

    Bibliography: p.
    Includes indexes.

    1. Languages—Psychology. 2. Communication.
3. Learning, Psychology of. I. Danks, Joseph H.,
joint author. II. Title.

    DNLM: 1. Psycholinguistics. BF455 G567e
P37.G5   401.9   75-2408
ISBN 0-470-30840-0

Printed in the United States of America

To Our Parents

Contents

Preface

Our conceptions of human cognitive functioning have changed radically in the last twenty years. The faith and conviction that perception, thinking, and language usage could ultimately be understood in terms of relatively simple stimulus–response mechanisms have given way to the current view of man as a relatively complex information-processing system. Within cognitive psychology, Donald Broadbent and Ulric Neisser were among the early important influences in this direction. Noam Chomsky and George Miller played similar roles among students of language. The message carried by these writers and by many others is that cognitive functioning in general and language behavior in particular involve rich and complex systems for perceiving, organizing, and using information. Earlier models of human functioning as a stimulus–response mechanism used the mechanical analog of a telephone switchboard. In contrast, our contemporary mechanical analog is the high-speed digital computer. Perhaps we always choose the most complicated machine we know of as our model of the human mind.

This shift in metaphors for mental activity does not necessarily involve abandonment of experimental psychology's traditional empiricist philosophy. Our orientation throughout this book is empirical in the broadest sense of the word. Psycholinguistics began with attempts to test the empirical validity of various formal linguistic concepts. A prototypical study in this genre was "The Psychological Reality of X," where X represented such concepts as the phoneme, deep structure, or case relations. This research strategy has lost some of its popularity. Developments in linguistic theory have contributed partially to this change. Psycholinguists no longer have just one type of linguistic model from which to borrow their concepts because one type of model no longer dominates the linguistic scene as transformational-generative grammars once did. Second, we have come to realize that linguistic models do not provide models of language competence. We may gain valuable insights about the properties of language from linguistics and hypotheses about language processing as well, but just as computer simulation programs need not be isomorphic with how people behave, linguistic theories need not be isomorphic with how people speak or understand speech.

This is the task of psycholinguistics: to discover how people produce and comprehend speech. This encompasses virtually all aspects of psychology, including perceptual, conceptual, and social processes. We have tried to capture the flavor of this approach to the psychology of language by describing the major contemporary issues, problems, and phenomena being dealt with in laboratories and in field studies, and by trying to make sense of the data we have. We have not tried to deal exhaustively with any one issue in linguistics or in psychology. We have tried to integrate our knowledge of language and language behavior so that someone entering the field has an intelligible framework with which to start.

Chapter 1 deals with rather broad questions about the nature of language and communication and so it is necessarily loose and speculative. Here, more than anywhere else in the book, we try to make explicit our communication-based bias toward the study of language behavior. Chapter 2, in contrast, deals with an area in which substantive empirical and theoretical advances have been made—speech perception and the sound systems of languages. Here we can tell a more detailed and coherent story. In Chapter 3 we return to less well-marked terrain—semantics and word meanings—and we must, perforce, leave many issues unresolved. Perhaps the most technical chapter from a student's point of view is Chapter 4, where we survey the attempts to understand how we comprehend sentences and larger units of discourse. It is here and in the following chapter on language learning (Chapter 5) that the interactions between psychology and linguistics have been at the same time the most fruitful and the most disappointing—the most fruitful because of the volume of empirical and theoretical work that has been generated and the most disappointing because neither psychologists nor linguists can agree with one another or among themselves on the most appropriate ways to characterize either language or speech. There is not even general agreement on whether language acquisition involves learning to any significant degree, although we present as strong a case as we can against premature and theoretically empty appeals to unspecified innate mechanisms. In the last two chapters we return to more global issues. We describe, in Chapter 6, the recent work on "nonstandard" dialects of American English and we present an analysis of the cognitive and social issues involved in planning and carrying out remedial education programs, especially in teaching reading. This leads to the last chapter (Chapter 7), where we discuss the relations between thought, language, and communication.

Throughout, we have tried to characterize where we have been and where we might go next. To the extent that we have been able to integrate the broad and variegated field of psycholinguistics, we thank our colleagues and our students for pushing us to the limits of our understanding. Two anonymous reviewers and two selfless colleagues—Jerry Homzie and David Pisoni—provided invaluable critiques of the entire manuscript. Tom Trabasso, Carl Sherrick, Irene Vogel, Deborah Harrison, and Carol Vasquez were especially helpful with Chapters 1, 2, 5, 6, and 7, respectively, and Jim Dooling with Chapters 5, 6, and 7. We also thank two undergraduate classes in language and thought at Kent State, who used early drafts of the manuscript as lecture notes and who were quick to point out problems. Our wives always let us know when we drifted into obscurity and trivia, and we probably didn't heed their advice often enough.

Portions of the book were written while SG was a visiting professor at the University of Sussex, and we thank Stuart Sutherland and William Muntz for the administrative and intellectual support provided. Monica Robinson and her secretarial staff were most helpful, not only as typists but as literate critics. The final draft was typed with efficiency and dispatch by Joan Daviduk and Sharon Olsen, who also detected nonsensical sentence structures and unintelligible phrases. Bodhan Porytko deserves our thanks for his thorough check of the references and bibliography. We are indebted to Trudy Glucksberg for her illustrations and art work, and to Charlotte Carlson for the technical drawings.

Neither of us can be identified any longer for any single chapter because we have constantly revised one another's work. We could not even decide on order of authorship and so we flipped a coin. Finally, our children deserve thanks for showing us how language learning can come about in the real world where phonology, semantics, syntax, and cognition are inseparable.

SAM GLUCKSBERG
JOSEPH H. DANKS

1

Communication Systems and the General Properties of Human Language

How is speech produced and understood in the context of everyday communication? This is the central problem for psycholinguistics and the focus of this book. Every communicative act involves at least four components:

1. something to be communicated, such as an idea or a thought;
2. a speaker's intention to transmit that idea or thought to someone else;
3. a message in the form of speech which represents that idea or thought;
4. a listener who intends to comprehend the message and who interprets that message.

Each of these components involves complex mental processes, and none is fully understood yet. We do, however, have some understanding of the major processes involved in communicative acts, and some notion of the general properties of natural human languages.

HOW IS A THOUGHT COMMUNICATED?

How do people start with a thought and produce a sequence of sounds that, when heard by someone else, elicits a second thought that is roughly equivalent to the original one? This question is the concern of the branch

1

of psychology and linguistics called PSYCHOLINGUISTICS: the study of language production and comprehension. Finding an answer to this question is difficult because the things we are interested in are not directly observable. We hear speech, but how is that speech produced? We need to understand the mental operations which start with an idea or thought, and ultimately produce a message which represents that idea or thought. Similarly, we usually know when a person understands something, but this understanding is also an end product of a set of mental operations that takes the sounds arriving at the ears and ultimately produces an idea or thought. What kinds of mental operations are involved in speech production and comprehension?

Speech Production: An Overview

A number of steps or operations must occur in a typical communication. Assume that I want to express the proposition represented by the sentence

(1)   Koala bears make good imaginary
       playmates for lonely children.

Several different kinds of operations must be performed in progressing from the proposition to speech. We can identify each of these, even though we do not yet understand how they are integrated into the smoothly flowing process of speech production.

One operation involves generating or constructing the basic linguistic format for the sentence. We must select the appropriate words from the many thousands of words stored in our mental dictionary. We also have to decide how the words are to be ordered so that they do express the thought we began with. These two sets of operations are called, respectively, semantic and syntactic. The SEMANTIC OPERATIONS select the words according to intended meanings, and the SYNTACTIC OPERATIONS select the appropriate sentence structures as well as such function words as *but, and, or,* and *as*. A third set of operations—PHONOLOGICAL—transforms the message into speech sounds produced by the articulatory system—the tongue, lips, larynx, and the like. (An alternative here would be to write or type the message.)

These three sets of operations—semantic, syntactic, and phonological—will be called a GRAMMAR. They are logically sufficient to produce speech. They are not sufficient to produce successful communication because, for any given idea one wants to express, there are hundreds of potential speech messages. To take an extreme case, I know two languages, English and French. Which one will I use on any given occasion? When I am speaking to someone who knows only French, I will use French, and I will use English for English-speaking listeners. The same kind of choices are made even when we speak only one language. If I am talking to a young child, the words I use will be words I think he would understand. I would be far less limited in my choice of words if I were talking to an adult. The adults I talk with also differ considerably from one another. Some are good friends and share an immense amount of knowledge with me. Others are strangers and need to have things spelled out in much greater detail. In all cases, we select one particular way of saying something from a set of many alternative ways.

This process can be referred to as SOCIAL EDITING, and is dealt with in linguistics as part of the pragmatics of a language. Like the semantic, syntactic, and phonological operations, social editing involves decisions that are usually unconscious and are executed automatically. We usually are not aware of hunting for the right word or turn of phrase when we talk casually with other people. Unlike writing, speaking seems to function spontaneously and freely. The complexities of the mental operations and the decisions involved in speaking are masked.

These four major classes of mental processes act in concert to transform a thought into speech. Figure 1.1 is a rough approximation of how these four sets of processes might interact in a typical communicative act. The idea or thought to be communicated—what it is that is talked about, the REFERENT—may be a simple visual image or a complex logical proposition. Whatever it is, appropriate words and sentence structures are chosen so that a listener will have, in some sense, an equivalent idea. This general description applies to all human languages, even though the languages of the world vary widely in terms of their syntactic, semantic, and phonological characteristics. The social editing component may also differ among languages, and among individuals speaking the same language, as well.

As mentioned before, of the four components involved in a speech act, the first three—semantic, syntactic, and phonological—comprise the grammar of a language. Most people understand the term "grammar" as a PRESCRIPTION of how a language should be spoken. For example, we often hear that someone has "bad grammar," and we then attribute this to a deficiency in that person's education or intellect. In contemporary

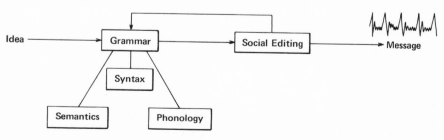

FIGURE 1.1   Stages in a speaker's formulation of a message (see text).

linguistics and psychology, the grammar of a language is not a standard to be lived up to. Instead, it is an explicit DESCRIPTION of the language. A grammar specifies and describes three aspects of a language. The first aspect is the set of words in that language and how they can be integrated by syntax. This is the semantic component of the grammar. The second describes the particular word orders, inflections, and relationships among words used in the language, and this is the syntactic component. Third, the sound system of a language is described by the phonological component of the grammar. For example, the semantic component of a grammar of English would include *dog* as one of the words in the language, but would not include *prif*. The syntactic component of that grammar would specify that *I hit the dog* is an acceptable sequence, or string of words, and that this string is a sentence of the language. The string *hit the I dog* is not acceptable and is not a sentence of the language. The phonological component would specify that *I hit the dog* (as normally pronounced by a native speaker) is acceptable, and that *ah heet su dok* is not. The phonological component also specifies that a sound combination like *prif* is acceptable in English, even though it is not a word, and that a sound combination like *tlib* or *srate* is not (Brown & Hildum, 1956).

To these three linguistic components we have added a fourth, social editing. Depending on the social context, a speaker will tailor his speech so that it is appropriate for the particular listener and the situation. Consider sentence (1) as an example. If I were talking about playmates for children instead of koala bears, I might say

(1a)   Good imaginary playmates for lonely
        children are koala bears.

Or, if I were discussing lonely children, I might say

(1b)   Lonely children find koala bears to
        be good imaginary playmates.

Those two different sentences reflect two different topic emphases. Both mean about the same thing and both are acceptable sentences.

Speech Comprehension: An Overview

The four global sets of operations involved in speech production—phonological, syntactic, semantic, and social editing—have their counterparts in speech comprehension. First, you must "know" a language before you can actually hear it. When you hear someone speaking English, you hear separate words and phrases, even though the actual sound arriving at your ears is a continuous stream. Figure 2.5 (Chapter 2, page 37) is a visual display of an actual speech signal. Where are the silent spaces between the words that we do, in fact, hear? The spaces are created by our phonological processing systems. We operate on the incoming sounds and segment the speech appropriately. If we hear a language we do not know, we hear a continuous stream of sound, not separate words or phrases. Whatever phonological processing does, it must be capable of doing at least this.

Semantic and syntactic components must also be involved. Consider an utterance beginning

(2a)   The ball was . . .

The words *the* and *was* can usually be interpreted immediately. The word *ball* cannot be. As we hear the utterance, we must defer interpreting *ball* until we hear what comes next. If the utterance continues

(2b)   . . . hit sharply over the net.,

then *ball* refers to a spherical object used in games like tennis, ping-pong, or volleyball. If the utterance continues

(2c)   . . . one of the social highlights of
         the year.,

then *ball* refers to a particular kind of event and not to a round spherical object. The word *ball* cannot be assigned a specific meaning until its semantic and syntactic contexts are known.

Sentence fragment (2a) is ambiguous at a lexical level because it involves two quite distinct words—*ball* as the name of a physical object and *ball* as the name of an event. Another type of ambiguity is syntactic ambiguity, displayed in sentence (3):

(3)   Taunting policemen can be dangerous.

This sentence could be interpreted to mean either that people who tease policemen may be injured, or that policemen who challenge crowds may provoke violence. The word *taunt* retains its core meaning in both interpretations. It refers to the same kind of action or behavior. Its syntactic properties in the two interpretations are different. In the first case it functions as a verb, denoting an action, and in the second case it denotes the same action but in adjectival form, modifying the noun *policemen*. Any adequate explanation of human speech comprehension must be able to deal with the kinds of decisions involved in dealing with sentences like these.

How do we make such decisions? One kind of information we use is knowledge of what the speaker is talking about and the inferences we make on what he is trying to say. This is a comprehension counterpart to the social editing component of the production process. When someone is talking about how students in a demonstration should behave, then sentence (3) would be interpreted in one way. Most likely, it would refer to the possibility that people who taunt policemen might get hurt. If, on the other hand, someone is talking about police tactics for handling riots, then sentence (3) would probably be interpreted to refer to the behavior of policemen and to their safety. Speakers usually expect their listeners to apply social interpretive criteria to what they say. When someone passes you in the hall and says "How are you?," he usually does not want to know the details of your health at that moment. He would be quite surprised and dismayed if you told him in exquisite detail of your various and innumerable aches and pains. Just as we automatically tailor what we say so that we will be understood by others, so do we automatically infer what people intend to tell us, and this contributes to our interpretations of speech. When I come home at night and my wife says "*I* took the garbage out this morning," we both understand what her message is. The same utterance by a proud seven-year-old represents a different message.

We have discussed, in very global terms, the processes that must be involved in human language behavior. Before we consider what those processes are in any detail, we should consider the general properties of human language.

GENERAL PROPERTIES OF HUMAN LANGUAGE

We all "know" what a language is, just as we all "know" what "justice" is. Nevertheless, people disagree on the definitions of "language" just as we disagree on the definitions of "justice." What behaviors qualify as exemplars of language? From a linguistic viewpoint, very few, if any, utterances qualify as exemplars of the concept "language" because a LANGUAGE is an idealized abstraction.

A central figure in the development of modern linguistics was Ferdinand de Saussure, whose lectures were published posthumously by his students in 1916. De Saussure introduced a distinction between LA LANGUE (language) and LA PAROLE (the actual utterances one can hear). The linguist, according to Lyons (1968), describes *la langue,* which is the language system. This language system is inferred from *la parole,* the utterances produced by people.[1] What are the relationships between utterances—what

---

[1] De Saussure's distinction between *la langue* and *la parole* is closely related to Chomsky's (1965) distinction between linguistic competence and linguistic performance. For a discussion of the latter distinction, see the relevant section in Chapter 4 (pages 85–86).

people say—and language? This issue has not yet been resolved satisfactorily, but most linguists and psychologists would agree that all people who speak a particular language share a common system despite wide individual variations. It is this generalized system presumably shared by all members of a speech community that constitutes the language. What properties are common to all human languages, over and above the immense differences among the utterances of people around the world?

Roger Brown has elegantly and succinctly summarized the most commonly accepted properties of language. All human languages display the following design features:

> Fewer than one hundred sounds which are individually meaningless are compounded, not in all possible ways, to produce some hundreds of thousands of meaningful morphemes . . . [for example, words] . . . which have meanings that are arbitrarily assigned, and these morphemes are combined by rule to yield an infinite set of sentences, having meanings that can be derived. All of the systems of communication called . . . [human] . . . languages have these design features [Brown, 1965, p. 248].

The three important properties referred to in this passage are (a) productivity (for example, an infinite set of sentences can be produced); (b) duality of structure (for example, some units are meaningless, others "have meaning"); and (c) arbitrary symbolic reference (for example, meanings are arbitrarily assigned). These three properties are not the only ones that have been proposed [see Hockett (1960), who lists 13 design features], but these are the most relevant for our purposes. Let us consider each of these properties in turn.

Productivity

All languages in principle are PRODUCTIVE. It would be impossible to memorize all the utterances we may produce or hear in the course of our lives. Despite this, we are able to produce and understand an infinite number of utterances including those we have never heard before. In this sense, the productive nature of language implies that it is creative. Language is also productive in a related sense. Although we may have more or less difficulty in expressing various thoughts, all languages have the potential to express all thoughts or ideas. As we shall see later, this open endedness is specific to human languages. Though other animals produce an unlimited variety of symbolic acts, no other animal communication system has the potential to express an unlimited number of ideas or concepts.

Duality of Structure

The second property of language is DUALITY OF STRUCTURE. This refers to the organizational structure of language. All human languages are organized on at least two levels. For example, we can analyze an utterance as a sequence of words, each of which has a meaning. Thus, the utterance

(4)   We went to town.

can be described as a sequence of the four words *we, went, to,* and *town*. We can also analyze the same utterance in a second way. Each of the word units can be described as a sequence of sounds—phonological units—that have no meaning in and of themselves.

Why is this feature important? Duality of structure is one of the reasons why language is productive. With only a small set of meaningless speech sounds (approximately 50 for English, and never more than 100 in any language), the number of possible combinations is so large that, for all practical purposes, the number of possible words in any one language is unlimited. Furthermore, if we now combine words to form sentences, the number of possible sentences is very large indeed. If each speech sound did have meaning, then the number of useful combinations would be drastically limited in much the same way that a picture-writing system is limited in contrast to an alphabetic system.

These two aspects of language—productivity and duality of structure—are not unique to natural languages. We could describe music or mathematics in the same way, for example. A single note of the scale is analogous to an individual speech sound. That note can be combined with others to produce a melodic theme, such as the opening bars of Beethoven's Fifth Symphony:

This is analogous to a word. This "word," combined with a second "word"

produces a "sentence." Indeed, this is often described as the opening statement of the symphony. These opening bars of the symphony can be described on two levels: as individual notes (the sound, or phonological level) and as thematic elements (the meaning, or semantic–syntactic level).

Is language indistinguishable from formal musical or mathematical systems? The "words" of music or mathematics are abstract. They refer to nothing in particular, and derive their "meaning" only in the context of their formal relations with other "words." They are not *symbolic*. They need not, and usually do not, represent or stand for something outside the musical or mathematical system. Language, in contrast, does display this symbolic feature. All human languages have words that represent or stand for nonlinguistic entities—objects, events, relationships. Meaningful units of language function as referential signs or symbols. The units of mathematics or music do not.

The symbolic–referential relations within a language are primarily arbitrary, even though some words are iconic (or onomatopoeic, in literary terms). ICONIC words are like an image or a picture. They sound like the things they refer to, such as the *quack* of a duck, the *moo* of a cow, or the *gurgling* and *babbling* of a brook. Some linguists have extended the notion of iconic relationships to encompass a wider range of words. The sounds of many common words, particularly the vowels of these words, may be directly related to the semantic properties of the word. This relation is referred to as PHONETIC SYMBOLISM. For example, *little, tiny,* and *mini* have short, high vowels, whereas *huge, large,* and *macro* have long, low vowels. Apparently, small-sounding vowels are usually associated with small objects, as are big-sounding vowels with big objects. Similar relations have been reported for other languages (Brown, Black, & Horowitz, 1955), even though there are exceptions, such as *small* and *big*. Nevertheless, phonetic symbolism is a minor aspect of language structure. Iconic words of any kind are the exception rather than the rule.

Arbitrary Symbolic Reference

Most relations between things and words are ARBITRARY. There need be no relationship whatsoever between the sound of a word and its referent—the thing symbolized. The relation between the word *cow* and its referent—the animal we call a cow—is purely arbitrary. Cows could just as well be named *mulls,* provided people agreed to do so. The arbitrary assignment of meanings, like duality of structure, is one of the properties of language which contribute to productivity. If the sound of a word had to resemble the concept to which it referred, then how could we possibly have words like *possible?*

These three properties of language—productivity, which in turn depends upon both duality of structure and arbitrary symbolic reference—enable languages to fulfill their primary function: communication of a potentially infinite number of ideas. Animal communication systems do not have these properties of human languages and are limited in a variety of other ways. As we explore these limitations, we will also deal with the classic question: Do animals other than humans have language?

ANIMAL COMMUNICATION:
BEES AND CHIMPANZEES

What Is Communication?

All animals communicate with one another—within species, between species, and with humans—at least to the extent that the behavior of any animal can affect the behavior of another. An amoeba can attract the attention of a scientist or a biology student, and the student can affect the behavior of the amoeba. This "interaction" between amoeba and student is not what we typically mean when we think of communication. Usually, communication implies more than the mere transmission of information among organisms and more than interorganism influences. The behavior of an amoeba under a microscope influences a scientist in the same way as a comet seen in a telescope. The scientist observes the amoeba and the comet for the same reasons—both are interesting. Neither the amoeba nor the comet could care less about what the scientist does, and the behaviors of both the amoeba and the comet are completely unaffected by the scientist's actions.

Contrast this state of affairs with the behavior of a friendly dog that nudges your hand when you stop scratching his head and then stops nudging when you scratch him again. Your behavior can be considered to be the "target" or goal of the dog's behavior. What you do or do not do directly influences what the dog does. We are tempted to infer that the dog is "trying to tell you something." After all, he does not nudge your toe when your hand is doing the scratching and when it seems that the dog wants to be scratched. Wanting and intending, unfortunately, are fuzzy and crude concepts, especially when applied to nonhumans, and it is not wholly satisfactory to try to use these concepts as criteria for communication.

As a first approximation we can characterize a COMMUNICATIVE ACT as an interaction between two or more organisms, where (a) the behavior of one is directed toward the other; (b) the other's behavior is influenced by the first; and (c) the initiator's subsequent behavior is influenced by the response originally elicited. Put simply, the behavior of both organisms is maintained and influenced in a reciprocal fashion. Dogs do not wag their tails at marble statues; birds do not preen and sing to flowers; lions do not growl at rocks; people do not usually talk to filing cabinets. If a person is talking to someone and the listener pays no attention whatsoever, the speaker will stop talking within one minute and say something like "what's the matter with you?" Try this, if you are able to, the next time someone talks to you. Give no sign whatever that you are listening. Do not nod; do not make eye contact. When your unsuspecting partner becomes angry, try to explain your "experiment." Communication, to be maintained, requires the cooperative interaction of the participants.

Despite our difficulty in defining communicative behavior, it is relatively easy to identify those behaviors that are communicative. It is quite another problem to infer the mechanisms or processes underlying those behaviors. We tend to believe that we are aware of how and what we communicate to one another, yet we are seldom aware of the many ways we can let other people know how we feel and what we feel about them. Much of this communication is nonverbal, involving gestures, facial expressions, body orientation, and eye movements (see, for example, Hall, 1969; Wiener, Devoe, Rubinow, & Geller, 1972). With respect to our intuitive beliefs about animals, we often infer motives, feelings, and thoughts that are like those of humans. These beliefs, though intrinsic to our concept of human communication, can be mistaken.

The classic case of Clever Hans is a sobering reminder of the dangers of generalizing our beliefs about humans to animals. Clever Hans was a horse that apparently could read numbers and then add or multiply them. For example, his owner would show him the digits 4 or 5 and then ask Hans to add them. Hans then would tap his hoof nine times. Careful analysis of this performance by Pfungst (1911) demonstrated that Hans was not as clever as he seemed. He could not read numbers, nor could he do arithmetic, but he was clever enough to attend to subtle cues unconsciously provided by the people who set the problems for him. The horse would start tapping when asked to add or multiply, and then stop when his questionner glanced expectantly in anticipation of an error. In some way the horse had learned to detect what people did when they expected him to stop, and he used this information quite effectively. When the person giving the problem to Hans did not know the answer, then Hans failed completely. Hans' owner was quite unaware of the cues he had been giving, and he sincerely believed that his horse could read and do arithmetic. Communication certainly took place, but far more subtly than it had appeared.

Different animals employ widely different communication systems, just as people (and horses) employ a variety of communication systems. To what extent does any nonhuman communication system share the criterial properties of human language? Among the many animal communication systems we know about, two are particularly interesting: those of the honeybees and the great apes.

Bees

Karl von Frisch, a German scientist and recent Nobel prize recipient, spent thirty years studying bees and analyzing their "dances," which he called the "language of the bees" (von Frisch, 1962, 1967). When a foraging bee returns to its hive, it may perform an intricate pattern of movements that looks like a dance. The details of the dance will vary from time to time and depend on the location and the quality of the nectar it has found. Obviously, if other bees in the hive could understand the dance, it would be to their advantage. They need not go hunting for nectar; they could fly directly to the source.

Whether the bees in the hive can read the dance or not, the dance does contain useful information. When the nectar source is less than 100 yards from the hive, the bee does a round dance (Figure 1.2a). When the source is farther away, the bee does a waggle dance in a figure eight (Figure 1.2b): there is a long straight portion in the middle, and the bee alternates turning left and right. The dance reflects three kinds of information. The direction of the straight-line portion of the waggle dance corresponds with the direction from the hive to the nectar source, relative to the sun. While traveling through the straight-line portion of the waggle dance, the bee waggles its abdomen, and the richer the nectar source, the faster it waggles. Finally, distance information is reflected by the traveling speed of the bee. The nearer the source, the faster it moves, and the more figure eights it completes per minute. Specific details of the dance vary from species to species, but the basic dance has been found in all species of honeybee observed to date.

Is this dance communicative? If the dancer is a bee and the observer is a human being who knows the code, then it certainly is, although the dancing bee is not influenced by what the observer does subsequently. It is not clear whether other bees use all the information contained in the

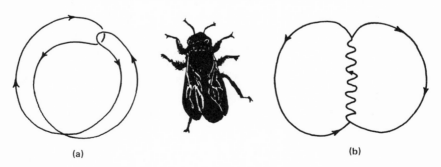

(a)   (b)

FIGURE 1.2   The round dance (a) and the waggle dance (b) performed by honey bees after returning to the hive from a nectar source.

dance. Some studies (Wenner, 1967; Wenner & Johnson, 1967) suggest that the bees in the hive do not. Instead, they use chemical cues, such as odors, and this informs them that a new source of nectar has been found and nothing more. What appeared to be a fairly intricate communication system might be far simpler than it had appeared.

Even in its intricate form, the dance of the honey bee shares none of the properties of human language systems. It is not productive, since the set of messages is quite limited. The organization of the dance is simple—there is no duality of structure. Each element—the straight portion, the frequency of waggling, and the rate of travel—always bears the same relationship to the other elements. Insofar as each "has meaning," each always means the same thing, irrespective of context. Finally, the symbolic reference, such as it is, is not arbitrary. If it were arbitrary in the sense that referential relations in human languages are arbitrary, then which referred to what would be optional and variable. The referential relationships between the dance of the bee and the information symbolized are obligatory. It is built into the bee and cannot be changed. The dance of the honeybee provides a clear example of a communication system that is complex and intricate, yet quite unlike human language systems. As complex as it is, the "language" of the bees is extraordinarily limited in terms of what can and cannot be "talked about."

Chimpanzees

The most likely candidate for a nonhuman language of any complexity is with the higher primates, our closest evolutionary neighbors. The great apes are not only the most intelligent of infrahuman animals; they also display complex communication behaviors in their natural habitats.

The most extensive study of chimpanzees in the wild has been done by Jane van Lawick-Goodall (1971). Among other aspects of chimpanzee behavior, Goodall included details of their communications with one another. Several vocalizations appear to be specifically communicative. A drawn-out, high pitched "wraaa" is a threat cry signaling a potential attack. A low "hoo" occurs when a chimp appears frightened in the presence of a strange object. Hooting seems to be a call for chimps to gather together, and friendly chimps seem to use panting grunts as people would use words of greeting to one another. The repertoire of vocalizations is quite small, but chimps also employ gestures and facial expressions. Chimps reassure one another by embracing and kissing, and a dominant chimp responds with a gentle touch to another chimp that displays the appropriate submissive gesture. As we shall see later, gesture may be the primary mode of communication among chimps.

In the wild, the topics of communication are relatively limited. Very little of the communication seems to be about the physical environment, such as food or predators. Most of it seems to be concerned with social interactions, and, in particular, social dominance relationships. Is this very different from human communication? Van Lawick-Goodall (1971) expresses her opinions quite vividly:

In the Shadow of Man:
JANE VAN LAWICK-GOODALL

Chimpanzees do have a wide range of calls, and these certainly serve to convey some types of information. When a chimp finds good food he utters loud barks; other chimps in the vicinity instantly become aware of the food source and hurry to join in. An attacked chimpanzee screams and this may alert his mother or a friend, either of whom may hurry to his aid. A chimpanzee confronted with an alarming and potentially dangerous situation utters his spine-chilling "wraaaa"—again, other chimps may hurry to the spot to see what is happening. A male chimpanzee, about to enter a valley or charge toward a food source, utters his pant-hoots—and other individuals realize that another member of the group is arriving and can identify which one. To our human ears each chimpanzee is characterized more by his pant-hoots than by any other type of call. This is significant since the pant-hoot in particular is the call that serves to maintain contact between the scattered groups of the community. Yet the chimps themselves can certainly recognize individuals by other calls; for instance, a mother knows the scream of her offspring. Probably a chimpanzee can recognize the calls of most of his acquaintances.

While chimpanzee calls do serve to convey basic information about some situations and individuals, they cannot for the most part be compared to a spoken language. Man by means of words can communicate abstract ideas; he can benefit from the experiences of them without having to be present at the time; he can make intelligent cooperative plans. All the same, when humans come to an exchange of emotional feelings, most people fall back on the old chimpanzee-type of gestural communication—the cheering pat, the embrace of exuberance, the clasp of hands. And when on these occasions we also use words, we often use them in rather the same way as a chimpanzee utters his calls—simply to convey the emotion we feel at that moment. "I love you, I love you," repeats the lover again and again as he strives to convey his overwhelming passion to his beloved—not by words but by his embraces and caresses. When we are surprised we utter inanities such as "Golly!" or "Gosh!" or "Gee Whiz!" When we are angry we may express ourselves with swear words and other more or less meaningless phrases. This usage of words on the emotional level is as different from oratory, from literature, from intelligent conversation, as are the grunts and hoots of chimpanzees [pp. 248–249].*

This passage implies that chimpanzees, as lovable and as bright as they are, do not use language as we do, and are incapable of doing so (although we humans are capable of chimpanzee-like communication!). Until quite recently, the evidence unequivocally supported this conclusion. A number of people had tried to teach human language to chimps in captivity. All these early attempts ended in virtual failure, including the two best known, one by the Kelloggs, the other by the Hayes.

The Kelloggs (Kellogg & Kellogg, 1933) raised a chimp named Gua along with their own son, Donald. They tried to treat Gua and Donald as equals, making no special efforts to teach Gua to speak or to understand English. Donald, of course, learned to talk as any normal child does. Gua never produced any distinctly human speech sounds—only the vocalizations usually made by chimps in captivity. Gua did use some communicative gestures, and she also could respond appropriately to about seventy words. She could not understand sequences of words in combinations. In short, Gua's accomplishments were not qualitatively different from a well-trained dog.

A second attempt was made several years later by the Hayes, who raised a chimp named Viki for three years (Hayes, 1951). Viki finally managed to produce three utterances that could be identified as "words." These three words were *papa, mama,* and *cup.* The words were used appropriately, but were quite unclear and could not easily be recognized as words by strangers. Her speech comprehension was vastly superior, and with practice she could understand some word combinations. However, the practice had to be quite specific because she rarely would understand new combinations of old words. This last point is crucial since it is one of the most important properties of human language.

What is the reason for these failures? One possibility is that chimps simply do not have the cognitive abilities to master a human-like communication system. Another possibility is that chimps may have the requisite cognitive abilities, but we were asking them to do something for which they are poorly equipped, namely, speaking. If one looks carefully at chimps in the wild, their vocal repertoire is quite small, but they use gesture continually. Could it be that chimps might be able to handle a far more complex communication system if they could use gestures instead of vocalizations?

* Copyright © 1971 by Hugo and Jane van Lawick-Goodall. Reprinted by permission of Houghton Mifflin Company.

Allen and Beatrice Gardner argued that chimps could not learn to speak as humans do because the chimps' vocal apparatus is quite different (see Lieberman, 1972; Lieberman, Crelin, & Klatt, 1972). Therefore, the Gardners felt that the earlier failures demonstrated primarily that chimps could not learn to speak, that is, use their vocal apparatus. Their communicative or linguistic competence had not really been tested.

On these grounds they decided to teach a female chimp named Washoe the American Sign Language (ASL), a communication system used by deaf and mute people in the United States (Gardner & Gardner, 1969). The results to date have been overwhelming. Here is a portion of their first-hand report:

Teaching Sign Language to a Chimpanzee:
R. ALLEN GARDNER AND BEATRICE T. GARDNER

The youngest infant that we could obtain was a wild-born female, whom we named Washoe, and who was estimated to be between 8 and 14 months old when we began our program of training. The laboratory conditions, while not patterned after those of a human family (as in the studies of Kellogg and Kellogg and of Hayes and Hayes), involved a minimum of confinement and a maximum of social interaction with human companions. For all practical purposes, the only verbal communication was in ASL, and the chimpanzee was maximally exposed to the use of this language by human beings.

It was necessary to develop a rough-and-ready mixture of training methods. There was evidence that some of Washoe's early signs were acquired by delayed imitation of the signing behavior of her human companions, but very few, if any, of her early signs were introduced by immediate imitation. Manual babbling was directly fostered and did increase in the course of the project. A number of signs were introduced by shaping and instrumental conditioning. A particularly effective and convenient method of shaping consisted of holding Washoe's hands, forming them into a configuration, and putting them through the movements of a sign.

We have listed more than 30 signs that Washoe acquired and could use spontaneously and appropriately by the end of the 22nd month of the project. [See Table 1.1.] The signs acquired earliest were simple demands. Most of the later signs have been names for objects, which Washoe has used both as demands and as answers to questions. Washoe readily used noun signs to name pictures of objects as well as actual objects and has frequently called the attention of her companions to pictures and objects by naming them. Once acquired, the signs have not remained specific to the original referents but have

been transferred spontaneously to a wide class of appropriate referents. At this writing, Washoe's rate of acquisition of new signs is still
accelerating.

From the time she had eight or ten signs in her repertoire, Washoe
began to use them in strings of two or more. [For example, Washoe
hopping up and down outside a closed door might make three signs
meaning *door open hurry.* The meaning is clear, no matter what the
order of these signs.] During the period covered by this article we
made no deliberate effort to elicit combinations other than by our
own habitual use of strings of signs. Some of the combined forms
that Washoe has used may have been imitative but many have been
inventions of her own. Only a small proportion of the possible combinations have, in fact, been observed. This is because most of Washoe's
combinations include one of a limited group of signs that act as com-
biners. Among the signs that Washoe has recently acquired are the
pronouns "I/me" and "you." When these occur in combinations the
result resembles a short sentence. In terms of the eventual level of
communication that a chimpanzee might be able to attain, the most
promising results have been spontaneous naming, spontaneous transfer to new referents, and spontaneous combinations and recombina-
tions of signs [p. 672].

There is no question that Washoe's signing employs arbitrary symbolic
reference. Furthermore, her use of the sign system resembles in some important ways the early language use of human children. This is especially
noticeable in two-sign combinations, which resemble the early, two-word
combinations used by children. Many early human utterances consist of
two words, one of which combines regularly with many other words
(Braine, 1963). For example, the word *my* would be combined with a
large number of other words to form two-word utterances like *my milk,
my mommy,* and *my hat.* Many of Washoe's combinations are like these.
The sign for *go* would be combined with other words to produce

> . . . 'go in' or 'go out' (when at some distance from a door), 'go
> sweet' (for being carried to a raspberry bush), 'open flower' (to be
> let through the gate to a flower garden), 'open key' (for a locked
> door), 'listen eat' (at the sound of an alarm clock signaling mealtime),
> and 'listen dog' (at the sound of barking by an unseen dog). All but
> the first and last of these six examples were inventions of Washoe's
> [Gardner & Gardner, 1969, p. 671].

Is Washoe then at an early stage of language development analogous
to an early stage of human language development? One problem with

TABLE 1.1

Signs Used Reliably by Chimpanzee Washoe within
22 Months of the Beginning of Training[a,b]

Signs	Context
Come-gimme	Sign made to persons or animals, also for objects out of reach. Often combined: "come tickle," "gimme sweet," etc.
More	When asking for continuation or repetition of activities such as swinging or tickling, for second helpings of food, etc. Also used to ask for repetition of some performance, such as a somersault.
Up	Wants a lift to reach objects such as grapes on vine, or leaves; or wants to be placed on someone's shoulders; or wants to leave potty-chair.
Sweet	For dessert; used spontaneously at end of meal. Also, when asking for candy.
Open	At door of house, room, car, refrigerator, or cupboard; on containers such as jars; and on faucets.
Tickle	For tickling or for chasing games.
Go	While walking hand-in-hand or riding on someone's shoulders. Washoe usually indicates the direction desired.
Out	When passing through doorways; until recently, used for both "in" and "out." Also, when asking to be taken outdoors.
Hurry	Often follows signs such as "come-gimme," "out," "open," and "go," particularly if there is a delay before Washoe is obeyed. Also, used while watching her meal being prepared.
Hear–listen	For loud or strange sounds: bells, car horns, sonic booms, etc. Also, for asking someone to hold a watch to her ear.
Toothbrush	When Washoe has finished her meal, or at other times when shown a toothbrush.
Drink	For water, formula, soda pop, etc. For soda pop, often combined with "sweet."
Hurt	To indicate cuts and bruises on herself or on others. Can be elicited by red stains on a person's skin or by tears in clothing.
Sorry	After biting someone, or when someone has been hurt in another way (not necessarily by Washoe). When told to apologize for mischief.
Funny	When soliciting interaction play, and during games. Occasionally, when being pursued after mischief.
Please	When asking for objects and activities. Frequently combined: "Please go," "Out, please," "Please drink."
Food–eat	During meals and preparation of meals.
Flower	For flowers.
Cover–blanket	At bedtime or naptime, and, on cold days, when Washoe wants to be taken out.
Dog	For dogs and for barking.
You	Indicates successive turns in games. Also used in response to questions such as "Who tickle?" "Who brush?"
Napkin–bib	For bib, for washcloth, and for Kleenex.
In	Wants to go indoors, or wants someone to join her indoors.
Brush	For hairbrush, and when asking for brushing.

(continued)

TABLE 1.1 *(continued)*

Signs	Context
Hat	For hats and caps.
I-me	Indicates Washoe's turn, when she and a companion share food, drink, etc. Also used in phrases, such as "I drink," and in reply to questions such as "Who tickle?" (Washoe: "you"); "Who I tickle?" (Washoe: "Me.")
Shoes	For shoes and boots.
Smell	For scented objects: tobacco, perfume, sage, etc.
Pants	For diapers, rubber pants, trousers.
Clothes	For Washoe's jacket, nightgown, and shirts; also for our clothing.
Cat	For cats.
Key	Used for keys and locks and to ask us to unlock a door.
Baby	For dolls, including animal dolls such as a toy horse and duck.
Clean	Used when Washoe is washing, or being washed, or when a companion is washing hands or some other object. Also used for "soap."

[a] The signs are listed in the order of their original appearance in her repertoire.

[b] Adapted from Gardner and Gardner (1969, pp. 668–669). © 1969 by the American Association for the Advancement of Science.

Washoe is that she seemed to be quite insensitive to word orders, and until recently it was generally believed that young children were highly sensitive to word orders. More recent work has shown that, at a very early stage (approximately 18 to 24 months of age), this need not be true, particularly when children are learning a language in which rigid sequential word orders for certain meanings are not used (Brown, 1973). Careful comparison of Washoe's accomplishments with that of these young children lead Brown to conclude that "the evidence that Washoe has . . . language is about the same as it is for . . . [these young] . . . children" (Brown, 1973, p. 43). The criteria for this early child speech are discussed in the context of human language development (see Chapter 5). For now it will suffice to characterize the evidence in these simple terms: Washoe and young children produce constructions (sign combinations) that can be interpreted in context, and these utterances express semantic relations which appear to be universal—they occur in all human languages. Among such relations are possession (for example, *my hat*), recurrence (for example, *more sweet candy*), and nonexistence (for example, *no more*). These examples are taken from children's speech as illustrative of semantic relations in general. That Washoe displayed such competence suggests that her communication system is comparable to at least an early stage of human language.[2] Whether Washoe or her successors will achieve more is an open question.

[2] To validate this conclusion we need to know how a deaf, but otherwise normal, child acquires American Sign Language. The relevant data are not yet available, although Klima and Bellugi (1972) have begun to study the development of sign language.

Washoe has developed, and is still developing, the most impressive communication system ever displayed by a chimpanzee. Her accomplishments are closely rivaled by another chimpanzee named Sarah, who has also acquired an elaborate conceptual system. Sarah is a chimpanzee trained by David Premack (1971). Premack started with the same question asked by the Gardners: Can apes be taught language? He characterized language in terms of a set of fundamental elements: some of these elements were linguistic, such as "words" or "sentences"; other elements were metalinguistic, like the concept of naming, and others nonlinguistic, having to do with logic. Among these was the *if–then* relation and the concept of negation.

Premack's interest in training Sarah lay not so much in developing communicative competence as it was in assessing her conceptual capacities. His training procedures were therefore quite unlike the Gardners'. Unlike Washoe, Sarah was restricted to a laboratory cage, and she was given a carefully programmed sequence of tasks to learn. The units of her communicative system were "words" made of plastic forms. The forms varied unsystematically in size, shape, and color, and each had a metal backing so they could be stuck to a vertical magnetized board. Sentence-like combinations of words consisted of appropriate forms arranged vertically on the board. One of Sarah's "sentences" is shown in Figure 1.3. This communication system served only one purpose. It enabled Premack to know what Sarah had learned. Sarah did not use the system spontaneously to ask questions or to make requests.

What did Sarah learn to do? Among other things she acquired a vocabulary of over 60 nouns, 20 verbs, and 30 other words, including adjectives and adverbs. Some of the training procedures were relatively simple and straightforward. The plastic form for apple was made available, together

FIGURE 1.3 Example of the physical basis of Sarah's language—a set of pieces of plastic that vary in color, size, and shape. Each piece is a word, and each is backed with metal so that it will cling to a magnetized slate. Sentences are written on the vertical. The "sentence" means "Sarah take apple." (After Premack, 1971, p. 809. © 1969 by the American Association for the Advancement of Science.)

with other plastic forms, and an apple was shown to Sarah. Sarah had to pick out the correct plastic form and put it up on the board. If she did so, then she got a piece of the apple. After Sarah had learned to pick the correct forms for two things, like apple and banana, she could be given a more complicated task, like learning the concept *name of*. The plastic form representing this concept was placed between the plastic form for *apple* and a real apple. The form for *not name of* was placed between the plastic form for *apple* and a real banana. After several trials with only these two pairs of exemplars (apples, bananas, their respective "names," and the two concepts *name of* and *not name of*), Sarah was tested on new forms and objects. She responded correctly about 80% of the time.

Other concepts were taught similarly. The logical connective *if–then* involved teaching Sarah that she would get a piece of chocolate when she picked up a piece of an apple, but not when she picked up a piece of banana. She liked apples and bananas equally well, but chocolate was a real treat. She quickly learned to pick apple, so Premack inferred that she had mastered the relation, "if apple, then chocolate." The next step was to attach a "name"—a particular plastic form—to this concept. Sarah had to learn to insert the appropriate plastic form in the following sentences: "Sarah take apple? _____ Mary give Sarah chocolate" and "Sarah take banana? _____ Mary no give Sarah chocolate." This proved to be a difficult task for Sarah, particularly when she did not get her chocolate, as when the *if–then* contingency referred to taking some banana and not getting her chocolate. Eventually she did learn and transferred her knowledge to other contexts.

Unlike Washoe, Sarah did not acquire a usable communication system, even though her "speech" involved arbitrary symbolic reference. Premack's primary interest was in finding out what linguistic and conceptual material Sarah could master, not in giving Sarah a usable "language." As a result, the effective productivity of Sarah's "language" is extremely limited for at least two reasons. First, Sarah communicated by selecting one word at a time from a set of from two to eight alternatives. These alternatives were selected and made available by the experimenter. The experimenter therefore controlled Sarah's usable vocabulary for any given situation and also controlled the kinds of mistakes Sarah might make. Sarah was, and is, effectively prohibited from communicating spontaneously in the ways that people (and Washoe) do. Second, the plastic form system does not involve duality of structure. Each "word" is a unit in and of itself. It is not composed of "meaningless" smaller elements in any systematic way. For every new "word" Sarah learned she had to learn the relation between a new plastic form and its referent. This effectively and drastically limited the total number of words that Sarah might be expected to learn and also limited her effective production vocabulary at any given time.

Consider the problems we would have if every word we knew were to be represented by plastic chips which varied unsystematically in shape, size, and color. In addition to the memory load associated with such a system, we would find it too time consuming to rummage through our vocabulary every time we wanted to say something. Even if we only had 100 "words" at our disposal, how would we go about finding the right one when the set is completely unorganized? Sarah, of course, never faced this problem because she never was expected to "talk about" anything at any time. She was always given a specific "topic" and a very small set of alternatives from which to choose.

The differences between Washoe and Sarah represent a difference between two views of what a human language is. For Premack, a language is characterized by a set of explicit criteria. These criteria are revealed by a list of "exemplars, things an organism must be able to do in order to give evidence of language" (Premack, 1971, p. 808). Among the exemplars chosen by Premack were selected aspects of words, sentences, questions, and both class and logical concepts. Why these exemplars were chosen rather than certain others is not clear. For example, one might argue that an organism must express a variety of semantic relations in order to give evidence of language, as Roger Brown and other students of child language development have done (Brown, 1973). Similarly, one might take the Gardners' viewpoint and argue that an organism must be capable of spontaneous communicative interactions as evidence of language. For Premack, neither the primacy of semantic relations nor the use of a "language" for communicative interactions is critical. Within Premack's terms, Sarah gives evidence of language.

Washoe, on the other hand, gives evidence of language usage that is indistinguishable from that of young children's. Which criteria should we use to characterize "language"? From a psychological viewpoint, in contrast to that of theoretical linguistics, it seems to us that human language usage provides the more useful set of criteria. The three properties of language summarized by Brown—productivity, duality of structure, and arbitrary symbolic reference—are important because they make it possible for language to fulfill its function as a communication system. Sarah, even though she displays an impressive set of language-like exemplars, is without a usable communication system. Washoe, even though she did not display some of the language-like exemplars listed by Premack (for example, the *if–then* logical connective), does have a usable communication system, and she uses it throughout her daily life. Perhaps we should stop asking the question, What is human language?, and ask, instead: How do people use language, and what properties of languages make it possible for us to do what we do? As we shall see when we discuss the problem of language acquisition, this way of defining the question has led to the first real successes in understanding how children use and acquire their first language. In order to clarify our usage throughout this book, we use LANGUAGE to refer to that verbal communication system developed and used by humans.

SUGGESTED READINGS

Words and things (Paperback edition, New York: Free Press, 1968), the recent classic by R. Brown, first published in 1958, helped to rekindle psychology's interest in linguistics and in language. The preface to the paperback edition reviews the growth of the field from 1958 to the late 1960s. In A. L. Blumenthal, *Language and psychology: Historical aspects of psycholinguistics* (New York: Wiley, 1970), the historical roots of psycholinguistics are traced from Wilhelm Wundt to Noam Chomsky, with generous samples of original texts. Rereading Wundt reminds us that the classic problems remain unresolved.

The volume edited by R. A. Hinde, *Non-verbal communication* (Cambridge, England: The University Press, 1972), is a report of a Royal Society study group on nonverbal communication in animals and humans. It contains discussions of the nature of language and of communicative processes in general, as well as analyses of various animal communication systems.

There has been a virtual explosion of interest in chimpanzee communication with humans following the Gardners' and Premack's work with Washoe and Sarah, respectively. Much of this work is still in progress with little reported in detail. Perhaps the most concise background on this topic can be found in a volume edited by Allan Schrier and Fred Stollnitz, *Behavior of nonhuman primates* (Volume 4. New York: Academic Press, 1971). Both the Gardners and Premack report on the then-current progress of Washoe and Sarah in more detail than is usual in journal articles, and both of their chapters are well worth reading.

GENERAL SOURCES

The current literature in psycholinguistics can be found in a number of professional journals. Among the more well known are:

> *Cognition: An International Journal*
> *Cognitive Psychology*
> *Journal of Experimental Psychology: Human Learning and Memory*
> *Journal of Experimental Psychology: Human Perception and Performance*
> *Journal of Psycholinguistic Research*
> *Journal of Verbal Learning and Verbal Behavior*
> *Memory and Cognition*
> *Perception and Psychophysics*

The *Annual Review of Psychology* periodically has reviews of psycholinguistic research. The latest is by P. Johnson-Laird, 1974.

2
Speech Sounds and Speech Perception

In our discussion of animal communication systems we were not concerned with the units or elements of any given communication system. This reflects a characteristic of many nonlinguistic communication systems. They are not organized in terms of hierarchically related units such as sounds, words, phrases, and sentences. The communication system we call human language has, as one of its most salient characteristics, a hierarchical organization of units. The word is one of those units, and words can be described in at least three ways. One description concerns the meanings any given word "has." In the next chapter we consider the semantic properties of words and how words are organized in our mental dictionaries. A second property of words concerns their syntactic functions and how words may be combined to form a larger unit, the sentence. These syntactic properties of words are discussed in Chapter 4, where we consider sentences and sentence meanings. The third aspect of words is the sounds they are composed of. In this chapter we describe the sound systems of human languages, taking English as our example, and the speech perception process.

There are at least two reasons for beginning with the sounds of a language. One is the intuitive feeling that one should begin with the smallest units of a system and then proceed to the larger, more complex ones. A more important reason for starting with the sound system and speech perception is that work in this area has progressed much farther than work in semantics or syntax. Because of this, speech perception illustrates three important principles of language behavior applicable to all levels of language processing.

Rule Governing.   First, language behavior is RULE GOVERNED. A rule describes regularities in the sequencing and patterning of linguistic units. These units may be speech sounds, words, or sentences. When these units are ordered and combined according to a rule, a larger acceptable unit is formed. In English, for example, we have rules that enable us to form the past tense of a verb. *Talk* becomes *talked, listen* becomes *listened,* and so on. We also have rules that enable us to generate sentences with tag-question endings, like

(1)   He went to the store, didn't he?

(2)   He didn't go to the store, did he?

One rule governing tag questions specifies that, if the first part of the utterance is affirmative (*he went*), the tag question is negative (*didn't he?*) and vice versa.

The sound system of English (or any other language) is also rule governed. It is systematic, and every speaker of the language follows the same implicit set of rules to produce the acceptable sounds and sound sequences of the language. Rules are "known" to every speaker in the sense that we obey them when we speak. They are not "known" in the sense that we are explicitly aware of them, or that we are able to explain them to anyone. Few of us are aware, for example, of the rules which specify that (3) is correct and (4) is not:

(3)   I bought a large red Turkish truck.

(4)   I bought a Turkish red large truck.

Nevertheless, even though we never explicitly think of the correct and incorrect ways to order adjectives, we generally order them correctly. We behave as if we knew and applied the rules.

Context Dependence.   A second general principle of language behavior is that the units of a language are CONTEXT DEPENDENT. Any given word cannot be interpreted unambiguously unless we know the context in which the word appears. Similarly, many speech sounds are context dependent in that a given sound pattern will be heard differently in different sound-pattern contexts. Sentences also require a context if they are to be interpreted. In the sentence *they are visiting relatives* it is not clear who is doing the traveling without context. Likewise, how would you interpret the utterance

(5)   A canary has skin,

if someone says that to you as he passes you in the hall and then just continues walking on? With no context for that remark one simply does not know what the sentence means (or, more precisely, what the person meant to tell us). As we shall see, the role of context is important in the interpretation and perception of speech sounds as well as larger units of language such as words and sentences.

Categorization.   Third, all units of speech are members of categories, and we perceive them as such. Whenever we use a word, we symbolize a category of events, things, or relationships. At the level of speech sounds a unit of sound itself, the phoneme, is really a category of speech sounds that are functionally equivalent. Our ability to discriminate between categories is extremely good; our ability to discriminate among members within the same category is quite poor. This principle is clearly demonstrated in speech perception, and is also applicable to our perception and interpretation of larger speech units.

In this chapter we refer to each of these three general principles of language behavior in the context of the sound system of English and the facts and theories of speech perception. We shall see later that these three principles apply with equal force to word, sentence, and message processing.

SOUNDS AND PHONEMES

Every human language has a relatively small set of sounds that is unique to that language. Languages sound different from one another, but the differences we hear are not caused by different orderings or sequences of the same set of speech sounds. Instead, different languages use different sets of sounds, each set consisting of a relatively small number of phonemes. A PHONEME is defined as the smallest unit in a language that makes a meaningful difference to people who speak that language. Listen to the initial sounds of the words *bad* and *pad*. The only difference between them is in their first sound. Since this difference in the initial sounds produces two different words, the difference is a meaningful one. This meaningful difference, or contrast, defines /b/ and /p/[1] as two different phonemes. Similarly, *bad* and *bid* are two different words. Hence, the difference between /æ/ and /ɪ/ is a meaningful difference, and so /æ/ and /ɪ/ are two different phonemes, as well. Finally, one can contrast *bad* and *bat* to discover that /d/ and /t/ are also two different phonemes. Two speech

---

[1] Phonemes and phonemic transcriptions typically are written between slashed lines.

sounds are defined as different phonemes if, when one is substituted for the other in a word, the result is two different meaningful words.

Why do we take so much trouble to define phonemic differences? Why can't we simply say that two speech sounds are different if they sound different? The problem here is that people who speak different languages perceive the speech sounds differently. Two speech sounds that sound very different to people who speak English may not sound different to people who do not speak English. We clearly hear the difference between *rice* and *rise* and between *ice* and *eyes*. Ignoring the vagaries of English spelling, these pairs of words differ only in their final sounds. The first word in each pair ends with the phoneme /s/, and the second ends with the phoneme /z/. People who speak Spanish may not hear this difference because the Spanish language does not distinguish words on the basis of the difference between /s/ and /z/. These two sounds are not different phonemes in Spanish, even though they are different phonemes in English.

All languages are selective in their choice of phonemes, and English is no exception. English does not use certain sound differences to distinguish one word from another, and English speakers may not hear the difference between certain phonemes of another language. Pronounce, and then compare, the initial sounds in the words *keep* and *cool*. To most of us the initial /k/ sounds are identical, and in English they are treated as such. In Arabic, these two /k/ sounds are different phonemes because they produce different words. For example, /kalb/ means *dog* and /qalb/ means *heart,* where /k /is the same as in *keep* and /q/ is as in *cool* (Gleason, 1961). Although we may fail to hear the difference, we can feel it. The /k/ sound is made by touching the back of the tongue to the roof of the mouth to momentarily stop the flow of air. In pronouncing *cool,* the point of contact is farther toward the back of the mouth than that used in pronouncing *keep.* This apparently trivial difference in place of articulation produces enough of a difference in sound for speakers of Arabic to hear the difference quite plainly, even though we may not.

This is not an isolated and exotic example. In other languages differences are used that are not used in English, and if we, in our own language, do not use a difference to distinguish among words, then we may not even hear that difference. Consider the /p/ sounds in *spin* and in *pin.* They may sound identical, but hold your hand about two inches in front of your lips and pronounce *spin* and *pin.* The puff of air that you feel when you say *pin* is quite strong and obvious; very little air is expelled when you say *spin.* The /p/ in *pin* is aspirated (pronounced with a rush of air), whereas the /p/ in *spin* is not. Indeed, if you force yourself to aspirate the /p/ in *spin,* it sounds very much like a Russian speaker speaking English. In English, words are not differentiated by the presence or absence of aspiration on the phoneme /p/, so whether we pronounce that /p/

sound with or without aspiration makes no difference in our interpretation of the word. In some other languages, such as Hindi, aspiration does yield meaningful differences.

These examples show that a phoneme is not a single speech sound, but a category of sounds that are treated as functionally identical. The single, individual sounds of a language are called PHONES. Any given phoneme consists of a set of phones that are treated as identical, and often even heard as identical. For example, the English phoneme /k/ is a category of sounds that includes, among others, the two phones [k] and [q].[2] The English phoneme /p/ is a category of sounds that includes both the aspirated and unaspirated [p] phones. The set of phones categorized as a single phoneme are called ALLOPHONES of that phoneme. The phones [k] and [q] are two allophones of the English phoneme /k/. This categorization becomes so automatic that we may never really hear the differences among the allophones.

This automatic categorization is one of the reasons why we often find it difficult to learn a foreign language. If you were learning Arabic, one of the things you would have to learn is to hear the difference between [k] and [q]. You would also have to learn when to pronounce one and not the other, since, if you get them mixed up, you would not be saying the word you meant to say. A set of phonological problems is inherent in each language for speakers of other languages because each language has its own unique sound system. What is the nature of this sound system?

English Phones and Phonemes

The phones and phonemes of a language can be organized into a reasonably coherent system in at least two ways. One basis for defining and organizing sounds is the ACOUSTIC properties of the sounds themselves, where the acoustic properties refer to the measurable properties of the sound waves involved. A second basis for dealing with speech sounds is their ARTICULATORY properties, where articulatory refers to the positions and movements of our vocal apparatus when we produce those sounds. Because the acoustic properties of speech sounds are relatively complex, let us begin with the articulatory properties of English speech sounds.

Figure 2.1 is a cross-sectional diagram of the human vocal tract. The vocal tract is essentially a pathway through which air is expelled. There are two major ways to modulate the resulting sound. The first is to obstruct the air stream in one way or another. These obstructions may range from a complete closure to a minor or partial closure, and they may be placed

---

[2] Phones and phonetic transcriptions are indicated by square brackets in order to distinguish them from phonemes, since the same characters are usually used to represent both phones and phonemes.

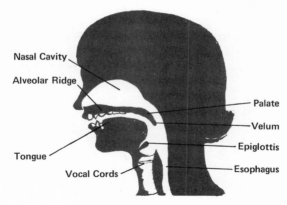

Nasal Cavity

Alveolar Ridge

Palate

Velum

Epiglottis

Tongue

Vocal Cords

Esophagus

FIGURE 2.1 Cross-sectional diagram of the vocal tract and speech apparatus.

anywhere between the vocal cords and the lips. The second way to shape the sound is to alter the shape of the cavities in which sound may resonate. The two largest cavities are the oral (mouth) and nasal (nose) cavities. All the speech sounds we make are produced by varying the amount and place of closure and by varying the resonant characteristics of the oral and nasal cavities. Consonants can be generally characterized by the place and type of obstruction introduced in the air stream. In contrast, vowel sound qualities are dependent primarily upon the resonance properties of the oral and nasal cavities.

Consonants. Langacker's (1968) description of consonants is representative of most linguistic descriptions, and Table 2.1 is a summary of his description. The places in the vocal tract where the obstruction occurs are listed along the top of the chart. The type or manner of obstruction is listed down the side.

The easiest consonants to describe are the STOPS: [p, b, t, d, k, g] as in *pat, bat, tack, dig, cat,* and *get.* A stop involves a brief but complete blocking of the air stream. This blocking may occur at the lips (where it is called bilabial) as for [b, p], at the ridge just behind the teeth (alveolar) for [d, t], or at the back of the mouth (velar) for [g, k]. In addition, the first of each pair is voiced, and the second voiceless. If the vocal cords start vibrating immediately after the stop is released, the sound is voiced. If there is a short delay, it is voiceless. To feel this difference clearly, place your fingers lightly on your larynx or "Adam's apple" while repeating the syllables *ba* and *pa.* You should feel vibrations earlier with *ba* than with *pa.*

Another set of consonants is the FRICATIVES. These are formed by a partial occlusion that does not completely stop the air flow, but creates

TABLE 2.1
English Consonants Classified by Manner and
Place of Articulation

Manner of articulation		Bilabial	Labiodental	Dental	Alveolar	Palatal	Velar	Glottal
					Place of articulation			
Stops	Voiceless	p (pat)			t (tack)		k (cat)	
	Voiced	b (bat)			d (dig)		g (get)	
Fricatives	Voiceless		f (fat)	θ (thin)	s (sat)	š (fish)		h (hat)
	Voiced		v (vat)	ð (then)	z (zap)	ž (azure)		
Affricatives	Voiceless					č (church)		
	Voiced					ǰ (judge)		
Nasals		m (mat)			n (nat)		ŋ (sing)	
Liquids					l (late)	r (rate)		
Glides		w (win)				y (yet)		

turbulance. There are nine fricatives in English: [f, v, θ, ð, s, z, š, ž, h] as in *fat, vat, thin, then, sat, zap, fish* (the final consonant), *azure* (the first consonant), and *hat*. As with the stops, the fricatives can be paired according to place of articulation, and (with the exception of [h]) each pair can be distinguished by voicing. Labiodental fricatives [f, v] have their point of articulation between the lower lip and the upper row of teeth. For dental fricatives [θ, ð], the tongue tip touches the teeth; for alveolar fricatives [s, z], the tongue tip touches the alveolar ridge; and for palatal fricatives [š, ž], the back of the tongue is raised against the palate. The glottal fricative [h] is produced by a very slight constriction of the vocal cords without vibration.

The AFFRICATIVES [č, ǰ], as in *church* and *judge,* are produced as a combination of a stop and a fricative. This is accomplished by first blocking the air flow as in a stop and then releasing to a fricative position causing turbulance. The pair is distinguished by voicing.

All stops, fricatives, and affricatives are oral consonants. When they are produced, the nasal cavitiy is closed off by the velum (see Figure 2.1). The NASALS are produced by closing the oral cavity and opening the nasal cavity by dropping the velum. The oral cavity may be closed either by the lips, producing [m] as in *mat,* or by the tongue against the alveolar ridge, [n] as in *nat,* or by the tongue against the velum, [ŋ] as in *sing* (the terminal consonant, spelled with the letters *ng*).

The last four consonants are closely related to vowels and are frequently combined with vowels to produce diphthongs. The LIQUIDS or LATERALS, [l, r] as in *late* and *rate,* never completely stop the air flow, nor cause turbulance. The [l] is produced by blocking the air in the center of the mouth and letting it escape along the sides. The [r] involves forming a cup with the tongue, but with no closure. The English [r] is unusual. In many languages (for example, Spanish, French, and German) [r]-like sounds are produced by trilling or flapping the tongue. The glides, [w, y] as in *wow* and *you,* are formed by the rapid movement of the articulatory apparatus as it glides either into or out of position for a vowel. The glides are often called SEMIVOWELS.

All possible sounds are not used in English for the simple reason that it would be very difficult to hear all of the fine differences. This is not to say that most English speakers do not produce these other sounds in one context or another. For example, remember the allophones of /k/ in *keep* and *cool.* The [k] in *keep* is actually a palatal voiceless stop and the [q] in *cool* is a velar voiceless stop. However, this difference is only allophonic, not phonemic, because in English one does not depend on palatal versus velar stops to distinguish any pair of words.

There are other articulatory properties that are not functional in English, but are used in other languages. ASPIRATION (whether a stop is released with a puff of air [pʰɪn] or not [spɪn]) is important in some languages. LABIALIZATION, when the lips are rounded during consonant production, is another functional property in some languages. English labializes stops when they precede a [w], as in *twig, dwarf,* and *quick,* but this feature is not phonemic in English. We do not have contrasting words like *twig* versus *t'wig* or *dwarf* versus *d'warf,* where the lips are not rounded for [t] and [d]. The number of consonant phonemes in any language are sufficient to produce any number of words in combination, yet the number is not so large as to make learning and discriminating among them too difficult.

Vowels. Whereas consonants are produced by relatively discrete movements, vowels are more continuously variable in mode of production. Vowels are produced by vibration of the vocal cords and are shaped by modifications in the length, size, and shape of the cavities through which

	Front	Center	Back
High	i (b<u>ee</u>t) ɪ (b<u>i</u>t)	ɝ (b<u>i</u>rd)	u (b<u>oo</u>t) ʊ (b<u>oo</u>k) o (b<u>o</u>de)
Middle	e (b<u>a</u>by) ɛ (b<u>e</u>t)	ə (sof<u>a</u>)	ɔ (b<u>o</u>ught)
Low	æ (b<u>a</u>t)	ʌ (b<u>u</u>t)	a (p<u>a</u>lm)

FIGURE 2.2   Chart of English vowels.

the sound passes. All English vowels are produced with the nasal cavity closed off by the velum, so we are primarily concerned with the position of the tongue. In Figure 2.2, the vowels are classified according to two dimensions related to the position of the tongue (see Langacker, 1968; Miller, 1951). The tongue can be held high, low, or somewhere in between. High means that the tongue is very close to the roof of the mouth; low means that it is compressed against the floor. Various parts of the tongue may also be raised, starting from the tip to the back or base of the tongue. Figure 2.3 shows the tongue in three relatively extreme positions, yielding the vowels in three corners of the chart in Figure 2.2.

A better feel for the two dimensions can be gotten by slowly repeating the series of vowels along the perimeter of Figure 2.2. Compare [i, ɪ, e, ɛ, æ] by saying only the vowels in *beet, bit, baby, bet,* and *bat.* You should feel your tongue fall, especially the tip. Now say only the vowels in the series [u, ʊ, o, ɔ, a] as in *boot, book, bode, bought,* and *palm.* Here you should feel the back of your tongue fall away from the velum. Finally, say

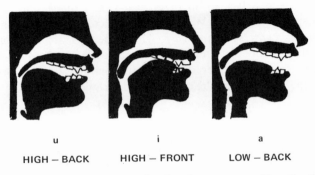

u   i   a

HIGH – BACK   HIGH – FRONT   LOW – BACK

FIGURE 2.3   Cross-sectional diagram showing the tongue position for three vowels.

the vowels [æ, ʌ, a] as in *bat, but,* and *palm.* You should feel your tongue move from front to back, but the movement is quite small because the tongue is being compressed against the floor of your mouth.

The vowel [ə], as the final vowel in *sofa,* is often called "schwa." It is a neutral vowel, as is indicated by its position in the center of the chart. The [ə] is used exclusively in unaccented syllables, and the other vowels are often pronounced as [ə] in rapid speech. There is a tendency for all vowels to move toward this neutral position except when one is speaking in a formal, distinct manner.[3]

Some vowel sounds are combinations of two phones, usually a vowel and a glide. These combinations are called DIPHTHONGS. The most common of these are [ey, ow, ay, ɔy, aw], as in *bait, boat, eye, boy,* and *cow.* The first two of these [ey, ow] are much more common than the single vowels [e, o]. Some linguists have proposed that the vowels [i, e, u, o], as described here, are not separate unitary phonemes at all, but are diphthongs of neighboring vowels and should be represented as [ɪy, ɛy, ʊw, ɔw] [see Gleason (1961) for a relatively complete presentation of this position]. Though there is disagreement among linguists as to the correct description, the one presented here seems to be the simplest.

As with consonants, there are aspects of vowel production that are important in other languages, but are not phonemically important in English. One is whether the vowels are nasal or oral. All English vowels are ORAL; whenever we produce a vowel, the velum closes off the nasal cavity. Many other languages have NASAL vowels in which the nasal cavity is not blocked off. The most familiar example for most Americans is French. Any of the English vowels we have described can be nasalized simply by opening the velum. A second characteristic is the position of the lips. Pronounce the vowels [i, u], as in *beet* and *boot,* in succession. In addition to the change in tongue position, the lips protrude and become rounded for [u] in contrast to [i]. This is called ROUNDING. Though all the vowels in the English vowel chart could be either rounded or not, only the back vowels [u, ʊ, o, ɔ] are rounded. Thus, rounding is not phonemic in English, whereas in other languages, such as French, it is.

Suprasegmentals.   A final category of speech sounds to consider is the SUPRASEGMENTALS. These are not separate units in English, but are attached to other phones, primarily vowels. Some of the common suprasegmental forms are stress, length, and tone. Only stress is phonemic in English, as illustrated by the pair *black'bird* and *black bird'.* The former refers to a particular species of bird and the latter refers to a bird that is black.

---

[3] See Labov (1972) for a description of regularities in phoneme variation as a function of social class and social situation. This study provides an excellent example of social editing at the level of phonology.

This stress contrast is phonemic because it produces a meaningful difference. Vowel length can be adjusted by varying the time that the vocal cords are vibrated before continuing to the next sound. In English, *bed* has a slightly longer vowel than *bet,* but this vowel-length difference is not phonemic. In other languages, vowel length may be used to discriminate among words. A third characteristic is the tone contour, or pitch of a word. The "same" sounds can be produced with a high pitch or a low pitch. In a tonal language, such as Chinese or Vietnamese, these pitches result in different words with completely different meanings. In English, stress and pitch combine to produce different intonation patterns across phrases and sentences. For example,

(6)   You want to go home

can be interpreted as a declarative statement, a question, an imperative, or an exclamation, depending on the intonation contour used.

Acoustic Properties and Distinctive Features

Since we can describe speech sounds in terms of their articulation, there must be a very close relationship between articulatory configuration and the acoustic signal. Just as an acoustician can predict what a new music hall will sound like, so can a phonetician predict what the acoustic signal will be from the movement, shape, and placement of the articulators. The reverse correspondence is not as simple, however, because there are usually several different ways to produce a particular sound. Because the relationship among the acoustic properties, articulatory configurations, and perceived phonemes is so complex, some workers have attempted to design a simplified description in terms of distinctive features (Jakobson, Fant, & Halle, 1963). One purpose of distinctive features is to describe each phoneme in terms of a bundle of smaller acoustic and articulatory elements. A DISTINCTIVE FEATURE is a unitary property of the acoustic signal or articulatory configuration that differentiates one phoneme from another. One of the easiest features to hear is STRIDENCY, the presence or absence of a noisy rush of air created by an obstacle in the air stream. The fricative and affricative consonants [f, v, s, z, š, ž, č, ǰ] are strident. The other consonants and vowels are nonstrident. Another distinctive feature corresponds to the presence or absence of VOICING. We hear a brief "buzz" with a voiced strident consonant and a "hiss" with a voiceless one. To hear this difference clearly, pronounce [v] and then [f] for about a second each.

How many features are needed to describe all the sounds of a language? Halle (1962, 1964) listed only 11 distinctive features to describe 36 speech sounds of English. Later, Chomsky and Halle (1968) listed 46 English speech sounds that could be described in terms of just 13 features. For all the speech segments (sounds) that occur in all the languages of the world, linguists estimate that only about 20 to 30 features would be necessary (Stevens & House, 1972). The utility of distinctive features is obvious. They enable us to describe or represent the sound system of any language quite economically. They also enable us to summarize the regularities or rules of the sound system.

Phonological Rules

Linguistic rules summarize and describe the regularities within a language. The sounds and sound sequences acceptable in English (or any other language) are described by a subset of the linguistic rules of that language, namely, the phonological rules of the language. These rules are not simply an exhaustive list of all the acceptable sequences. Such a list would not reveal very much about the nature of the sound system, and would also be far too long and cumbersome. Instead, the rules specify how certain classes of phonemes may or may not be sequenced. For example, when two or more consonants occur together in a string, they are either all voiced or all voiceless. English words may begin with /sp--/, /st--/, or /sk--/. English words may not begin with /sb--/, /sd--/, or /sg--/. Instead of listing all the permissible and nonpermissible instances, a voicing rule can be used to summarize this feature of English phonology.

Another type of phonological rule describes the mapping between the phonemic and the articulatory systems. When we speak, we presumably start with a selection of phonemes as specified by the pronunciation of the words to be uttered. These phoneme sequences are then translated into neuromuscular commands. For example, one set of phonological rules would specify that the sequence of phonemes in the word *bag* (/bæg/) is permissible in English.[4] Another set of rules would specify how these three phonemes are to be put together in the articulatory system (see Figure 2.4). The vowel /æ/ is specified as low and front. This vowel is also oral and unrounded, and these qualities are specified by two phonological rules. One rule states that all English vowels are oral; the other states that all front vowels are unrounded. Similar types of rules specify the formation of the two consonants. Notice that these rules do not describe the neural mechanisms by which people actually produce speech. They simply describe the linguistic regularities of the language in terms of the sounds actually spoken.

[4] The semantic rules of English would specify that the sound sequence [bæg] is, in fact a word. The phonological rules specify that the sound sequence itself is permissible. The sequence [skæm] is phonologically permissible, but it is not a word.

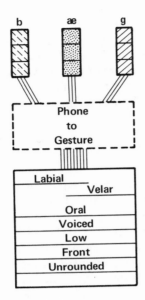

FIGURE 2.4 Schematic diagram illustrating the translation of phones into articulatory gesture. (Adapted from Liberman, 1970.)

SPEECH PERCEPTION

There are three phenomena that must be accounted for when we consider speech perception: (a) parallel transmission or the segmentation problem, (b) context-conditioned variation, and (c) categorical perception. A fourth feature of speech perception, a right-ear advantage for certain speech sounds, is considered in the context of categorical perception.

Parallel Transmission or the Segmentation Problem

A sound spectrograph is a device that converts sound energy into a visual display. Figure 2.5 is an actual spectrogram of the utterance *to catch pink salmon* (Liberman, Mattingly, & Turvey, 1972). Figure 2.6 is a schematic representation of this same spectrogram. These displays represent three properties of the sound signals. Frequency (or pitch) is represented in the vertical dimension. The higher the pattern in the display, the higher is the frequency (hence, the higher the pitch). Time is represented on the horizontal axis. Finally, the density or darkness of the display pattern represents the intensity (hence, the loudness) of the sound. Darker patterns are loud; lighter patterns are softer.

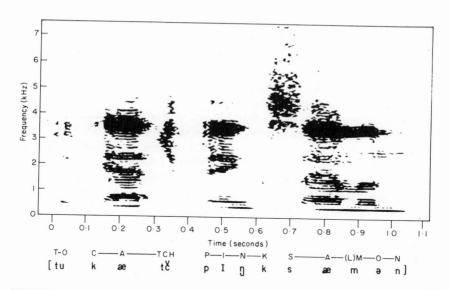

FIGURE 2.5 Sound spectrogram of a natural speech recording of *to catch pink salmon*. (After Liberman, Mattingly, & Turvey, 1972.)

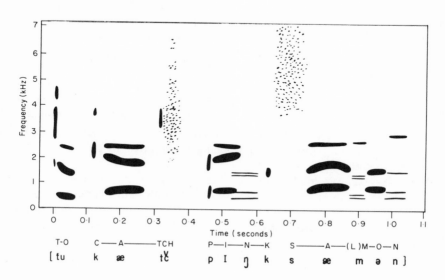

FIGURE 2.6 Schematic spectrogram for the synthesis of *to catch pink salmon*. (From Liberman, Mattingly, & Turvey, 1972.)

To illustrate the segmentation problem, compare the sound patterns in Figure 2.5 with the phonetic transcription printed below those patterns. There is no obvious one-to-one correspondence between the elements of the transcription and the acoustic properties of the sound waves. We cannot even identify the boundaries between words or between syllables. Individual sounds (phones) are not isolated in the pattern, and other noncorrespondences are present. For example, some sound bursts, such as [tč], appear to represent two phones, whereas other phones, for example, [k] and [n], seem to be represented by the absence of any sound.

Is the situation clearer when we construct a schematic spectrogram? Figure 2.6 is a picture of a schematic that can be "read" by a speech synthesizer, a machine that produces sound by "reading" instructions to produce specified frequencies of sound at specified intensities for specified time periods. If the appropriate frequency, time, and intensity information is provided, the machine produces sounds that are reasonable approximations to natural human speech. Even though it sounds somewhat artificial, it is quite intelligible.

The schematic spectrogram in Figure 2.6 can instruct a speech synthesizer to produce the utterance *to catch pink salmon*. We still find failures of correspondence between the sound patterns and the perceived speech. Compare, for example, the [æ] sound in *catch* with the "same" [æ] sound in *salmon*. The spectrogram patterns are not the same. Each of the [æ] sounds is produced by three FORMANTS (patterns of sounds varying in frequency contour over time). The first (bottom) and third (top) formants are virtually identical in the two [æ] patterns, but the second formants are quite different. The second formant for the [æ] in *catch* is concave upward; the corresponding formant for the [æ] in *salmon* is turned down. This difference is not accidental. It reflects the consonants that occur on either side of the vowels. Notice that the consonants surrounding the vowel in *catch* (the [k] and [t]) have very little sound associated directly with them. Actually, the acoustic information leading the listener to hear these consonants is contained in the vowel formants. Both vowel and consonant information is being transmitted in parallel by the vowel-associated formants.

A simpler example might be useful here. Consider the word *bag*, which consists of three phones [bæg], and is schematically represented in Figure 2.7 (Liberman, 1970). If these two formants are fed into a speech synthesizer, a recognizable word is produced (*bag*). We must, however, feed the information in as a unit. We could not divide the information, as shown in the schematic representation, into three separate sections and still get the three phones. If we wished to change the [b] into a [g] to produce *gag*, we could not do so by changing just the first third of the schematic. We would have to change over 60% of the information, as indicated in

FIGURE 2.7 Schematic spectrogram of the syllable [bæg], illustrating the phenomenon of parallel transmission. (After Liberman, 1970.)

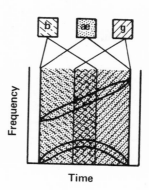

the diagram by the dashed diagonal hashing. Similarly, if we were to change the [g] to [d] to produce *bad,* we would have to change the last 60% of the acoustic signal (the solid diagonal hashing). Note that the first and third consonant information overlap in the acoustic signal. Finally, if we wanted to change the vowel to form *big,* we would have to change the entire signal since information about the vowel extends throughout the syllable. It is now clear why the two [æ]'s in Figure 2.6 are different from one another. The formants that produce each [æ] sound are also involved in producing the preceding and following consonants, and if these consonants are different, then the acoustic signal for the vowel must also be different. Because any given acoustic signal usually carries information about more than one phone, there is said to be PARALLEL TRANSMISSION of information in acoustic signals.

Context-Conditioned Variation

The phenomenon of parallel transmission leads to another property of speech perception. A single phone is represented or encoded differently in different contexts (Liberman, 1970; Liberman, Cooper, Shankweiler, & Studdert-Kennedy, 1967; Liberman, Mattingly, & Turvey, 1972). Variation in one phone that is controlled by the nature of the surrounding phones is called CONTEXT-CONDITIONED VARIATION. This phenomenon is illustrated by the two schematic spectrograms in Figure 2.8. One of these produces the syllable [di] on a speech synthesizer; the other produces the syllable [du]. There is no difference between the first formants of these two syllables since both [i] and [u] are high vowels. The frequency of the second formant encodes the front–back dimension of vowels, and this represents the major difference between [i] and [u]. Now consider the first 50 milliseconds of the second formant. The tips are turned in opposite directions, yet both

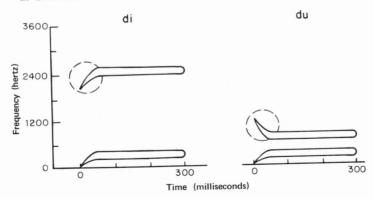

FIGURE 2.8 Simplified spectrographic patterns sufficient to synthesize the syllables [di] and [du]. (After Liberman, 1970.)

produce the [d] sound. If either tip were turned in the other direction, we would not hear a [d] sound. In these contexts, each tip must be pointed toward an imaginary sound at 1800 hertz (cycles per second). The acoustic stimulus for [d] is clearly not invariant, but is conditioned by the following vowel. If we clip the second formant at 50 milliseconds so that only this tip is read by the synthesizer, we do not get a [d] sound in either case. Instead, we get a short chirping sound that does not even sound like speech (Mattingly, Liberman, Syrdal, & Halwes, 1971). An essential part of the acoustic signal for the [d] sound is transmitted in parallel with the vowel information that follows. The particular form of the signal needed to produce the [d] sound is thus context dependent.

Categorical Perception and the Right-Ear Advantage

In general, people can discriminate among a very large number of physical stimuli. For example, we can discriminate among approximately 1,200 different pitches, and among a wide variety of colors. We are also aware that such stimuli as pitches and colors vary continuously and smoothly along particular dimensions.

Certain speech stimuli do not behave in this way (Liberman, Harris, Hoffman, & Griffith, 1957; Studdert-Kennedy, Liberman, Harris, & Cooper, 1970). Although the physical stimuli may vary continuously over a fairly wide range, we do not perceive this variation. Consider the continuous series of changes in the second formant of a simple English syllable, shown in Figure 2.9. These sound patterns produce the syllables [ba], [da], and [ga] when fed into a speech synthesizer. The first three syllables are

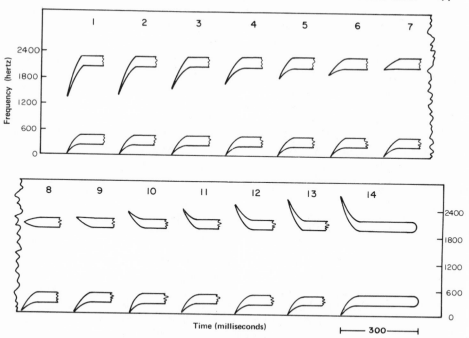

FIGURE 2.9 Series of schematic spectrograms sufficient to demonstrate the phenomenon of categorical perception. (Adapted from Liberman, Harris, Hoffman, & Griffith, 1957, p. 359. Copyright 1957 by the American Psychological Association. Reprinted by permission.)

heard as [ba], the next six as [da], and the last five as [ga]. People discriminate extremely well between these three "categories," but do not hear the differences within each category (Mattingly *et al.,* 1971). The three [b]'s all sound the same, even though there is continuous change along a single dimension. Between stimuli 3 and 4, listeners perceive a shift from [b] to [d]. This difference is always perceived as quite distinct, even though it is physically no more different than the difference between stimuli 2 and 3 or between 4 and 5.

The phenomenon of poor discrimination within categories and excellent discrimination between categories is known as CATEGORICAL PERCEPTION. This property of our speech perception system does not reflect our inability to discriminate among sounds per se.[5] If only the first bit of the second formant is played on a speech synthesizer, we no longer hear the sound as speech, and we then hear equally discriminable chirps along the whole range (Mattingly *et al.,* 1971). Apparently, the categorical nature of our

[5] Lane (1965) and others have argued that categorical perception is not limited to speech perception, but see the reply to Lane by Studdert-Kennedy *et al.* (1970).

perception reflects our learning to process speech sounds, and specific speech sounds at that. Categorical perception is not the rule for all speech sounds. Steady-state vowels (vowels without preceding or following consonants) are not perceived categorically. Instead, people discriminate among them just as they are able to discriminate among pure tones (Fry, Abramson, Eimas, & Liberman, 1962). Interestingly enough, though people can identify these synthesized vowels, they are not as consistent in their identifications as they are with stop consonants (Pisoni, 1973).

What is the source of categorical perception? Much of it must be learned, since different languages use different categories. Nevertheless, there is some evidence that our nervous systems are constructed in ways that at least predispose us to perceive certain kinds of sounds categorically. Some of this evidence comes from studies of the developing human infant, and some comes from studies of the localized functions of the adult human brain.

Young infants can be tested for their abilities to discriminate among various sounds by training them to suck on a nipple for some sounds, and not to suck for others. In one such study, four-week-old infants were given a range of synthesized speech stimuli. These stimuli would be categorized by English-speaking adults as [bæ] or [pæ], two syllables that are distinguished by voicing of the stop consonant. In the first category [bæ], the formants start immediately following release of air pressure of the stop (voiced). In the second [pæ], the formants start 25 milliseconds after the release (unvoiced). Surprisingly, these infants showed discrimination performance very much like adults. They were able to discriminate between the two syllable categories as defined by adult listeners (Eimas, Siqueland, Jusczyk, & Vigorito, 1971). This result suggests that categorical perception, at least of the voicing distinction, may be a direct function of our neural apparatus.

The second source of evidence for a specialized mode of speech processing comes from studies of laterality of brain function. Language functions tend to be localized in the left cerebral hemisphere of the brain (Broca, 1861). Since each ear has richer neural connections with the side of the brain on the opposite or contralateral side than with the ipsilateral (same) side, differences in perceptual performance between the two ears can tell us whether one hemisphere of the brain has more to do with speech perception than the other. Kimura took advantage of this feature of our anatomy by asking people to identify material presented simultaneously to both ears. In one study, she presented pairs of digits dichotically—one digit to each ear (Kimura, 1961). People were more accurate in identifying the digits presented to the right ear than to the left, displaying a RIGHT-EAR ADVANTAGE. Presumably, this result was obtained because the left side of the brain processes language materials. In a later study, Kimura (1964) presented different melodies dichotically, with one tune in one ear and another in the other ear. In this case, the material at the left ear was more accurately identified, suggesting that the right hemisphere is more involved with nonlinguistic material.

These results were extended to the perception of stop consonants and vowels by Shankweiler and Studdert-Kennedy (1967; Studdert-Kennedy & Shankweiler, 1970). Recall that stop consonants are categorically perceived, whereas vowels are not. When stop consonants are presented dichotically, a right-ear advantage is reliably found. When only vowels are presented, there is no longer a right-ear advantage.

From both the categorical perception findings and the right-ear advantage findings, we can conclude that some acoustic processing has been specialized for speech perception. What is the nature of this speech processing mechanism?

THEORETICAL MODELS OF SPEECH PERCEPTION

A number of lines of evidence point toward a special decoding system for the perception of speech. In particular, categorical perception and the right-ear advantage suggest that at least some classes of speech sounds are processed differently from most other auditory signals. Furthermore, we are able to process much more information in the speech mode than with other auditory material (for example, parallel transmission), and we use a localized area of the brain for such processing. Three general models of speech perception have been proposed. The first two—template matching and feature detection—are described briefly and are shown to be inadequate. The third model, analysis by synthesis, and a variant of it, the motor theory of speech perception, are considered more carefully, since this is the most adequate type of model currently available.

Template Matching

This type of theory or model takes its name from the draftsman's template—a pattern used to make exact copies of a particular form or shape. In perceptual theory, a TEMPLATE is a standardized representation of a category of items, say the letter "A." Imagine that, when you see a printed letter, you take that input and compare it to your mental "template" of the letter "A." If the two patterns match, you decide that the printed letter is, indeed, an "A." If they do not match, you try other templates until you find one that does.

A template-matching model for the recognition of written and printed letters assumes that each letter has at least one template that is used to match up with the letters on a page. This notion is simple and attractive, but poses some thorny problems. What might a template look like? Is the template for the letter "A" large or small? Is it upside down, or tilted? Is it general enough for all the type faces, upper and lower cases, and the varied handwriting scripts? A single template for each letter would be insufficient, and it also seems unlikely that we have a different set of templates for every type face and every handwriting style that we might encounter.

A template model for speech recognition faces the same general problem. According to such a model, whenever we hear speech, we match each successive sound to our templates of all the phonemes of the language. We would have templates for /k/ and for /d/, and, when we hear a sound like [k] or [d], we would compare or match the incoming signals to our templates of /k/ and /d/. In written language, there is no single invariant visual pattern that uniquely specifies any given letter. This problem is compounded for spoken language. There just is no single invariant acoustic pattern that uniquely specifies either /k/ or /d/. For example, do we have one template or three different templates for the three allophones of /k/ in *block that kick*? Do we have one or two templates for the /d/ in [di] and [du]? We would need many more templates than there are phonemes in a language, even if we ignore the individual differences among speakers. Males, females, and children speak in different pitches. Speakers also differ widely in dialect and accents, yet we have no trouble understanding them. Do we have different templates for each type of speaker? Far too many templates would be needed. Even if we could limit the number of templates, individual templates could not handle the phenomenon of parallel transmission, or of context-conditioned variation. For these reasons, a template model of pattern recognition in general, and speech perception in particular, is inadequate.

Feature Detection

Feature-detection models are somewhat more sophisticated than template-matching models. Instead of matching templates, which represent patterns for whole phonemes, a feature detector matches the distinctive features of phonemes. The feature detector has a set of "templates" for each distinctive feature in the sound system, and the features of each phoneme in the input signal are compared with those "templates." Thus, the "templates" are used to analyze each input signal in terms of its acoustic properties. When the appropriate set of features for a phoneme in the signal has been analyzed, that phoneme is identified. In order for a feature-detection model to function properly, there must be a one-to-one correspondence between acoustic cues and distinctive features. Such is not the case. A feature detector is functionally equivalent to a template matcher, except that the level of analysis is more fine grained. As such, it suffers from the same problems. A feature detector would encounter difficulties both with parallel transmission of information, and with context-conditioned variation.

Aside from these problems, either a template-matching or a feature-detection model would have great difficulty in accounting for nonphonemic and nonacoustic factors in speech perception. When we decode a speech signal, we use much more than just our knowledge of the sound system. We also use our knowledge of the phonological, semantic, and syntactic properties of the language, and our knowledge of what people usually say in familiar contexts. Words are perceived more accurately than nonsense syllables, even when the nonsense syllables conform to the phonological rules of English (Stevens & House, 1972). Frequent words are perceived more accurately than infrequent ones (Pollack, Rubenstein, & Decker, 1959), and words in sentences are easier to identify than those same words heard in isolation (Miller, Heise, & Lichten, 1951). Grammatical sentences are more intelligible than nongrammatical ones, and meaningful sentences are more intelligible than anomalous ones (Miller & Isard, 1963). Neither a template-matching nor a feature-detection system would be affected by the syntactic and semantic properties of the input signals. For these reasons, as well as those mentioned earlier, a more sophisticated speech perception mechanism must be assumed.

Analysis by Synthesis

An analysis-by-synthesis mechanism (Halle & Stevens, 1964) works by a trial-and-error procedure. When an acoustic signal is heard, the mechanism generates a SYNTHESIS or "replica" of what has been received. This synthesis represents the best guess, or first approximation, of the identity of the input signal. The synthesis then is compared with an encoded memory of the input signal. If the synthesis and the remembered input signal match, then the synthesis is accepted as an accurate interpretation of the input. If they do not match, another synthesis is generated. This process continues until a match is achieved (or, if no match can be generated, the input remains unrecognized). This kind of system could, in principle, handle the complexities that template-matching and feature-detection systems could not, including context-conditioned variation, parallel transmission of information, and the effects of syntactic and semantic expectations.

One form of this model is sketched in Figure 2.10, adapted from Stevens (1972). After some initial peripheral auditory analysis, the speech signal is stored in an auditory buffer or temporary memory store. At this stage,

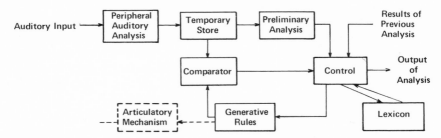

FIGURE 2.10   A diagram of an analysis-by-synthesis model of speech perception. (After Stevens, 1972, © 1972 by The Massachusetts Institute of Technology.)

most of the acoustic properties of the signal are retained. The signal is subjected to a preliminary phonetic analysis, which includes a direct analysis of those acoustic properties that are relatively invariant. Next, the control component produces (synthesizes) a phonetic sequence, using both the data from the preliminary analysis and information from preceding analyses. This information includes interpretations of the social and physical context, as well as expectancies about what might be coming next. Furthermore, the synthesized phonetic sequence conforms to the rules of English phonology. It is now compared (see *comparator* in Figure 2.10) with the signal held in the temporary memory store. If the synthesized sequence and the temporarily stored sequence match, the control transmits the message for higher-level processing, where full semantic interpretation will be conducted. If the synthesized and remembered sequences do not match, the process is repeated.

What is the representation used by the comparator? If it is in phonetic form, then some of the problems of template matching and feature detection would be problems here as well. To deal with this question, Stevens (1972) proposes that two procedures are used for phonetic identification. The first is a relatively direct analysis of the acoustic signal which extracts the simple speech sounds. For example, a direct analysis would be adequate for simple vowels because they are relatively context free and do not involve categorical perception (recall also that they do not show a right-ear advantage). Other phonetic properties of the signal could also be handled directly, provided that they were not subject to context-conditioned variation. The remaining phonetic segments would be analyzed by a second procedure, which involves the application of generative phonological rules. These rules apply to sequences larger than single phones, such as syllables. In this way, they could deal with both context-conditioned variation and parallel transmission.

In this model, the influence of semantic and syntactic expectancies would occur after the two levels of phonological analysis, but before the control produces a trial synthesis. Though the details of the process remain to be spelled out, a sophisticated analysis-by-synthesis model could, in principle, handle the data of speech perception. One variant of analysis-by-synthesis models has been elaborated in more detail than others—the motor theory of speech perception developed by Liberman and his associates at the Haskins Laboratories (Liberman, 1970; Liberman *et al.,* 1972; Studdert-Kennedy, 1974).

Referring back to Figure 2.10, note that the generative phonological rules lead directly to the articulatory mechanisms used for speech production. The synthesis produced by the control component is in a form that could produce an utterance, and this utterance would conform to the articulatory constraints of the speech production system. These articulatory constraints normalize the input to a standard form that can then be identified. The actual motor activities of speech production need not be involved, but the processes leading up to speaking are. We do not mimic a speaker overtly, nor need we engage in subvocal speech. The argument is this: the phonological rules and the articulatory organization of our vocal apparatus work together to generate a trial synthesis.

What is the advantage of this variant of an analysis-by-synthesis model? There are at least two advantages for identifying the articulatory system as a component of the speech decoder. First, it is easier to specify speech sounds in articulatory, rather than in acoustic, terms. Among these are those consonants that are heavily context dependent. Second, if the production system could serve the dual functions of speech production and perception, we would not have to develop a highly complex processing system just for the acoustic analysis of speech. All the available data tell us that a simple auditory analysis is inadequate for speech perception. A relatively simple solution is to use the already available articulatory system as a component of the special speech decoder. A separate acoustic system is, of course, possible, but it would be more efficient to use articulatory knowledge for speech perception.

Along with these advantages, a motor theory of speech perception does have some unresolved problems. For example, children apparently recognize and understand speech before they actually can produce it. The severity of this problem for such a motor theory is unclear, however, because we know very little about how much children can comprehend before they produce speech (Nelson, 1973). A second problem arises when we consider that we often can understand a foreign language before we can speak it with anything like accurate pronunciation. Whatever the contributions of the articulatory mechanisms might be, they must be more abstract than actual commands to the vocal apparatus. Finally, we have yet to specify how articulatory properties may be translated into acoustic form or how articulatory properties are abstracted from the acoustic signal. Until the necessary mechanisms are specified more fully, the motor theory cannot be assessed properly. The extent of our ignorance of speech perception is reflected in our inability to design and build a machine that can recognize speech, even though we have been able to build a machine to produce synthetic speech.

SUGGESTED READINGS

The book by R. W. Langacker, *Language and its structure* (New York: Harcourt, Brace and World, 1968), is an excellent introduction to the general field of linguistics. In addition, it provides a more extensive account of phonetics and phonological description than was given here.

The article by A. M. Liberman, F. S. Cooper, D. Shankweiler, and M. Studdert-Kennedy, "Perception of the speech code," *Psychological Review,* 1967, **74,** 431–461, provides a comprehensive summary of the technical literature on speech perception. The survey of this literature lead Liberman and his co-workers to develop the motor theory of speech perception. A. M. Liberman, in "The grammars of speech and language," *Cognitive Psychology,* 1970, **1,** 301–323, discusses the relation between speech processing and language processing in general.

K. N. Stevens, and A. S. House, "Speech perception," in J. V. Tobias (Ed.), *Foundations of modern auditory theory* (Vol. II. New York Academic Press, 1972, Pp. 1–62) and M. Studdert-Kennedy, "Speech perception," in N. J. Lass (Ed.), *Contemporary issues in experimental phonetics* (Springfield, Illinois: Charles C Thomas, 1974), both give sophisticated and current reviews of recent theory and research in speech perception.

3
Word Meanings and the Mental Dictionary

WORD MEANINGS

When we think of the concept of meaning, we usually think of word meanings. However, other units of language also "have" meaning. One of these meaningful units, the MORPHEME, is below the level of the word. A morpheme is the smallest meaningful unit in a language, and all words are composed of at least one morpheme. Such words as *black, blue,* and *berry* consist of one morpheme each. In these examples, the morpheme and the word are one and the same. These morphemes are called FREE MORPHEMES because they need not be combined with other morphemes—they can occur alone. They can also be combined with other morphemes to form other words, such as *blackberry* or *blueberry,* which are composed of two free morphemes each. The other type of morpheme is the BOUND MORPHEME. These cannot occur alone, but must be combined with other morphemes in order to form a word. The plural suffix *-s* is a bound morpheme that, when added to a noun (like *dog*), produces the plural form (*dogs*). Other examples of bound morphemes are *-ing,* as in *asking, -ed* as in *walked, un-* and *-ful* as in *uneventful.* All meaningful prefixes and suffixes are bound morphemes. Indeed, bound morphemes are meaningful precisely because they change one or more aspects of a word's meaning.

Units above the level of a word also "have" meaning. Among such units are phrases, clauses, sentences, and longer utterances. It could be argued that it is impossible to decide unequivocally what the meaning of a word is unless we have that word in context. Does the word *pen* refer to a writing instrument, a place to keep pigs, a prison, the action of writing, or the action of trapping animals in an enclosure? The word *pen* is by no means unusual in "having" so many meanings. Linguists differ in their estimates of the ambiguity of single isolated words, but all agree that ambiguity is the rule rather than the exception. For example, "J. J. Katz . . . has recently remarked that 'practically every word in a natural language is ambiguous.' It does appear to be the case that at least fifty percent of a reasonably adequate English lexicon is constituted of either homonymous or polysemous entries" (Ziff, 1967, p. 403). *Pen* (the writing instrument) and *pen* (the prison) are HOMONYMS—they are identical in sound, but they represent different meanings that are totally unrelated to one another. POLYSEMOUS simply means multiple meanings. Most of the words we use can be interpreted in more than one way, and if we include metaphorical usage, then virtually all words can be interpreted in more than one way. Any given word, in principle, can be assigned more than one meaning.

This problem is compounded when we consider that there are several aspects of word meaning. We shall consider four of these: referential, denotative, associative, and affective. Each of these refers to a different component of meaning, or a different aspect of a person's reaction to a word. We adopt the view that meaning refers to a set of interpretations generated by a listener (or reader) when a message is heard (or read). The set of possible meanings of any given word is the set of possible feelings, images, ideas, concepts, thoughts, and inferences that a person might produce when that word is heard and processed. This implies that word comprehension, like speech perception, is an active constructive process that is highly sensitive to both linguistic and social–physical contexts. The meaning of an utterance is the interpretation of that utterance by a listener in a given situation. The four aspects of word meanings referred to above are components of the interpretations generated by listeners (and, hopefully, intended by speakers). For simplicity we talk about these aspects of meaning as if they were properties of individual words. It should be kept in mind that we are really referring to people's interpretations of words in contexts. Words (or sentences) do not have meaning. It is the people who use them who have the meanings in mind—the speaker's intended meaning and the listener's interpreted meaning [for a related viewpoint, see Olson, (1970)].

Referential and Denotative Meaning

The REFERENTIAL MEANING of a word is the particular object, event, or relationship specified by that word. The referential meaning of the word *dog* is, in most contexts, a particular animal or a class of animals. Referential meaning is highly specific, and is heavily dependent upon context. What is being referred to by any particular word can never be determined unless the context is known. Consider the sentence

(1a)   Washington was President.

In this sentence the word *Washington* refers to a particular man. The word *President* refers to that same man. Therefore, the referential meanings of these two words are identical in this context.

The DENOTATIVE MEANING of a word is the generic idea or concept represented by that word. Consider the denotative meanings of the two words *Washington* and *President*. They are quite different from one another, and this difference is revealed when we try to substitute one for the other in sentence (1a). If we did so, we would have

(1b)   Washington was Washington.

(1c)   President was President.

(1d)   President was Washington.

None of these sentences makes any sense because we no longer are expressing interpretable relationships between concepts or referents, and so it is unclear what we are referring to. The denotative meanings are more general in that they remain more constant across a variety of sentence or utterance contexts.

Whereas the referential meaning of a word (or phrase or sentence) is the particular thing we are talking about, the denotative meaning of a word is the concept represented by that word. The denotative meaning of the word *dog* includes our knowledge that a dog is an animal, it is domesticated, has fur, barks, and so on. This meaning can be described in two different but equivalent ways. We can specify the relation of a word with other words, or we can specify its relevant semantic features or attributes.

Words can be denotatively related to one another by a classification system that illustrates the relations among the concepts represented by those words. A classification system is illustrated in Figure 3.1 that includes the word (concept) *dog*. This classification is by no means complete, but the concept represented by the word *dog* includes all the information illustrated in the diagram, and more. Omitted from the diagram is the information that dogs are four legged, have paws rather than hooves, sometimes wag their tails, often chase cars and bicycles, can be housebroken, and come in many shapes, colors, and sizes. All of these facts about dogs are represented by the word *dog*.

An equivalent way of describing the concept *dog* is to list the semantic features or attributes that distinguish the concept from all other concepts in the language. Semantic features are "the means by which we can decompose the meaning of one sense of a lexical item into its atomic concepts, and thus exhibit the semantic structure *in* a dictionary entry and the semantic relations *between* dictionary entries" (Katz & Fodor, 1963, pp.

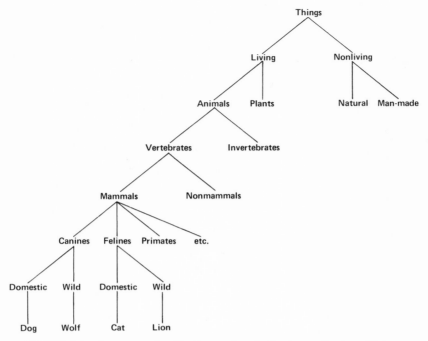

FIGURE 3.1   A concept classification system in the form of a tree diagram.

TABLE 3.1
A Concept Classification System in the Form of a
Semantic Features Table[a]

Features	Concepts						
	Dog	Wolf	Cat	Fish	Snail	Rose	Rock
Living	+	+	+	+	+	+	–
Animal	+	+	+	+	+	–	0
Vertebrate	+	+	+	+	–	0	0
Mammal	+	+	+	–	0	0	0
Canine	+	+	–	0	0	0	0
Domestic	+	–	+	–	–	±	0

[a] A plus sign (+) indicates that a concept is described by that feature; a minus sign (–) indicates that it is not; a zero (0) indicates that the feature is not relevant.

185–186). Semantic features are analogous to phonological distinctive features in that they function as atoms of meaning that distinguish words, just as phonological distinctive features are the characteristics that distinguish phonemes. In principle, the denotative meaning of a word could be specified by listing a set of distinctive features for that word. This list would include all those features that differentiate one word from all others. For example, the words *man* and *woman* would share all their defining semantic features except one. Both have the features *animate, human, adult,* but they differ on the feature of *sex*. Table 3.1 is a distinctive feature classification that includes the concept *dog,* and it is formally equivalent to the tree diagram in Figure 3.1. Both methods of representing the word *dog* allow us to assess the similarity of a concept to other concepts. *Wolf* and *dog* are more similar to one another than are *dog* and *snail,* and this is reflected in the number of shared features. *Wolf* and *dog* are alike on five of the six features listed, whereas *snail* and *dog* are alike on only two features. The number of shared features corresponds roughly to our intuitive judgments of the similarities among concepts.

Most of us would agree that neither Table 3.1 nor Figure 3.1 does full justice to the denotative meanings of the words listed. Nevertheless, a semantic feature analysis is an improvement over the entries we find in dictionaries. Katz and Fodor (1963), in an influential paper, "The Structure of a Semantic Theory," argue that the distinctive-feature approach is essential to any adequate theory of semantics (see also Katz, 1967, 1972). They propose that a semantic theory must be able to describe three things: the dictionary, semantic rules, and semantic interpretations. Semantic rules and semantic interpretations are involved in deriving the meanings of sentences, once we have at least partially interpreted the meanings of individual words. We consider these aspects of semantic processing in Chapter 4. The dictionary component of a semantic theory has to do with individual words. For each word in our language we have an entry in our mental dictionaries that is quite unlike the kinds of entries we find in ordinary printed dictionaries. Contrast the typical dictionary entry for the word *bachelor* with a semantic feature representation (Figure 3.2). Katz and Fodor argue that an adequate semantic theory must have entries in the form illustrated by the tree graph in Figure 3.2. Is this also the appropriate form for the entries in our mental dictionary? Is this the way concepts are represented in our minds?

A semantic feature entry provides more information about the word (or words) represented by the string of letters, *bachelor,* than does the dictionary entry. It tells us which features are shared by which senses or interpretations of the word, for example, *human* versus *animal* or *male* versus *unspecified*. The semantic feature representation also tells us something about the relationships among the set of words we might mean when we

Dictionary Entry

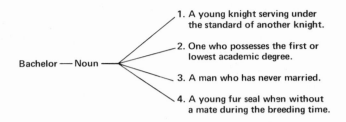

Bachelor — Noun

1. A young knight serving under the standard of another knight.

2. One who possesses the first or lowest academic degree.

3. A man who has never married.

4. A young fur seal when without a mate during the breeding time.

Semantic Feature Representation
(Tree Diagram)

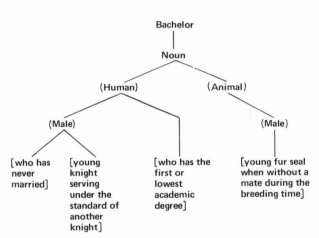

FIGURE 3.2 A dictionary entry for *bachelor* contrasted with a tree graph, each listing four possible meanings. (After Katz & Fodor, 1963.)

say or write *bachelor*. An ordinary dictionary entry does not do so. We thus can conclude that one type of dictionary entry is better for some purposes than another type of dictionary entry. In *Roget's Thesaurus* words are classified according to topic; in rhyming dictionaries words are classified according to their sounds. Both are better than other types of dictionaries for their specialized purposes. None of these is intended to be a model of the psychological processes involved in speaking or listening, or the ways that words are organized in our mental dictionary. Our subjective organization of concepts (and the words we use to represent those concepts) may or may not be analogous to any particular dictionary system.

Katz and Fodor's analysis of the word(s) *bachelor* provides an excellent case in point. Theoretically, *bachelor* in the sense of a degree holder and *bachelor* in the sense of an unmarried male are related to one another in a particular way (see Figure 3.2). Both are subordinates of the super-ordinate category *human*. Psychologically, these two senses of *bachelor* may be no more related to one another than *pen* (writing instrument) and *pen* (enclosure for pigs) are related to on another. They might be two entirely different words that happen to be spelled and pronounced in exactly the same ways.

There is another danger in interpreting a particular kind of dictionary entry as a model for mental structures. We have already suggested that the relations among particular entries in the dictionary might not reflect the psychological relations among those items or entries. We should also consider the likelihood that the form of the relationships among words or concepts might vary, depending on the semantic domains involved (Fillenbaum & Rapoport, 1971). A semantic feature analysis suggests that words and concepts are organized hierarchically. We shall see that some sets of words are organized in this way, but that others are not.

These considerations leave us with three unsolved problems for a seman-tic feature analysis of denotative meaning.[1] First, the particular classifica-tion schemes and the lists of relevant features are chosen more or less arbitrarily. Why use the distinction *living–nonliving* instead of *organic–inor-ganic*? Why isn't the contrast between *short* and *tall* just as important? How are we to decide which feature contrasts are relevant and which are not? Referring back to our feature table and tree diagram, how are we to judge the relative similarities of *dog, cat,* and *wolf?* Many people would say that *dog* and *cat* are more similar to one another than *dog* and *wolf,* but our diagram and feature table do not reflect this. One reason may be that we have selected an inappropriate set of distinctive features. Had we chosen a different set, then *cat* and *dog* could be defined as more similar to one another than *wolf* and *dog.* For example, if there were a feature like *household pet,* a shared feature could be added to the pair *dog–cat.* Unfortunately, we have no firm criteria for deciding which feature contrasts are necessary. We do not even know whether any finite set of features can be chosen so that they reflect universal properties of semantic systems.

A second unsolved problem of distinctive feature systems has to do with the relative importance of features. We have assumed that all those features that are included are equally important. However, if we could assign differ-ential weights to selected features, then we could weigh the feature *domes-tic* more heavily than *canine* in Table 3.1, and so have *cat–dog* as more similar than *wolf–dog.* No doubt, it is possible to assign differential weights to selected features, but there are no *a priori* grounds for doing so. We could argue that in one context, say in talking about animals that amuse

[1] These problems of semantic feature analyses are discussed in detail by Bolinger (1965), who also deals with purely linguistic considerations.

children, a *pet* feature is relevant and should be weighted heavily. In another context, say in talking about evolutionary processes in biology, the
feline–canine contrast is more relevant, and therefore should be weighted
more heavily. Aside from these quite general considerations, we have no
rules or guidelines for either selecting or weighting features, and certainly
no criteria for deciding upon any universal, context-free set of distinctive
semantic features, weighted or unweighted.

Finally, we must consider the problem of organization and dimension-
ality. This problem cannot be solved by alternative feature-selection or
feature-weighting systems. A distinctive feature system is inherently two
dimensional, and is also likely to be hierarchical (see Figure 3.1 and Table
3.1). For some sets of words, three or more dimensions may be necessary
to describe their denotative meanings. The words in the American English
kinship system, for example, are better represented by a three-dimensional
system than a two-dimensional one (see Figure 3.3). The three relevant
dimensions are sex, generation, and linearity of relation with respect to
self. This type of classification scheme is called a COMPONENTIAL ANALYSIS.
The relative importance of dimensions is still a problem, even though the
dimensions do seem to capture our intuitions about family relations. According to the diagram (Figure 3.3), *father* is to *mother* as *son* is to *daughter*. This implies that the psychological distance between *father* and *mother*
is equal to the distance between *son* and *daughter*. This is not the way

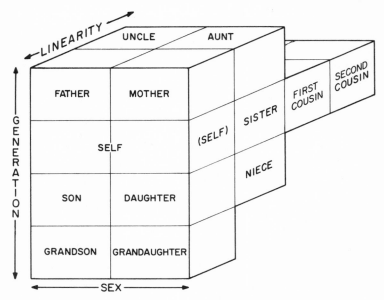

FIGURE 3.3 A partial three-dimensional model of the American kinship system.
Where would *grandfather* be placed? Where is *brother*?

most people feel. People judge the concepts *father* and *mother* as psychologically closer to one another than the concepts *son* and *daughter* (Romney & D'Andrade, 1964). Simply adding dimensions to a classification scheme can be useful, but it does not solve the other problems we have in describing denotative meaning.

If words are organized in different ways depending upon the particular semantic domain involved, then no single graphic or representational scheme could be adequate as a general or universal descriptive system. As we shall see later, different sets of nouns (for example, those that refer to parts of the body, color adjectives, and emotion names) are subjectively organized in quite different ways (Fillenbaum & Rapoport, 1971). Even if we ignore the influence of social and physical contexts, we need more than one kind of system to deal with denotative meanings. We also need to understand at least two other kinds of word meaning—associative and connotative meaning.

Associative Meaning

What is the first word that comes to mind when you hear the word *table?* Most people would say *chair*. Others might say *food, desk, cloth, breakfast,* or *floor*. The associative meaning of the concept represented by the stimulus word (for example, *table*) is "the sum total of all the things a given person thinks of" when he hears the word (Deese, 1970, p. 109). This kind of meaning—the pattern of responses to a word—is somewhat similar to denotative meaning, but is far less systematic. The denotative meaning of *paper* does not include the concept *pencil,* yet we often think of the word *pencil* when we hear the word *paper* in isolation, as in a free-word association test. One reason for associating *paper* and *pencil* is that the two words often occur together, as in *paper-and-pencil* test. Another is that the two objects represented by these words tend to go together in our experience. Returning to our problems with cats, dogs, and wolves, perhaps we feel that *cat* and *dog* are more similar to one another than *wolf* and *dog* because the former pair are more closely related to one another in our everyday lives. Our intuitive judgments of similarities might well be based in part upon such associative relationships.

How do associations between words develop? Two ways have already been suggested. Some words cooccur frequently in language usage: *pro* and *con; red, white,* and *blue; ham* and *eggs; liberty* and *justice; coffee, tea,* or *milk.* Other words may refer to things that tend to cooccur in our experience: *ham* and *eggs; paper* and *pencil; wine* and *cheese; table* and *chair; gas* and *oil; cigarette* and *smoke.* A third category of common associates consists of antonyms, words that are opposites of one another:

good–bad, black–white, fast–slow, left–right, up–down. A fourth category involves common word sequences, with the response word intuitively completing an incomplete unit: *ding-dong, national debt, cough drops.*

These four kinds of word associations are direct. When you hear one word, you think of the other. Associative relations between words can also be indirect. *Woman* and *lady* are similar in denotative meaning, and in associative meaning as well, even though neither word makes you think directly of the other. *Woman* is not a common associate to *lady,* and *lady* is not a common associate to *woman.* What they have in common is a similar set of associations. When *lady* is used as a stimulus word, we get a set of responses that overlap considerably with the responses we get for *woman.* For example, either word might elicit *man.* In much the same way that we could estimate similarity of denotative meaning by the number of shared distinctive features, we can estimate similarity of associative meaning by the extent of associative overlap—the number of associations two words have in common (Deese, 1962, 1965). *Moth* and *butterfly* are similar in denotative meaning. They are also similar in associative meaning, as revealed by the set of associations common to both words, for example, *fly, insect,* and *wings.* In contrast, *dog* and *canine* are quite similar in denotative meaning, but very different in associative meaning. *Canine* and *dog* do not elicit similar sets of word-association responses.

These different kinds of associative relations are only a sample of those that can be identified. Since there are so many categories of associative relations, it is likely that the word-association process or mechanism is not one but several alternative processes. Consider what we must do when we take a word-association test. The stimulus word is given in isolation. Since virtually any word uttered out of context is ambiguous, the word may be interpreted in any one of several different ways. If the stimulus word is *table,* it could be understood as *table₁* (a four-legged piece of furniture), *table₂* (a graphic display of numbers), or *table₃* (the action of postponing a decision on a motion in a debate). This very first stage of producing word associations involves variability.

After the word has been interpreted in one particular way, then any one of a number of associative operations may be performed. Clark (1970) lists a number of possible ways in which an associative response may be selected. Each of these is characterized by a rule which uses semantic features to select a particular type of association. Take antonymous responses, for example: if a word has a common antonym, then people will select that antonym more often than any other word in a word-association task. This can be accomplished by an associative mechanism which selects a response word which contrasts minimally with the stimulus word. Clark calls this mechanism the "minimal contrast rule." Ideally, the stimulus word and the response word differ on one and only one semantic feature. The pairs *long* and *short, good* and *bad, man* and *woman* all have this property. Furthermore, Clark and others argue that the list of features for any particular word is ordered, and the last feature in the list is changed to its opposite. This accounts for the preference to respond to *man* with *woman,* rather than with *boy.* The feature *sex* is lower on the list than is the feature *age.*

It should be clear from our discussion of the problem of distinctive feature systems in general that associative rules based upon feature contrasts (or feature-deletion and preservation rules) pose the same kinds of problems. Which feature lists should we assign to any given word? What is the basis for ordering the features in any particular way? Some linguists argue that features can be ordered nonarbitrarily (see Bierwisch, 1967, 1970); others argue that semantic feature systems are inadequate to begin with (Weinreich, 1966).

Whether these issues can be resolved in the future or not, Clark's approach to the mechanisms underlying associations represents a valuable departure from the traditional view. It had long been supposed that associations were fundamental units of mental organization, and out of our associative knowledge grew our knowledge of language. Clark (1970; see also McNeill, 1966b; Clifton, 1967) takes the opposite viewpoint. We could not display the associative repertoires we do unless we already have a well-developed semantic and syntactic system. The mechanisms underlying language production and comprehension are the same ones that we use to produce associations, and those mechanisms do not arise out of associative learning (see Chapter 5). We would add one comment to this general view. Our knowledge of the world underlies much of our capability to use language, and this knowledge of the world must, in turn, influence our selection of associative responses. Word associations are undoubtedly produced by mental operations that depend upon both knowledge of the language and knowledge of the world. This interaction between language and cognition—between linguistic competence and knowledge of people and things in the experiential world—will concern us throughout our discussion of language, communication, and thinking.

With respect to the acquisition of associations, it is still not clear whether the patterns of associations people display reflect their language competence or their knowledge of the world. We know that word-association patterns among adults are quite homogeneous and predictable (Entwisle, Forsyth, & Muuss, 1964). We also know that young children's associations differ systematically from those of adults in at least two ways. First, children's word associations are far less homogeneous than are adults'. Perhaps children's early experiences vary widely, whereas most adults have gone through fairly similar educational experiences and have had enough time to experience a common set of situations. This alone would make adults resemble one another more than children resemble one another. Another possibility is that most adults who have been tested are college students, and so are a highly restricted and relatively uniform segment of the adult population. Children, in contrast, are usually tested in public school settings, and thus are a more representative and diverse sample of the population. Until these two possibilities are ruled out, we cannot evaluate the more interesting possibilities concerning the relation between conceptual and linguistic development on the one hand, and homogeneity of associative patterns on the other.

A second difference between adult and child word-association patterns is that children tend to give relatively more syntagmatic responses than do adults. A SYNTAGMATIC RESPONSE to a stimulus word is a word that would follow it in normal speech (for example, *run–fast, red–ball*). Adults tend to give PARADIGMATIC RESPONSES. These are response words that belong to the same form class as the stimulus word. If the stimulus word is a noun, then the response word is a noun; if the stimulus word is an adjective, then the response word is an adjective (for example, *table–chair, red–yellow*). Do these changes with age and experience reflect a shift in ways of thinking, a deeper mastery of the language, or both? The pitiful amount of evidence on this point is equivocal. In one study, adults learned a miniature artificial language in which certain nonsense syllables always occurred in either noun or verb positions in a variety of real sentences (Glucksberg & Cohen, 1965). Even these newly learned words elicited paradigmatic responses, provided that the people in the test were adults, and that the newly learned words were "plugged into" a well-learned language. It is still not clear why the syntagmatic-to-paradigmatic shift should occur at all. Presumably, a categorical form of organization represents a higher level of knowledge than a sequential form.

We now turn to a component of meaning that is partly associative, but involves responses to words that are not other words, but feelings and emotions instead.

Affective Meaning

Is a tree good or bad? Is a rock active or passive? Is music strong or weak? These questions, odd though they may seem, tap the emotional or affective quality of the words representing these concepts. How we feel about a concept is the AFFECTIVE or CONNOTATIVE MEANING of the words denoting that concept. Affective meaning can be measured by the Semantic Differential, a measurement technique developed by Osgood, Suci, and Tannenbaum (1957). The semantic differential consists of a set of rating scales, each composed of a pair of bipolar adjectives (adjectives that are opposite in meaning, as in Figure 3.4). A word representing a concept, like *music,* is listed at the top, and a person rates that concept on each of the scales listed on the page. The other pages of the semantic differential have the same rating scales, but different concepts are rated. The concept *music* might be rated as smooth rather than rough, good rather than bad, and relaxed rather than tense. The concept *dictator* might be rated as bad, tense, and rough. If a concept is rated as good, then it probably will also be rated as smooth. Because ratings on some scales tend to correspond to ratings on other scales (that is, they are correlated), Osgood and his colleagues were able (using factor analytic techniques) to condense the various scales to just three summary scales. These three summary scales are the *good–bad* scale, the *active–passive* scale, and the *strong–weak* scale. Each of these adjective pairs is the best exemplar of one of the three major dimensions of affective meaning: EVALUATION, ACTIVITY, and POTENCY. Since the rating of a concept on any one of these three dimensions is not necessarily related to its rating on either of the other two dimensions, the dimensions are theoretically independent. We can have a concept like *mosquito,* which might be rated as bad, active, and weak; or a concept like *honeybee,* which might be rated as good, active, and weak. Any combinations of evaluation, activity, and potency ratings are possible.

How general are these three dimensions of affective meaning? The semantic differential has been tested in many different cultures with many different languages, including American, English, Dutch, French, Finnish, and Japanese. The three major dimensions of affective meaning appear in every culture examined thus far, suggesting that these three dimensions are universal. All people seem to react emotionally in the same general ways. This is not to say that specific concepts are rated in the same ways.

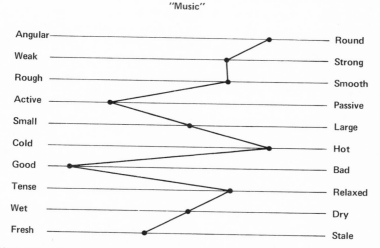

FIGURE 3.4 How one person rated the concept "music" on the Semantic Differential. How would you rate "music" on these scales?

We might rate the concept of *American* as good, active, and strong; others might rate the same concept as bad, active, and strong, depending upon the political and economic circumstances of the times. Both groups of people are still using the same three criteria represented by the three dimensions. The universality of the semantic differential is not in the particular concept ratings, but in the three implicit criteria we all seem to use.

These criteria and their corresponding dimensions are quite general and appropriate when concepts are judged out of context. When concepts are embedded in specific social and linguistic contexts, then other dimensions or criteria come to the surface. One context in which evaluative meaning is especially important is in the area of personality-trait adjectives. Here, several evaluative criteria emerge. One way to find out what criteria people use to judge specific trait adjectives is to construct a semantic map which represents the closeness or similarity among words. People can be asked to judge how often two traits occur together in a single individual, and we then can use this to estimate the "distance" between words. Such a map, derived from a group of college freshmen, is shown in Figure 3.5 (Friendly & Glucksberg, 1970). Because these words were judged in a specified context, the three general dimensions did not appear here. Instead, the freshmen used two evaluative dimensions rather than one general good–bad scale. These two good–bad scales reflect a social evaluation and an academic–intellectual evaluation, respectively.

The position of a word on this map tells us something about its affective meaning. For example, the word *wonk* was denotatively defined as "an introverted student who studies all the time; generally considered to be physically unattractive" (see Table 3.2). The map adds information to this definition by telling us something about its affective meaning. The concept (trait) represented by the word is considered to be low on both social and academic scales, at least in the eyes of college freshmen in 1968. A map of these same words derived from the judgments of college seniors indicates that some affective meanings had shifted. The word *wonk* in Figure 3.6 is still low on the social evaluation scale, but is now high on the academic–intellectual scale. This position is more in line with its denotative definition given by college seniors. The word *practical* has also moved up on the evaluation scale for seniors, but *imaginative* and *intelligent* are far less "good" than they had appeared to freshmen. Is this a realistic shift in perceptions?

THE MENTAL DICTIONARY

Words can be characterized in various ways—acoustically, denotatively, associatively, and affectively, among others. Which of these aspects of words do we use in constructing, organizing, and using our vocabulary—

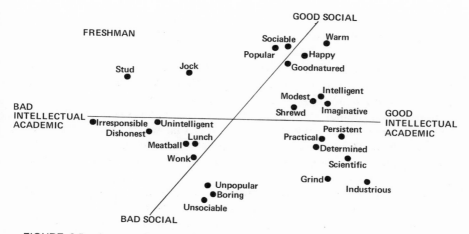

FIGURE 3.5 A semantic map of college-related words obtained from college fresh-men. The relative position of a word on either of the two scales is estimated by drawing a line from the word perpendicular to the scales.

TABLE 3.2
Lexicon of Some College Words

Word	Denotative meaning
Wonk	An introverted student who studies all the time; generally considered to be physically unattractive
Stud	A good-looking student who is successful with women; cool and detached
Lunch	A graceless, socially unattractive student
Meatball	Same as *lunch,* only more physically and intellectually unattractive
Grind	A student who studies diligently for long periods of time; a periodic *wonk*
Jock	An athlete

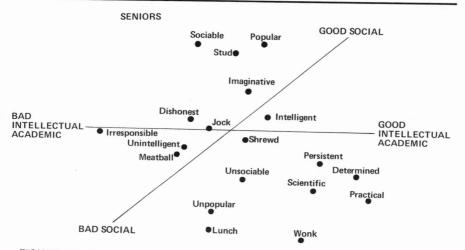

FIGURE 3.6 Semantic map obtained from college seniors. How does this differ from the map obtained from freshmen in Figure 3.5?

63

our mental dictionary? An ordinary dictionary organizes words alphabetically, and if we know its spelling, we can find a word by looking for it in the appropriate location. The words we know are part of our mental dictionary—sometimes called the SUBJECTIVE LEXICON—and they too must be stored and organized in such a way that we can find them when we need them. Furthermore, we must be able to find them very quickly, for every time we speak or listen to someone we must have immediate access to the words.

What is in the lexicon, how is the lexicon organized, and how do we go about finding items that are stored there? Are words stored in hierarchical fashion as represented in Figure 3.1, or are they stored in some semantic space with one, two, three, or more dimensions, as in Figures 3.3, 3.5, and 3.6? One way to begin answering questions like these is to find out what people do and do not remember about words in various kinds of situations.

Episodic Memory

Most memory tasks used in the laboratory call for EPISODIC MEMORY—memory for what occurred, when and where: "Episodic memory receives and stores information about temporally dated episodes or events and temporal–spatial relations among these events" (Tulving, 1972, p. 385). If you are asked to remember a list of words verbatim, then you must try to remember the precise identity of each word, and this includes its sound. Synonyms or closely related words just will not do. Episodic memory tasks generally lead people to encode words in acoustic–articulatory formats for just this reason. People tend to make errors that sound like the original to-be-remembered items (Conrad, 1964). This indicates that when the original items had been presented, their acoustic–articulatory properties had been attended to, encoded, and stored in memory. If *goat* were one of the original items, then *coat* or *boat* would be a more likely confusion error than *cow* or *sheep*. If the letter *E* were to be remembered, then *G*, *C*, or *D* would be more likely errors than *H* or *F*, even though these latter two letters look like *E*. This happens when the original presentation is either auditory or visual. Even when people read the items and do not hear them, the sounds of the items, not their visual appearance, are remembered and are potential sources of confusion. The preferred mode of encoding a short list of unrelated items seems to be auditory rather than semantic or visual (Conrad, 1964).

Do all episodic memory tasks foster this kind of encoding strategy? The answer is "no" because people can remember any or all aspects of words if required to do so. Along with every word in our mental dictionary are the following: how the word sounds, how it is to be articulated (spoken), its denotative, associative, referential meanings, and its relationships to other words on each of these dimensions. Despite this, we often remember some aspects of words and forget others. One of the earliest studies to deal with this general issue was reported in 1939 by Gregory Razran. Razran used a classical conditioning technique to train people to salivate when they read a particular word, for example, *freeze*. Later, two test words were presented. One of the test words looked and sounded like the original training word (*frieze*); the other was similar in denotative meaning (*chill*). If people had been conditioned to the sight and sound of the original word *freeze*, then they should have generalized that conditioning to the sight and sound of the word *frieze* and thus should salivate to that word. On the other hand, if they had been conditioned to the meaning of *freeze*, then they should have responded to *chill* rather than to *frieze*. It turned out that the responses to *chill* were much more frequent and stronger than the responses to *frieze*, indicating that even in a simple conditioning situation, where words are experienced in isolation, people tend to remember the meaning of a word rather than its appearance or sound (Razran, 1939). The meaning of the word had been conditioned, not its physical attributes.

Razran conditioned the denotative meanings of words; the connotative or affective meanings of words and sentences can also be conditioned. Razran (1961) reported a Russian experiment in which a thirteen-year-old boy was conditioned to salivate to the word *khorosho* (which means *well* or *good*) and to inhibit salivation to the word *plokho* (*poorly, bad*). The boy was then tested on various words and sentences. If he had been conditioned to the affective meaning of *good*, then he should salivate to words and sentences that are "good" and inhibit salivation to words and sentences that are "bad." This is what happened (see Table 3.3). He salivated to "good" messages expressed by sentences like *The Soviet army was victorious,* and he salivated much less to "bad" news expressed by sentences like *Fascists destroyed many cities.*

These particular findings have yet to be replicated here, but similar results are obtained when simple memory tasks are used. Fillenbaum (1969) gave a list of 200 words to college students. They were asked to say "old" when any word appeared that had already been presented, and "new" whenever a word appeared for the first time. Some of the new words on the list were semantically related to words that had appeared earlier. For example, if *man* had appeared early in the list, then *male* or *woman* might appear later. Would people tend to think that *male* or *woman* was "old"? Similar words (like *male*) and antonyms (like *woman*) led to confusions. People often said "old" even though these words were new. Here, as in the conditioning experiments reported by Razran, the meanings of words were remembered far better than their visual or auditory characteristics.

TABLE 3.3
Some Responses of a Young Man Who Was
Conditioned to Salivate to the Word *Khorosho* (*Well,
Good*) and to Inhibit Salivation to the Word
Plokho (*Poorly, Bad*)[a]

Test word or sentence	Response[b]
Good	9
Bad	2
The Soviet army was victorious.	23
The pupil was fresh to the teacher.	0
The pupil failed to take the examination.	2
The pupil passed the examination with a mediocre grade.	10
The pupil studies excellently.	14
My friend is seriously ill.	2
The Fascists destroyed many cities.	2
The pioneer helps his comrade.	23

[a] After Razran (1961, p. 101). Copyright 1961 by the American Psychological Association. Reprinted by permission.
[b] Drops of saliva per 30 seconds.

Indeed, the people in Fillenbaum's experiment tended to forget what the "old" words had sounded or looked like, but did remember what they had meant.

This does not mean that we do not remember what a word sounds like or looks like in print. We must remember what words sound like and what they look like in print; otherwise, we would not "know" the word and could not extract its meaning when we hear or see it. In one common episodic memory task, three or four items are presented (J. Brown, 1958; Peterson & Peterson, 1959). Immediately following this presentation the person counts backwards by threes for three to twenty seconds, starting with a randomly chosen two-digit number. This counting activity can effectively prevent rehearsal or any other mnemonic strategy. At the end of a designated retention interval, say 20 seconds, the original items are to be recalled, in correct order. In this kind of task people usually perform very well on the first trial, then performance deteriorates after two or three more trials, dropping from 90% correct on trial 1 to about 35% correct on trial 3 (Keppel & Underwood, 1962). This deterioration in performance can be attributed to PROACTIVE INHIBITION (PI), the interference from prior items on recall of later items. This interfering effect of PI can be eliminated, however, if different kinds of items are used on a later trial. For example, if people are asked to remember letters on trials 1 through 4, their performance on trial 4 is relatively poor. If, however, numbers are used instead of letters on trial 4, then memory performance improves markedly. This effect of changing the material to be remembered resulting in improved performance is called RELEASE FROM PI (Wickens, Born, & Allen, 1963).

What kinds of changes are effective in releasing the effects of PI? Presumably, only those changes which are relevant to the ways in which people ordinarily code the material for memory. Thus, we can use release from PI to infer how people do code material for memory in this task. Some changes are effective, and some are not [see Wickens (1970, 1972, 1973) for summaries of the extensive literature in this area]. When we change semantic categories, we invariably get release from PI. For example, shifts from words to numbers, from masculine words to feminine words, from one category of things (like foods) to another (like articles of clothing), and even from good things to bad things (as rated on the semantic differential) produce some release from PI. This indicates that people do code semantic information in this kind of memory task. In contrast, shifts from one syntactic category to another generally do not have any effects. For example, shifting from verbs to nouns or from singular nouns to plural nouns does not produce release from PI, indicating that people to not usually code syntactic information when they try to remember short lists of isolated words.

However, when people listen to material like prose passages, then their episodic memory performance reveals that they remember meaning far more than they do individual words or sentences (Sachs, 1967). We generally remember the gist of what we read or hear, not the particular words or sentences. Episodic memory, then, is not limited to particular aspects of words or utterances. It simply refers to what we ask people to do—remember what was said at a particular time.

Semantic Memory

SEMANTIC MEMORY is "a mental thesaurus, organized knowledge a person possesses about words and other verbal symbols, their meanings and referents, about relations among them, and about rules . . . for the manipulation of these symbols, concepts, and relations" (Tulving, 1972, p. 386). There are two major questions to be asked about semantic memory:

1. What are the characteristics of our mental representations of words?
2. How are those mental representations organized and related to one another?

The first of these questions was addressed by Brown and McNeill (1966) in an ingenious study of the tip-of-the-tongue phenomenon. How often have you tried to remember a person's name or think of a word that you are sure you know, but just cannot remember? The name or the word is right on the tip of your tongue. This happens at one time or another to most people. Words that sound like the word we are struggling for may come to mind, as well as words that are close in meaning, but not the target word. We may even be able to identify the first letter of the elusive word, but the word is still, at least for the moment, just out of grasp. Brown and McNeill brought this familiar experience into the laboratory by deliberately inducing tip-of-the-tongue states. They gave people dictionary definitions of relatively infrequent words. For example, what is "a navigational instrument used in measuring angular distances, especially the altitude of sun, moon, and stars at sea"? People who felt that they knew the word but could not remember it were usually in a tip-of-the-tongue state. For this word, nine of fifty-six people tested found themselves in this irritating state. These nine people were asked questions about this word they felt they knew but could not remember. The questions were designed to reveal what aspects of the "lost" word they could remember.

Some general semantic properties of the word were available and accessible to them. They knew that words like *astrolabe, compass, dividers,* and *protractor* were conceptually related to the known but momentarily lost target word. This is not surprising if we consider that they do have a definition that is related to these words. They also knew that words like *secant, sexton,* and *sextet* sounded like the target word. They could even judge that *secant* sounded less like the target word than did *sexton* and still not recall the target itself. This sort of information could not be supplied by the definition, and neither could information about orthographic (visual) properties of the target word, yet people could often remember that the word started with the letter S and/or ended with a T without remembering what the middle letters were. All these fragmentary properties of the target word, *sextant,* could be recognized or remembered even though the word itself eluded conscious recall. Similar results occurred with other definitions and target words. Most people found themselves in a tip-of-the-tongue state on one occasion or another, and could usually report partial semantic, auditory–articulatory, and visual properties of the word that was on the tip of the tongue.

This elegant demonstration shows that multiple features of words are stored in memory and that they may be differentially accessible. Every tip-of-the-tongue word is immediately recognizable, even though it cannot be recalled. Like an ordinary dictionary, our mental dictionary lists a number of properties for each entry. Among these properties are how a word is pronounced, what part of speech it is, and what other words it is related to. The ordinary printed dictionary is organized on an alphabetical basis. *April* and *apron* both start with letters A and P, and so they are entered close to one another. Words that sound alike (*know* and *no*) or words that are similar in meaning (*infant* and *baby*) are entered in different places. Are our mental dictionaries organized in this way? In part, they are. We can, if we are asked to do so, gain access to words in our mental dictionary via their spelling. Almost anyone who can read could recite a list of words beginning, say, with the letter B. Success at games like Scrabble also depends on alphabetic access, but, unlike a printed dictionary, we have other ways of finding the words in our vocabulary. For example, we can use acoustic organization to produce rhymes just as easily as we can use alphabetic information to produce words that start with a given letter of the alphabet.

Our most important organizing principles must be neither alphabetical nor acoustic, but semantic. We rarely are asked to list words starting with a given letter or words that rhyme. We are always finding words to express intended meanings when we speak, and finding the meanings of words when we listen to someone else speak. When we speak, we start with the meaning (what we intend to express), then find the appropriate words and finally put these words into articulatory formats (or orthographic if we are writing). When we listen (or read), we do the reverse. If we can find words on the basis of semantic properties, then words must be organized according to some set of semantic principles. Words could not just be randomly scattered throughout our minds like Sarah's (Premack's chimpanzee, see Chapter 1) assortment of plastic shapes.

How are the semantic properties of words organized in our mental dictionaries? Several answers to this question were implied by our discussion of the different kinds of "meaning." For example, the entries might be distributed in a space along the dimensions derived from the Osgood *et al.* (1957) semantic differential. This organization by itself is hardly adequate, however, since we express denotative meanings as well as affective meanings. Others, like Deese (1965), have suggested that the dictionary is like a network in which the nodes are words and the connecting paths are associations. This associative concept leaves the meaning of the nodes unanalyzed and represents only the relations. As we have seen, even these relations cannot be adequately classified. A third type of organization, based on a semantic feature analysis, has enjoyed popularity in recent years, primarily because two key concerns are embodied in a single concept. First, the entries of the dictionary are analyzable into component features. Hence, the contents of each entry can be specified. Second, the semantic features provide implicit connections to other entries. For example, if *dog* is marked with the feature *animate,* not only do we know a characteristic of dogs, but we also know that dogs are in the same class as other entries marked *animate,* such as *cat, cow, horse,* and *elephant.*

Closely related to the notion of semantic features is the hierarchical organization of entries. If *dog* is marked *animate,* then dog must be included in the class of animals. Since *animal* is marked *physical object,* animals are included in the class of physical objects along with *plants* and *minerals,* but not with *love, ideas,* and *education.* A hierarchical system of categories like this was proposed and tested by Collins and Quillian (1969). Their theory of the contents and organization of semantic memory was based on a computer-based system devised by Quillian (1967, 1969).

Each word in semantic memory is represented by a node in a network of connections among nodes. These connections are "pointers" to other words in memory. A representative portion of the system is illustrated in Figure 3.7. This system has some interesting characteristics. As the memory capacity of a computer is severely limited compared with people's memory capacities, the system was designed to minimize memory load by avoiding duplication of information. Two kinds of "pointers" are involved. One kind represents property relations. *Canary* is a member of the superset (the category) *bird,* and *bird* in turn is a member of the superset *animal.* Sentences that refer to these category relations—for example, *a canary is a bird*—are called SUPERSET SENTENCES. A canary also has certain properties. A canary is yellow, it can sing, it has wings, and it can fly. Sentences that represent this kind of information are called PROPERTY SENTENCES. Because of the storage space limitation, no information is stored in more than one location. Because of this, properties common to all birds are stored only with the superset (category name) *bird.* Thus, the facts that canaries can fly, have feathers, and have wings are not stored with *canary,* but are stored instead with *bird.* Similarly, the general properties of fishes are stored with *fish,* but not with *salmon.*

This economy of storage is bought at the cost of the time it must take to find information. Information is found by "traveling" through the system

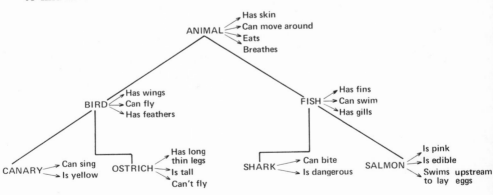

FIGURE 3.7   Illustration of the hypothetical memory structure for a three-level hierarchy. (After Collins & Quillian, 1969.)

along paths represented by the pointers. Assuming that it takes time to follow any pointer, moving from one node to another (say, from *canary* to *bird*) and moving from a node to a property stored at that node (say, from *canary* to *can sing*) takes time. If this is so, then the time needed to decide whether a sentence is true or false should depend on the number of steps required to find the relevant information. It is as if all questions about sentences are answered by traveling through the diagram in Figure 3.7 until one arrives at the place where the relevant information is stored.

Accordingly, there are three kinds of superset (*S*) sentences. All three refer to superset relations, but they vary in terms of the number of nodes one must travel through. A sentence like *A canary is a canary* can be verified without traveling at all, and this is referred to as an *S0* (*S*-zero) sentence. A sentence like *A canary is a bird* can be verified only by traveling from one node to another node one step away, and so this would be an *S1* sentence. Finally, a sentence like *A canary is an animal* involves traveling through two nodes—from *canary* to *bird* to *animal*—and this would be an *S2* sentence.

Property (*P*) sentences can also require different numbers of moves from node to node. *A canary can sing* is a *P0* sentence because the sentence can be verified without moving to a new node (see Figure 3.7). *A canary has wings* requires one move, so this is a *P1* sentence; *A canary has skin* is a *P2* sentence because it requires two moves between nodes.

Obviously, if one has to travel through the hierarchy along the paths laid down by the pointers in order to locate information, then the times taken to verify the various kinds of sentences should vary systematically. *S* sentences should be verified faster than *P* sentences; zero-node sentences should be faster than one-node sentences; and one-node sentences should be faster than two-node sentences.

Collins and Quillian tested these predictions by measuring the time taken to decide whether such sentences were true or false. Their results, shown in Figure 3.8, are consistent with a hierarchical organization of concepts and their properties. It takes longer to decide that a sentence like *A canary has skin* (*P2*) is true than a sentence like *A canary can fly* (*P1*), which in turn takes longer than *A canary can sing* (*P0*). Do these results mean that our memories, like that of a computer, are organized to minimize storage loads at the cost of extra retrieval operations? This might be the case, but why should it be so if our memories are not as limited as computer memories are? Might other mechanisms account for results like these?

Collins and Quillian assume that, in order to decide that the sentence *A canary can sing* is true, we need to contact the information stored in one location only. The property denoted by the words *can sing* is stored in the same place as the concept denoted by the word *canary*. In contrast, to decide that the sentence *A canary can fly* is true, we must make an

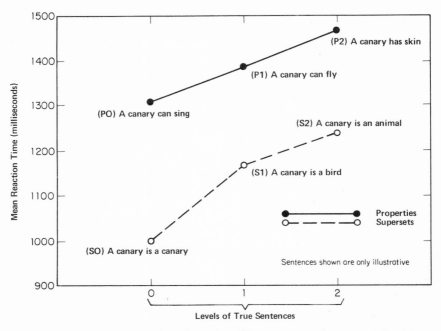

FIGURE 3.8   Average reaction times for different types of sentences in three experiments (the sentences shown are only illustrative). (After Collins & Quillian, 1969.)

inference, and the only way to do that is to consult information stored in two locations. A canary is a bird; a bird can fly; therefore, a canary can fly. Must this proposition, *a canary can fly,* be inferred every time the question is asked, or can it be directly "known" in the same way that *a canary can sing* is directly "known"? Surely, it must be possible to learn and remember that a canary can fly so that every time one hears the sentence, one does not have to search through the hierarchy in order to make the appropriate inference. One way might be to store useful information in strategic locations, even though such information would be duplicated. Perhaps it would be more economical to store the property *can fly* wherever it is useful—with *bird,* to be sure, but also with *canary, robin, eagle, hawk,* and with all other ordinary and familiar bird names.

A direct test of the economy of storage hypothesis was conducted by Conrad (1972). Conrad's reasoning parallels our argument for the utility of multiple storage locations for concept properties. If a concept (for example, *eagle*) and a property (for example, *can fly*) are frequently used together, then they should be stored together. This implies that sentences expressing familiar (relatively high frequency) properties like *a shark can move* should be processed faster than sentences expressing unfamiliar (low-frequency) properties like *a salmon has a mouth.* Each of these sentences is a *P2* sentence, so both would require equivalent inferences according to Collins and Quillian's model. Conrad repeated their experiment using high- and low-frequency sentences, and found no support for the notion of cognitive economy in semantic memory. When familiarity or frequency is controlled, the level of information required (number of nodes to be travelled through) had no effect on the time needed to decide that a sentence is true. Meyer (1970) makes the same point: ". . . at least two kinds of information about semantic categories, *names* of categories . . . and representations of their *attributes* [properties], are stored in memory and do not require 'computation' [inferences] [p. 243; bracketed terms and italics ours]." This should not be surprising. Perhaps, unlike computers, the human mind is constructed to facilitate fast processing at the expense of storage economy.

This revision of Collins and Quillian's model leaves the hierarchical organization intact. How general is this form of organization? Is semantic memory invariably hierarchical? Some classes of words, such as concrete nouns, do seem to be hierarchically organized. On the other hand, many semantic domains are not easily represented as hierarchies because the entries do not fall neatly into mutually inclusive subsets of one another. Consider abstract nouns. What are the superset categories for *love, idea,* or *education*? The supersets are not obvious, so these nouns cannot be easily organized. Even for those nouns that can be organized hierarchically, no more than four levels can be identified unequivocally. And then people may not necessarily agree with one another on what the "correct" arrangement of the hierarchy is for any given set of words, even when they might agree that there are discrepancies between objective and subjective realities. For example, it takes less time to decide that *a horse is an animal* than it does to decide that *a horse is a mammal* (Rips, Shoben, & Smith, 1973). In the subjective lexicon, this means that *animal* is closer to *horse* than *mammal* is. In a biological hierarchy, this cannot be so—*animal* is a superset that includes *mammal,* and *mammal* is a superset that includes *horse*. Hence, *mammal* must be closer to *horse* than *animal* is.

A third problem for any hierarchical model of semantic memory concerns the mechanisms for deciding that a sentence is false. How do we go about deciding that *a canary is a fish* is false? Do we travel through the hierarchy until we find a connection between *canary* and *fish* incompatible with the sentence? If so, then it should take longer to find an incompatible connection between two very different concepts (like *a canary is a tree*) than an incompatible connection between two more closely related concepts (*canary* and *fish*). That the opposite results would actually be obtained is suggested by experiments by Schaeffer and Wallace (1969, 1970), using a different but closely related procedure.

There are two ways to deal with these problems. One is to abandon the assumption that process and structure are interdependent. In principle, one could have a knowledge structure that is hierarchically organized along with memory search and decision procedures that do not follow the paths of the hierarchy. This system would help us to deal with the problem of how we decide that a sentence is false. For example, one could "hop" directly from one concept to another, and if the distance traveled exceeded some preset criterion, then the statement would be false. For example, a hop from *canary* to *tree* is a long one, so a *canary* is not a *tree;* the hop from *canary* to *fish* is shorter, but still too long, so a *canary* is not a *fish.* It takes longer to make a decision about the latter pair of concepts because the hop length is closer to the decision criterion.[2] The trouble with this kind of reasoning is that it could explain anything. Our measurements of decision times could not be used to make inferences about structure in any clear way. In fact, this system is functionally equivalent to one that is not hierarchical at all, but consists of associations determined ad hoc. This would seriously undermine contemporary research in memory and psycholinguistics because much of that research is based upon the assumption that process and structure are interdependent. How we go about retrieving information from memory is presumed to depend, at least in part, upon how that information is organized in our memory. Before abandoning this assumption we should consider a second and more likely alternative.

The second alternative is that different organizational principles are involved in different semantic domains. What might some of these principles be like? Fillenbaum and Rapoport (1971) have provided some answers to this question in a research monograph, *Structures in the Subjective Lexicon.* They constructed word lists from each of the following domains (sets): (1) color names; (2) kinship terms; (3) pronouns; (4) emotion names; (5) prepositions; (6) conjunctions; (7) verbs of the *have* family; (8) verbs of *judging;* and (9) *good–bad* terms. For each of these lists they asked people for a variety of similarity judgments among pairs of words within a domain.

Using these similarity judgments and a variety of analytic techniques, Fillenbaum and Rapoport found that words are organized in all kinds of ways: "the kinds of structures that may characterize a semantic domain can be quite various, and it must be obvious that the sorts of examples mentioned . . . viz., linear, cross-classificatory or paradigmatic structures,

---

[2] Smith, Shoben, and Rips (1974) attempt to resolve this issue by postulating two stages in deciding whether such sentences are true or false. The first stage involves a similarity judgment, and the less similar two concepts are, the easier it is to decide that a sentence is false. The second stage involves a comparison of defining features. By postulating one kind of structure and two kinds of mental operations on this structure they are able to handle much of the data on semantic memory.

nominal class structures, and taxonomic structures do not, even in combination, exhaust all the possibilities" (Fillenbaum & Rapoport, 1971, p. 239). They concluded that different semantic domains are structured differently.

The domain of color terms is best represented by a two-dimensional "map" that corresponds to the familiar color space (Figure 3.9). The color names are arranged very much like the colors themselves would be. The structure here is neither hierarchical nor taxonomic. It is two-dimensional. One dimension corresponds to hue; the other to saturation. Recall that kinship terms were also organized in *n*-dimensional terms, akin to the structure shown in Figure 3.3 (page 56). Fillenbaum and Rapoport obtained an organization for kinship terms quite similar to those suggested by componential analyses, with some minor differences in details.

Other semantic domains were best represented by a hierarchical organization. For example, prepositions could not be arranged in an interpretable space, but they could be organized into interpretable clusters or groups. For example, *behind, down, below,* and *under* formed one cluster, whereas *across, over, up,* and *on* formed another. Other semantic domains defied analysis. Emotion names could not be organized in any clear-cut way. Either we do not have a commonly shared interpersonal set of organizing principles for emotion names, or the analytic techniques tried thus

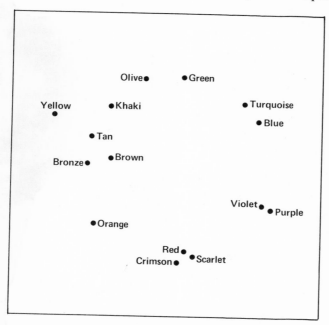

FIGURE 3.9 Organization of color names. (After Fillenbaum & Rapoport, 1971.)

far are inappropriate for discovering a common underlying structure for this semantic domain.

We are faced again with the question: Do findings and analyses like these reflect the organization of word meanings, or do they reflect our knowledge of the world (or both)? When people are asked to judge similarities of color names or of emotion names, what do they base their judgments on? Do they judge one or more aspects of the names, or do they simply judge the concepts to which the names refer? In the domain of color, "the circular configuration resulting from an analysis of the similarities among color names was very similar to that yielded by an analysis of the similarities among the colors themselves" (Fillenbaum & Rapoport, 1971, p. 106). Similarly, the failure to discover a structure for emotion names parallels our failures to classify and organize emotions and feelings themselves. How can we separate properties of referents (what words denote) from properties of the words per se? In the context of semantic theory this problem has not been solved, and the current trend is to include knowledge of all kinds within semantics.

For example, Collins and Quillian (1972) equate "knowledge of the world" with semantic memory. Lindsay and Norman (1972) tend toward the same conclusions. This leads to models of semantic memory with very few, if any, structural constraints. The mental dictionary now is represented as a complex network in which many different kinds of connections and relationships among words and concepts can exist. Super- and subordinate relations, as in Collins and Quillian's earlier (1969) hierarchical model, are now only two of the many possible relations among concepts. A nose is *part of* the face, but it is also *close to* the eyes. A child *precedes* (is father to) the man. A grocer *sells* dairy products. Is there no limit to the number of possible relations, or is there a relatively small set of fundamental relationships?

Until we can answer these questions, our models of the mental dictionary do little more than describe what we know and how we can generate knowledge. We know that *a camel is an animal*. We also know that *an animal has a liver*. Both of these relationships are stored in semantic memory, and so we know them directly. The knowledge that *a camel has a liver* is probably not stored directly (at least for most Americans), but it can be inferred from the knowledge that is stored once the question is raised. Indeed, after one or two occasions when you do think of it, the knowledge *camels have livers* probably will be stored directly, making future inferences unnecessary.

Our mental dictionary begins to look like a mental encyclopedia. It includes our knowledge about things in general, as represented by words. About the only things it does not explicitly include are motor skills ("knowing how to" play the piano or ride a bike) and information stored in sensory–perceptual formats (tastes, smells, sounds, sights, and so forth). In principle, these could be incorporated as well. Given that this "knowledge" is important for understanding how people use words, should we continue to treat semantic memory as part of our language system, separate and distinct from other forms of knowledge? What are the limits of a theory of semantics? We return to this issue in our discussions of sentence comprehension and communication processes, where meaning is represented by units larger than single words.

SUGGESTED READINGS

The paper by A. M. Collins and M. R. Quillian, "How to make a language user," in E. Tulving and W. Donaldson, (Eds.), *Organization of memory* (New York: Academic Press, 1972, pp. 309–351), is representative of the recent trend to incorporate knowledge of the world into a theory of semantic memory. Contrast this approach with the more traditional view expressed by J. Deese, *The structure of associations in language and thought* (Baltimore: Johns Hopkins Press, 1965).

For a lively perspective on issues concerning semantic theory, see D. D. Steinberg and L. A. Jakobovits, (Eds.), *Semantics* (Cambridge: Cambridge University Press, 1971). D. Olson, in "Language and thought: Aspects of a cognitive theory of semantics," *Psychological Review,* 1970, **77**, 257–273, argues that word meanings are best understood in the context of communicative interchange, and that the distinction between referential and denotative meaning is at best useless and usually misleading. E. E. Smith, E. J. Shoben, and L. J. Rips provide a review of research and theory in semantic memory in their paper, "Semantic memory and psychological semantics," appearing in G. H. Bower (Ed.), *The psychology of learning and motivation,* Volume 8 (New York: Academic Press, 1974).

4
Sentences: Syntax, Meaning, and Comprehension

In this chapter, we are concerned with how people process sentences. How are word meanings integrated with the structural meanings of sentences? Above and beyond the sounds and the meanings of the individual words in a sentence are the relations among the words. We cannot derive the meaning, or meanings, of a sentence from the meanings of the individual words alone. One aspect crucial in many languages, including English, is WORD ORDER. Consider

(1)   Miles Standish loved Priscilla.

(2)   Priscilla loved Miles Standish.

Because the sequential order of words in a sentence is meaningful, sentence (2) is different from sentence (1). The two sentences are not synonymous, even though the words in the two sentences are identical. The meaning of each word interacts with the structural meaning of the sentence to yield the meaning of the sentence. The STRUCTURAL MEANING of a sentence is the syntactic form of the sentence abstracted from the particular words in that sentence. In sentence (1), we can replace the words with abstract symbols, yielding

(3)   noun$_1$ verbed noun$_2$.

In this particular sentence, *noun$_1$* is the agent, *verbed* is the action (past tense), and *noun$_2$* is the recipient of the action. In sentence (1), which is a particular exemplar of the general form (3), *Miles Standish* refers to a particular person, *loved* to a particular class of actions or states of feeling, and *Priscilla* to another particular person. Miles, as the grammatical subject of the sentence, is an agent—Miles performs the action. Priscilla is the grammatical object, and is the recipient of the action.

FORMAL GRAMMARS

Since the appearance of Chomsky's *Syntactic Structures* in 1957, linguists have been deeply concerned with the form or type of grammar that, in principle, could adequately describe a natural language. We have had arguments for and against phrase-structure grammars (Yngve, 1960), transformational-generative grammars (Chomsky, 1965), case grammars (Fillmore, 1968), and conceptual-dependency grammars (Schank, 1972). None of these "grammars" actually exists—each represents a proposal or prospectus for what might be developed into an adequate grammar.

We describe several of these formal linguistic grammars for several reasons. First, they have provided a major impetus for psychological research on language, particularly during the past ten years, when psychologists used them as tentative models of how sentences are processed. Further and more important for our purposes, each type of formal grammar reflects one or another important aspect of the structure of language.

Phrase-Structure Grammars

Phrase-structure grammars are among the simplest of the formal grammars. The central feature of these grammars is that they describe a structural analysis of a sentence in the order that the words actually occur. For this reason, they are also called SURFACE-STRUCTURE ANALYSES. Words are grouped together in successively larger segments according to grammatical function. These nested groupings reflect the hierarchical structure of a sentence. The nesting parentheses in sentence (4) are an example of a surface structure analysis:

(4)   ((The pterodactyl) (entertains (the lonesome child))).

This bracketing of the sentence can be represented by a labeled tree diagram, shown in Figure 4.1, that reveals the hierarchical structure more clearly. The DETERMINER (Det) *the* and NOUN (N) *pterodactyl* combine to form a NOUN PHRASE (NP), which is the subject of the SENTENCE (S). The predicate, or VERB PHRASE (VP), is composed of a TRANSITIVE VERB (V_t), *entertains,* and another noun phrase. The second NP is the direct object and is composed of a determiner *the,* an ADJECTIVE (Adj) *lonesome,* and a noun, *child.*

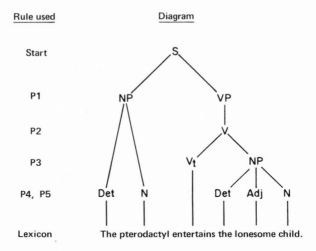

Rule used	Diagram
Start	
P1	
P2	
P3	
P4, P5	
Lexicon	The pterodactyl entertains the lonesome child.

FIGURE 4.1   Example of a phrase structure derivation using the grammar in Table 4.1.

The grammar itself, indicating how the analysis is conducted, is written in terms of phrase-structure or rewrite rules. An example of a phrase-structure rule is

$$S \rightarrow NP + VP.$$

This rule states that a sentence can be rewritten as a noun phrase plus a verb phrase. This can be done because a sentence can be composed of a noun phrase and a verb phrase. Another rule would be

$$NP \rightarrow Det + N.$$

This rule states that a noun phrase may consist of an article plus a noun.

TABLE 4.1
Some Phrase-Structure Rules for English[a]

PHRASE-STRUCTURE RULES:	LEXICON:
P1 $S \rightarrow NP + VP$	$N \rightarrow$ child, man, monster, pterodactyl, . . .
	$Det \rightarrow$ a, every, all, the, . . .
P2 $VP \rightarrow \begin{Bmatrix} be + Pred \\ V \end{Bmatrix}$ (Adv)	$V_i \rightarrow$ sleep, dance, . . .
	$V_t \rightarrow$ see, entertain, . . .
	$Adj \rightarrow$ lonesome, happy, . . .
P3 $V \rightarrow \begin{Bmatrix} V_i \\ V_t + NP \end{Bmatrix}$	$Adv \rightarrow$ today, . . .
P4 $Pred \rightarrow \begin{Bmatrix} NP \\ Adj \end{Bmatrix}$	
P5 $NP \rightarrow Det (+ Adj) + N$	

[a] Adapted from Thomas (1966).

Further specification of the units in the sentence can be made by a rule like

$$N \rightarrow \textit{boy, house, woman, street, etc. . . .}$$

which specifies that *boy, house, woman,* and *street* are nouns, and that wherever N appears in a statement, one could replace N with *boy* or *house,* etc.

A limited list of phrase-structure rules is given in Table 4.1. By starting with S, we can apply the rules to expand each symbol and so represent the phrase structure of an indefinitely large number of sentences. The parentheses and brackets in the rules signify optional elements. We can derive the following sentence as an example:

Rule used	Resultant sequence
Start	S
P1	$NP + VP$
P2	$NP + V$
P3	$NP + V_t + NP$
P5	$Det + N + V_t + NP$
P5	$Det + N + V_t + Det + Adj + N$

Now, by selecting appropriately from the lexicon we can generate

(4)   The pterodactyl entertains the
        lonesome child.

Note that, throughout the steps of the derivation, the ordering of elements in the final product (the sentence) is preserved. A complete set of phrase-structure rules like these would make up a phrase-structure grammar. This grammar could be complex enough to generate an infinite number of grammatical sentences. Would this grammar be adequate to describe other things we know about language?

Transformational-Generative Grammars

Consider the following sentences:

(5)   The boy hit the ball.

(6)   The ball was hit by the boy.

A phrase-structure analysis would not tell us that sentences (5) and (6) were related in any particular way. We know, however, that (5) and (6) are closely related to one another. They describe the same event, even though they are in different syntactic forms. One sentence is active; the other is passive. Since they both express the same propositions, they can be viewed as transformations of the same basic linguistic form, or DEEP STRUCTURE. Sentences (5) and (6) are two of the possible SURFACE STRUCTURES related to that deep structure. Operations that relate surface structures to one another and to their corresponding deep structures are called TRANSFORMATIONS. When we talk about the meaning of a sentence, we are talking about something more than the surface structure of that sentence, something more closely akin to the linguistic concept of deep structure. Active and passive sentences, like sentences (5) and (6), are related by a simple transform and therefore share the same deep structure. On conceptual grounds, the relations among the words are equivalent: *boy* and *ball* are agent and recipient, respectively, irrespective of the surface structure form.

How does a deep-structure representation, as exemplified by a transformational-generative grammar, accomplish this, whereas a phrase-structure grammar cannot? A transformational-generative grammar includes, among its rules for deriving sentences, rewrite rules similar to those in a phrase-structure grammar. These rewrite rules are used to generate a KERNEL corresponding to the deep structure. Kernels then are operated upon by transformations. These rules can be applied to strings of units as a whole, not just to one unit at a time. By rearranging groups of units, for example, a whole NP or VP, transformations can produce variations in surface structure. For example, a passive transformation would be

$$NP_1 + V_t + NP_2 \Rightarrow NP_2 + be + V_t + en + by + NP_2.$$

This rule interchanges the subject and object noun phrases, adds an auxiliary form of *be* and a participial affix to the verb, and introduces *by* for the concluding prepositional phrase.

Descriptively, transformational rules represent a major advantage over phrase-structure rules, since they can specify how sentences with differing surface structures, such as actives and passives, may be related to one another. They also can be used to specify how two sentences with identical surface structures can be quite different. The sentence

(7)   John is easy to please.

can be transformed (rewritten) to produce

(8)   It is easy to please John.

Both sentences make sense and mean the same thing. Sentence (9) seems to be, on the surface, similar to sentence (7):

(9)   John is eager to please.

but we cannot rewrite or transform sentence (9) as we did sentence (7):

(10)   It is eager to please John.

We do get a grammatical sentence (if *it* refers to, say, a dog), but its meaning is not the same as sentence (9). Here the surface structure and deep structure analyses differ. Sentences (5) and (6) have different surface structures but the same deep structures, and sentences (7) and (9) have the same surface structures but different deep structures.

"Semantic" Grammars and Artificial Intelligence

Transformational-generative grammars have been extremely popular in linguistics and have dominated the field for the past fifteen years. These grammars have been exclusively syntactic in that the meanings of words and sentences are not formally considered. A number of linguists have recognized this and have proposed alternatives to the purely syntactic approach of transformational grammars. Among these are Fillmore (1968), Chafe (1970), Halliday (1970), and Lakoff (1971). Though syntactic relations are still considered important, even more important are the conceptual-semantic relations represented in a sentence.

To take one example, Fillmore (1968) proposed a CASE GRAMMAR, which treats the verb of a sentence as the central organizing unit. The relation between the verb and the various nouns in a sentence are called CASE RELATIONS. Consider the sentence

(11)   Father carved the turkey at the
        Thanksgiving dinner table with his
        new carving knife.

One way to represent or describe this sentence is shown in Figure 4.2. On purely syntactic grounds, *father* is the grammatical subject of the sentence. In case-relation terms, *father* is also the agent, the one who performs the action of carving. *Turkey* is the recipient (or, technically, the patient) of the action; *knife* is the instrument; *dinner table* is the location; and *Thanksgiving* is the time or occasion. These cases—AGENTIVE, OBJECTIVE, INSTRUMENTAL, LOCATIVE, and TEMPORAL—represent what we "know" about the situation referred to by the sentence. They are not semantically empty categories as are noun phrase, subject, object, and verb phrase.

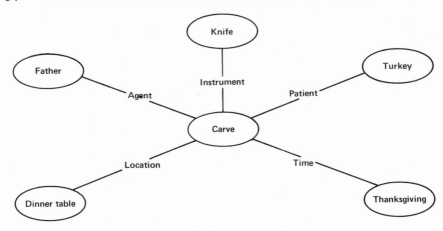

FIGURE 4.2 A pictorial representation of how a sentence would be represented using a case analysis of the grammar of the sentence.

What is the advantage of a case grammar over a transformational-generative grammar? One advantage is analogous to the relation between transformational grammars and phrase-structure grammars. Transformational grammars adequately describe some relations between sentences that phrase-structure grammars do not [for example, *John hit the ball* versus *The ball was hit by John,* and sentences (7), (8), (9), and (10), above]. Similarly, a case grammar can describe some relations among sentences that are difficult to handle on purely syntactic grounds. For example, Fillmore (1971) is able to account for the relationship between the words *me* and *I* in sentences (12) and (13):

(12)   John strikes me as pompous.

(13)   I regard John as pompous.

The words *I* and *me* share a common case relationship, that of EXPERIENCER. This analysis reflects our intuitions about sentences, and is also consistent with the ways in which people recognize sentences they have recently seen. Sentences similar to one another in terms of their case relations are more confusable than are sentences with the same nouns, and are also more confusable than are sentences with the same surface subjects and objects (Shafto, 1973). On both formal and psychological grounds, a case grammar has certain advantages over phrase-structure and transformational-generative grammars.

A second source of dissatisfaction with purely syntactic approaches to language analysis comes from the area of artificial intelligence, where people are trying to program computers to understand and produce natural language. The only successful approaches to date use programs that rely heavily on what we have been calling semantics and knowledge of the world, that is, what language is used to talk about. Winograd (1972) described one such system, which "understands" statements about blocks of various sizes, shapes, and colors. It responds by moving blocks about on a table according to directions like "put the large green block on top of the small red one and then put them both next to the blue one." The machine "knows" about the properties of solid objects, "remembers" what pronouns (like *them*) refer to, and asks questions if the instructions are ambiguous. Schank (1972) described a system with quite different syntactic processing rules, but which also relies heavily on "knowledge" and semantics. Like these admittedly simple artificial systems, natural language-processing systems may not be able to work, or even be usefully characterized, when syntactic processing is isolated from semantic and conceptual mechanisms.

Formal linguistic grammars for the analyses of sentences describe some aspects of sentences that conform to our intuitions about language. Do these grammars represent language processing as well? Must (or should) a theory of language production and comprehension be modeled after, say, a transformational-generative grammar, or any other formally adequate description of language?

Competence and Performance

In the sense that any adequate grammar captures what people "know" about a language, the grammar describes LINGUISTIC COMPETENCE. If the rules of a grammar can be used to describe formally all the grammatical sentences of a language and no ungrammatical ones, and if people can do the same thing intuitively, then in this sense the competence of the grammar is equivalent to the linguistic competence of the people who speak the language. But it does not necessarily specify how people go about producing the output, or LINGUISTIC PERFORMANCE. A grammar (or a computer program) may generate or describe sentences using one set of rules and principles and people might achieve equivalent results by using an entirely different set of rules and principles (see, for example, Sutherland, 1966).

Psychologists were once quite optimistic about the possibility of using competence grammars as models for language performance (see Deese, 1970; Slobin, 1971b). This optimism has all but disappeared. The main reason for this is that no single competence grammar proved adequate for the variety and complexity of the linguistic and other processing strategies people use when they deal with sentences. There is no single way that people perceive, remember, or comprehend any given type of linguistic material (Glucksberg, Trabasso, & Wald, 1973).

How we deal with any kind of informational input depends heavily upon what we are expected to do with it. If we are asked to find out if someone is in a room behind a closed door, we may listen at the door, detect the sound of people talking, and leave it at that. Little, if any, linguistic processing is performed beyond recognizing that someone is saying something. If we are asked to memorize a list of words or a list of sentences, we may do little more than memorize the material by rote without attempting to understand it. In contrast, when we are engaged in ordinary conversation we employ the full range of linguistic, cognitive and social skills available to us.

The same variability of processing occurs in psychological laboratories, where people are asked to do various things with language materials: to listen and detect certain sounds, remember words or sentences, judge whether some sentences are more or less grammatical than others, decide whether a sentence is true or false, and so on. In each case, one specific aspect of language processing would be more central to the person's performance than others, depending on the nature of the task and the materials used. In each case, the tasks and materials used must be carefully specified if we are to make appropriate inferences about our language processing mechanisms.

With this caution in mind, we turn to several aspects of sentence processing: sentence perception, sentence comprehension, sentence memory, and finally, comprehension and memory for related sets of sentences.

SENTENCE PERCEPTION

When we hear a sentence, the words come one after the other, in some sequential order. We usually begin to process a part of the sentence before the rest comes in, and this processing involves several kinds of operations. We assign meanings to words; we analyze syntactic and semantic relations; and we try to integrate information as quickly as possible so as to minimize the load on immediate memory. Most of the time this strategy works well, but it can go wrong if the first part of the sentence is interpreted incorrectly. Consider the sentence

(14)   I was going to take the plane to
Chicago but it was too heavy.

The phrase *take the plane* is ambiguous in isolation, and it is most frequently interpreted to refer to traveling by air rather than to carrying a wood-working tool. If this strategy can lead to misinterpretations of sentence segments, then why do we process sentences in this way? Why don't we wait until the whole sentence is available to start interpreting it?

Segmentation

One of the major performance factors involved in processing language is our memory capacities. We can crudely partition our memory system into two general components, WORKING MEMORY (or short-term, immediate memory), and LONG-TERM MEMORY. Our long-term memory comprises all of our knowledge, including episodic and semantic memory. Our working memory can be likened to what we are aware of at any given moment, and this component of our memory system is limited in terms of the total amount of material we can hold at any given moment. George Miller (1956) has suggested that the capacity of this working memory system is about seven (plus or minus two) "chunks" of information. We can hold seven letters, or seven numbers, or seven words. Notice that we can hold seven words or seven letters. When the letters can be organized (or "chunked") into words, then we can hold far more letters than when they are unrelated to one another.

Similarly, sentences consist of words, and if we could "chunk" or organize words into phrases, then we can handle far more material than just seven words. The important factor is our ability to segment fairly long sentences into interpretable "chunks" and thus be able to deal with more than seven or eight words at a time. When we are unable to do this, then sentences become very difficult to process indeed. Consider the following perfectly grammatical sentence:

(15a)   The plumber the doctor the nurse
         met called ate the cheese.

This is a self-embedded sentence without relative pronouns, and its structure is such that one cannot begin to interpret any segment of it until quite late in the string. If the sentence is actually made more complex from a formal-grammatical viewpoint, then it becomes easier to process. When relative pronouns are added, we can begin to segment the sentence appropriately and start interpretation much earlier:

(15b)   The plumber that the doctor that
         the nurse met called ate the cheese.

This is still difficult, but somewhat easier than sentence (15a), which is formally "simpler" (Hakes & Cairns, 1970; Hakes & Foss, 1970). If we modify the sentence to allow even earlier segmentation and interpretation, then it becomes easier still:

(15c)   The nurse met the doctor that called
         the plumber that ate the cheese.

Sentences (15a) and (15b) are center embedded. In a sense, they "start" in the middle and work toward both ends. Consequently, we cannot partition off a "chunk" at the beginning and deal with that. We have to wait for the end, and by that time our processing capacity has been overloaded. Sentence (15c) is right branching, and this allows us to work on manageable segments as the sentence comes in.

If this interpretation of sentence processing is correct, then we would expect people to forget a sentence segment that has just been processed. On this view, when a sentence is heard, the words are held in immediate memory until an interpretable segment is completed, then while the next sequence of words comes in, the first segment is processed. When the interpretative process is completed, the verbatim information is discarded to make room for the subsequent incoming material. Jarvella (1971) tested this notion by giving sentences like these to people:

(16a)   The confidence of Kofach was not unfounded. *To stack the meeting for McDonald, the union had even brought in outsiders.*

(16b)   Kofach had been persuaded by the international *to stack the meeting for McDonald. The union had even brought in outsiders.*

The italicized words in both pairs of sentences are identical. However, in sentence (16a), *To stack the meeting for McDonald* is the first part of the second sentence, whereas in sentence (16b) these words end the first sentence. If people are asked to recall as much as they can after they have heard the last word, *outsiders,* then their performance is far superior for passages like (16a), where the clause, *to stack the meeting for McDonald,* belongs to the last sentence heard, than for passages like (16b) where that clause belongs to the previous sentence. Jarvella (1971) suggests that, "After a sentence had been heard, and its meaning extracted . . . [verbatim material] . . . would be quickly lost . . . the . . . previous sentence would assume some abstract form from which only an approximation of the original unit could be reconstructed [p. 413]."

Segmentation between sentences clearly occurs when people are asked to remember and comprehend them. Do we segment within sentences as well? If we do, what governs the particular segmentations we impose? One way to examine these questions was developed by Bever, Fodor, Garrett, and their colleagues at the Massachusetts Institute of Technology. People were asked to listen to a sentence played in one ear and, at the same time, listen for a click played at some point in the other ear. They then wrote the sentence they heard and indicated where they thought the click had occurred. The logic behind this technique assumed that people would tend to "place" the remembered click between psychologically organized segments rather than within a unitized segment. In one such study, sentences like these were used:

(17a)   During prohibition because many
         were afraid to give open *support*
         drinking liquor was made illegal.

(17b)   During prohibition although a
         majority of people did *support*
         drinking liquor was made illegal.

The italicized portions of these two sentences are identical, but in sentence (17a) a major syntactic break occurs between the words *support* and *drinking,* whereas in sentence (17b) a break occurs between the words *drinking* and *liquor.* When clicks were superimposed over various parts of the sentences, they tended to be "misplaced" toward the appropriate boundaries in each of the two sentences (Garrett, Bever, & Fodor, 1966). We apparently have learned to segment sentences automatically and appropriately. As Johnson-Laird (1974) suggests, people take in as much of a sentence as they need to in order to make an interpretation of what is said, and interpret each segment in turn. Where the segmentation occurs sometimes can be predicted on the basis of one or another formal linguistic grammar, but in general, the segmentation seems to be governed by a complex set of factors, many of which are independent of linguistic theory (see Bever's paper, "The Cognitive Basis for Linguistic Structures," 1970).

These factors are related to the various strategies people use to interpret sentences in various contexts. In one context, a syntactic structure may be segmented in one way, while in another it may be segmented in another way. For example, sentences (18a) and (18b) have identical surface structures but different "deep" structures:

(18a)   The corrupt police can't bear
         criminals to confess very quickly.

(18b)   The corrupt police can't force
         criminals to confess very quickly.

In sentence (18a), clicks placed simultaneously with the word *criminals* are displaced to the "boundary" between *bear* and *criminals.* In sentence (18b), this does not happen (Bever, Lackner, & Kirk, 1969). Bever and his co-workers argue that the two sentences differ in their derivational history and so have different underlying structures. Therefore, the major syntactic breaks occur in different places. However, other investigators report results that are just the opposite of those found by Bever and co-workers

(Chapin, Smith, & Abrahamson, 1972). To add to the confusion, Reber and Anderson (1970) have shown that people misplace clicks toward the middle of any acoustic pattern, even when that pattern is just noise.

Whatever the determinants and details of the process, people seem to impose organization on just about everything they hear. This may be the result of generalizing from sentence-processing strategies to other acoustic patterns, or it may be a general characteristic of our auditory system. We need to know a good deal more about sentence processing in various contexts and about the mechanisms of our auditory systems before we will be able to reconcile the variety of experimental findings on click-within-sentence perception. In any case, the click studies show that people impose organizations upon sentences, and segment within sentences.

Sentence Organization

Jarvella's memory studies and the wealth of click-perception studies amply demonstrate that speech is segmented and organized as it is processed. Other memory studies have addressed this question: What are the resultant sentence organizations? In one such study, Weisberg (1969) asked people to memorize simple sentences like

(19a)   Slow children eat cold bread.

None of the words in this sentence is normally associated with one another. One way to reveal the organization of such sentences is to give someone a word from a memorized sentence and ask for the first other word from that sentence that comes to mind. If the sentence is organized in a simple linear, left-to-right fashion (as an associative chain), then *slow* should elicit *children, children* should elicit *eat, eat → cold,* and *cold →* *bread,* reflecting a sequential organization. When the five "words" of a sentence are nonsense syllables so that they form a list rather than a sentence, then we roughly get this pattern of responses. When real words form an acceptable sentence like (19a), the pattern is dramatically different from the list pattern. *Slow* does elicit *children,* but *children* just as reliably elicits *slow.* The effective "stimulus" for *eat* is the phrase, *slow children.* The word *eat* elicits either *cold* or *bread,* as if the unit *cold bread* is the appropriate "response" and *cold* and *bread* elicit one another. Furthermore, the same pattern of results appears even when the active sentence (19a) is transformed to passive voice:

(19b)   Cold bread is eaten by
         slow children.

Whatever the organizational pattern of a sentence is, it is not a left-to-right sequence, and the units are not only individual words. People do not encode sentences in the same ways they might encode lists or sequences of unrelated verbal items.[1] If sentences are not merely sequences of word pairs, then what are they? In the sentence

(20)   The [1] tall [2] boy [3] saved [4] the [5] dying [6] woman

the numbers between the words designate the transitions between the words. If people try to memorize a set of sentences like (20), which of these transitions is most difficult? Where would most errors occur? Would you expect that people would be more likely to forget what comes after *tall* (transition 2) than after *boy* (transition 3)? The probability that a word is forgotten, given that the immediately prior word is remembered, is the TRANSITIONAL ERROR PROBABILITY (TEP).

Neal Johnson (1965) gave people lists of sentences to be memorized and found that errors were distributed in certain ways. The patterns of transitional error probabilities would change systematically as the surface structure of the sentences was varied. Surface-structure diagrams of two sentence types (I and II) and their associated error patterns are shown in Figures 4.3 and 4.4, respectively. The two sentences have different phrase structures, and the errors correspond to transitions between phrases. For sentence type I most errors were made at transition 3, which is the end of the subject of the sentence and the beginning of the predicate. For sentence type II, most errors were made at transition 2. In general, Johnson found that errors tended to be made between the largest units or phrases, indicating that people had encoded the sentences as organized phrases rather than simple lists of words. Thus, the tree diagrams in Figure 4.3 not only describe the structure of the sentences in a particular abstract way, but also describe, to some extent, the way people code and remember the sentences.

We now have a plausible explanation for the Weisberg (1969) studies. People were not coding the sentences in terms of pairwise associations, but had imposed a phrase structure organization on the sentences. Weisberg's simple sentence is represented as a tree structure in Figure 4.5. Here

---

[1] Rejection of a linear associative model for sentence organization in no way implies that learning, broadly conceived, is not centrally involved in language acquisition and language use. Unfortunately, "learning" and "stimulus–response associations" have been inappropriately linked in the brief history of psycholinguistics. "Learning theory" is commonly taken to denote (*a*) *how* learning takes place and (*b*) *what* is learned. Learning supposedly occurs in ways analogous to classical and operant conditioning, and what is learned are stimulus–response associations. We do not deny that people can and do learn conditioned responses, and that people do acquire rather complex systems of associations. We also allow, however, that other modes of learning exist and that stimulus–response associations are not the only products of learning. Therefore, rejection of a conditioning model of language learning or language behavior does not in any way imply that language is not learned or that it is innate. We return to this issue in Chapter 5, where we discuss language development.

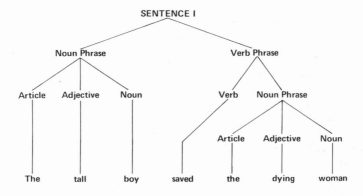

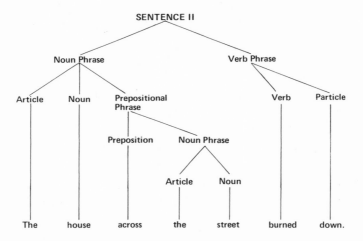

FIGURE 4.3 The surface-structure organization of the sentences used by Johnson (1965).

we can see that *slow* and *children* do indeed form a single unit corresponding to the first noun phrase (NP). *Cold* and *bread* also form an NP unit, which in turn combines with *eat* to form the verb phrase (VP). Both Johnson's error patterns and Weisberg's word-association patterns reflect this mode of organization.

As we shall see later when we consider memory for sentences in some detail, these patterns of organization are just some of the many possible ways that sentences can be segmented and represented in memory.[2] As

[2] For example, in a later series of experiments Weisberg (1971) demonstrates alternative sentence organizations.

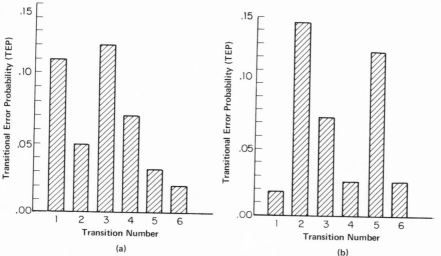

FIGURE 4.4 Where do people forget what comes next in a sentence? (a) Transitional error probabilities for sentences like *The tall boy saved the dying woman.* (b) Transitional error probabilities for sentences like *The house across the street burned down.* (After Johnson, 1965.)

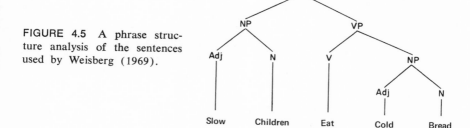

FIGURE 4.5 A phrase structure analysis of the sentences used by Weisberg (1969).

Jarvella's studies suggest, memory for a sentence may no longer include the verbatim record of the words themselves. Similarly, the patterns of organization of the words of a sentence may vary, depending on what people are asked to do with the linguistic material they get.

Processing Ambiguous Sentences

When we segment and begin to interpret a portion of a sentence, we are sometimes faced with the problem of choosing between two or more interpretations. Sentences may be ambiguous in one of two ways, lexical or syntactic. LEXICAL AMBIGUITY occurs when a word may be interpreted in two different ways, as in sentences (21a) and (21b):

(21a)   The sailors liked the port
         from Portugal.

(21b)   The sailors liked the port
         in Portugal.

The word *port* can be used to refer to a type of red wine or to a harbor. In sentence (21a), the more likely interpretation would be the red wine, whereas in sentence (21b), the more likely interpretation would be the harbor. SYNTACTIC AMBIGUITY occurs when a sentence can be organized in two different ways, as in sentences (22a) and (22b):

(22a)   They (are visiting) relatives
         in Chicago.

(22b)   They are (visiting relatives)
         from Chicago.

In the first example, the word *they* does not refer to the relatives, and the word *visiting* functions as a verb. In the second, *they* does refer to *relatives,* and *visiting* is used as a modifier of *relatives*.

What do people do about such sentences? Do we wait until enough of the sentence is completed to remove the ambiguity, or do we tentatively compute two interpretations and hold both in memory until the ambiguity is resolved? In either case, we should find that ambiguous sentences are harder to process than unambiguous sentences. In the first case, ambiguous sentences should impose a relatively greater load on working memory, and in the second case two interpretations must be made and remembered rather than just one.

One way to assess the relative difficulty of processing various types of sentences is to ask people to listen to a sentence and, at the same time, listen for the occurrence of a specified speech sound within that sentence (Foss, 1970). The logic for this phoneme-monitoring task assumes that people have a finite capacity for handling linguistic information, so if it takes more "mental work" to process a more difficult sentence, then it would also take slightly longer to detect a target sound in the more difficult sentence. Foss used sentences like the following to assess the relative difficulty of ambiguous and unambiguous sentences:

(23a)   The new men started to drill
         before they were ordered to do so.

(23b)   The new men started to march
         before they were ordered to do so.

People had to press a button as soon as they heard the phoneme /b/.

When the sentences were ambiguous, like (23a), it took longer to respond appropriately, presumably because of the extra processing involved in dealing with the ambiguity of a word like *drill*. Similar results were obtained when people were asked to complete ambiguous and unambiguous sentence fragments (MacKay, 1966). It takes longer to think of an ending to an incomplete ambiguous sentence than an unambiguous one, even though people are rarely aware of the ambiguity.

If we do generate two or more interpretations of an ambiguous word or phrase, how long do we hold onto both interpretations? Do we retain both only until the ambiguity is resolved and then "dump" the inappropriate interpretation, or do we retain both even after one can be clearly rejected? If people do generate two interpretations and retain both, then we should not feel tricked by "garden path" sentences like (14) on page 86:

(14)   I was going to take the plane to
        Chicago but it was too heavy.

If both interpretations had been made and retained, then the phrase *but it was too heavy* should not surprise us. Since it does surprise us, it is unlikely that we had generated and retained both interpretations of the phrase *take the plane*. It is far more likely that we generated only the most probable interpretation, namely, traveling by air. This hypothesis, that we generally make or retain only one interpretation of ambiguous phrases, and that the one we retain is the most likely or probable interpretation, was tested in an experiment where people had to decide upon the truth of sentences relative to pictured events. A sentence was given, followed by a picture. If the sentence and picture matched, then the correct response was "yes." If they did not match, then a "no" response was made, and both types of responses were timed. Consider the following sentence:

(24)   The boy is looking up the street.

This sentence is usually interpreted as referring to a boy who is gazing toward one end of a street or road. If it is followed by a picture of a boy standing in a road, "yes" responses are relatively fast. The sentence is also true relative to a picture of a boy holding a map as if he is looking up an address. When this picture follows the sentence, "yes" is still the correct response, but it takes more time to make the decision (Foss, Bever, & Silver, 1968). These data are consistent with the notion that the more probable interpretation was the only one made and retained; when the less probable interpretation is required by the picture, the person has to backtrack, come up with that second interpretation, and then decide that the sentence and picture do indeed match.

The strategy of generating two interpretations and then discarding one is a reasonable one for people to use when confronted with either lexical or syntactic ambiguity (Bever, Garrett, & Hurtig, 1973). This strategy would minimize memory load, and also enable us to minimize the number of times we generate just one incorrect interpretation and then have to backtrack to generate a more appropriate interpretation. On the other hand, the evidence for this two-interpretation strategy is equally compatible with another alternative. People could postpone interpretation of ambiguous sentence segments until the ambiguity could be resolved. This alternative strategy would also make ambiguous sentences more difficult to process because the amount of uninterpreted material held in memory would be greater than that for unambiguous sentences. Hence, the relative difficulty of ambiguous sentences may be attributable to either or both of two possibilities: the need to generate two tentative interpretations instead of just one, and/or the increased load on memory if interpretation is delayed until sufficient material has been obtained to resolve an ambiguity.

SENTENCE COMPREHENSION

Once a sentence has been perceived and interpreted, we may do various things with the resultant product. In general, we consider that a sentence has been understood or comprehended when we are able to use the information derived from the sentence in some appropriate way. One way to assess sentence comprehension was developed by Lee McMahon (1963), using an ingenious adaptation of the successive matching paradigm. Two events, A and B, were presented sequentially. The task was to decide whether or not A and B match—were they the same or different given a specified criterion? Events A and B could be in any format—two color patches, a color patch and a word, two geometric shapes, two pictures, or a picture and a sentence. If A was a picture and B was a sentence, one might be able to assess the relative difficulty of comprehending sentence B by measuring the time taken to decide if sentence B corresponded to the event represented by picture A. If A was a picture of a car hitting a truck (see Figure 4.6) and B was either sentence (25a) or (25b), then the correct decision would be "true" or "same":

(25a)   The car hit the truck.

(25b)   The truck was hit by the car.

Both of these sentences are true relative to the picture. Which sentence takes longer to "comprehend"?

In some early versions of Chomsky's transformational-generative grammar, passive sentences were considered to be more complex than active sentences, and so it was expected that sentence (25b) would be psychologically more complex and thus take longer to process. This expectation

FIGURE 4.6   How would you describe this picture?

was confirmed in a number of studies motivated by transformational-generative grammars (McMahon, 1963; Gough, 1965, 1966; Slobin, 1966). Each of these experiments used a variant of McMahon's successive matching task, and they found that passive sentences took longer to verify than did active sentences. In some of the later versions of transformational grammar, passive and active sentences were considered to be equally "complex" in that both required the same number of transformational steps in their formal derivations. Since linguistic theory no longer provided a rationale for the relative difficulty of active and passive sentences, other reasons for their relative difficulty had to be uncovered.

The place to find such reasons is in the demands of the particular successive-matching task itself. Figure 4.7 is an illustration of the steps people go through in deciding whether or not two events match (Clark & Chase, 1972; Trabasso, 1972). In Stage 1 the first event (A) is encoded and

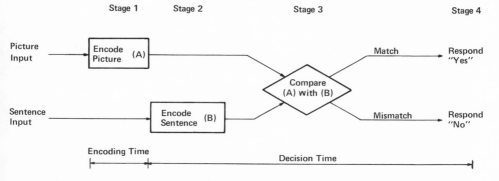

FIGURE 4.7   A schematic diagram of a four-stage model of sentence verification proposed by Clark and by Trabasso.

represented in memory so that the information can be compared later with the information in event B. If this first event is a picture, then it must be represented (or coded) in some format so that it can be compared with the second event. It could be coded and remembered as a visual image, but if a sentence is expected next, the picture would probably be represented in terms of a sentence (Tversky, 1969). In the absence of any particular linguistic or experiential context, the most likely sentence format would be in the active voice. If the picture involves a car hitting a truck, as in Figure 4.6, then the most likely mental description of that picture would be

(25c)   car hit truck.

In Stage 2 the second event, a sentence, is available and the information is taken in. Since the person doing the task is under instructions to perform as rapidly as possible, the most likely coding is verbatim. The next step is to compare the picture and sentence representations. In this third stage, active sentences and the active-format representation of the picture are perfectly congruent. Both have the "words" in the same order—*car hit truck*. The decision to respond "true" can be made rather quickly. What happens if the second event, the sentence, had been in passive voice? In this case, one would have to compare the memory of the picture—*car hit truck*—with the sequence of words—*truck hit by car*. If we assume that people compare the two sequences one word at a time, going from left to right, then the comparison sequence runs into trouble. The first and last words in the two sequences do not match, and the person doing the task must spend some more time to decide that the syntactic form of the sentence is passive; if it is so, then the two sequences do indeed match.

This suggests that passive sentences are not basically more complex than active sentences. The important factor is the way people choose to remember the picture. We have assumed that people, in general, describe a picture in the active format, and also use that format to remember a picture. What would happen if we set up the problem in such a way that people would encode the picture (event A) in passive format? When do we normally use a passive contruction? If I were telling a story about a car, then I would describe the event in Figure 4.6 in the active voice. If I were telling a story about the truck, then I would probably use the passive voice. Olson and Filby (1972) manipulated the context in this way. First, they found that people did use the passive voice when the topic focus was put on the truck. Second, they found that when the focus was put on the recipient of the action (for example, the truck in Figure 4.6), passive sentences were easier than active sentences. On the left-hand side of Figure 4.8 we find a complete reversal of the relative difficulty of active and passive sen-

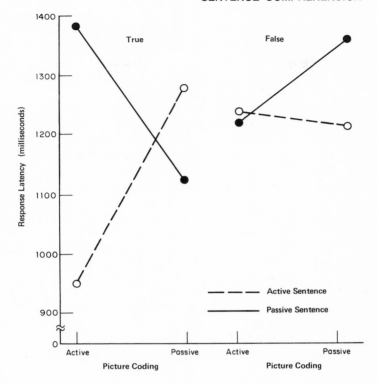

FIGURE 4.8   Response times to true and false active and passive sentences given that subjects have an active or passive coding of a picture. (After Olson & Filby, 1972.)

tences when the picture is coded in passive format. On the right-hand side analogous results are shown when the sentence is false relative to the picture. In general, when the sequential order of elements in a sentence is congruent with the sequential order of describing a picture, it is relatively easy to decide whether they match one another. When the sequential orders do not match, extra time is needed to compare the two representations.

The same kinds of effects of syntactic mismatches can be found when people are given sentences and then asked questions about them. Wright (1969, 1972) used sentences like

    (26a)   The crowd was held back by
            the police.

and then asked questions like

    (26b)   Was the crowd held back by
            the police?

When the syntactic form of sentence and question matched, fewer errors were made than when they did not match. If the sentence were in passive voice, then active questions like

(26c)   Did the police hold back the crowd?

were more difficult than passive questions.

In an elegant extension of Wright's experiments, Garrod and Trabasso (1973) gave people four sentences related to a single topic, then asked either active or passive questions and measured the time taken to answer. They, too, found that syntactic mismatches resulted in longer decision times, but only for the first and last sentences. When questions were asked about the middle two sentences, the syntactic form of the sentence and question had no effect. Garrod and Trabasso suggested that only the first and last sentence are held in surface (verbatim) form, presumably because it would overload short-term memory to hold all four sentences that way. The middle two sentences are interpreted and remembered in some "deep" or abstract form, and so their particular syntactic format is no longer retained.

These studies suggest that the syntactic form of a sentence has no direct effects upon sentence processing once the sentence has been encoded (perceived and interpreted). Is it more difficult to encode passive sentences than to encode active sentences? The earlier sentence verification work suggested that it is. In one of the best-known studies in this area, Slobin (1966) measured the time needed to decide whether a picture matched a previously heard sentence. Slobin used reversible sentences like

(27a)   The cat chased the dog.

as well as nonreversible sentences like

(27b)   The boy watered the flowers.

Sentence (27a) is reversible because the subject and object can be interchanged and still make sense, whereas sentence (27b) would not make sense if the subject and object were to be interchanged. Slobin found that active sentences were easier than passive ones, but only when nonreversible sentences were used. He also found that nonreversible sentences were easier than reversible sentences, regardless of sentence voice.

Why should this be so? One answer has been proposed by Glucksberg, Trabasso, and Wald (1973), who replicated and extended Slobin's experiments. First, they found that people did not need more time to read and encode passive and reversible sentences, when compared with active and nonreversible sentences. This suggests that the differential difficulty of passive and reversible sentences is not in the sentence-perception and encoding stage. The relative difficulty of passive and reversible sentences is in the comparison stage, and is entirely due to the particular strategies people use to compare the contents of a picture with the information represented by a sentence. If a sentence is nonreversible, and if it contains the verb and the two nouns that are in the picture, then the picture and sentence must match irrespective of sentence voice. Hence, active and passive nonreversible sentences are equally easy to compare with a picture.[3]

These analyses led Glucksberg and his co-workers to conclude that the relative difficulty of passive and reversible sentences has little to do with language processing or linguistic factors per se. The general form of the Clark and Chase and the Trabasso model (see Figure 4.7) can account for people's performance in sentence–picture verification tasks, and the particular effects of syntax can be attributed entirely to problem-solving and decision strategies developed by people during the course of each individual experiment.

The general conclusions to be drawn from the variety of studies using sentence–picture matching techniques turn out to be disappointing from a psycholinguistic viewpoint. First, because the bulk of linguistic processing takes place in the encoding stage and this is precisely the stage where virtually no linguistic effects occur. And second, because the linguistic effects that do occur can be easily manipulated by manipulating the ways people deal with the problems we set them (see, for example, Olson & Filby, 1972).

This conclusion seems applicable even to one of the more consistent and robust findings in the psycholinguistic literature, the effects of LEXICAL MARKING. Many pairs of comparative adjectives and prepositions are asymmetrical. In each of the following pairs, the first is considered unmarked, the second marked: *above–below, to–from, on top of–under, long–short, good–bad.* One of the defining characteristics of marking is the difference between the neutral member of a pair and the "biased" member. If someone asks, *how good is Alan?,* we do not assume that Alan is particularly good or bad. If, however, we hear the question *how bad is Alan?,* we usually assume that Alan is in fact bad. A second aspect of markedness has to do with the name of the scale or dimension referred to. *Good* is a comparative adjective and is also the label of the dimension, *goodness.* *Bad* is also a comparative adjective, but is not the label for the underlying scale. Hence, *bad* is considered to be "marked." Third, markedness can refer to the ways in which we normally perceive the spatial world. We usually measure from the ground plane as a reference point, so *above* and *tall* are unmarked (neutral?) and *below* and *short* are marked (Clark, 1973). Fourth, unmarked terms are more frequently used in the language

---

[3] This is true only if we assume that anomalous sentences, like *the flower watered the boy* never occur.

and are also more favorably rated on Osgood's semantic differential scales (Boucher & Osgood, 1969).

All of these characteristics differentiate marked and unmarked terms. Any one or several of them may be responsible for the general finding that sentences or phrases with unmarked terms are easier to process than those with marked terms (Clark & Chase, 1972; Seymour, 1973). One reason may be that people usually describe pictures or events by using the unmarked term in preference to the marked. When a picture of a star and a plus is shown, with the star above the plus, people normally describe the picture by saying "the star is above the plus." If this picture is shown, followed by a sentence to be verified like

(28a)   Star is above plus.

the decision is faster than if the equally true sentence

(28b)   Plus is below star.

is used. This finding is analogous to the findings for active versus passive sentences. Olson and Filby were able to reverse the relative difficulty of active and passive sentences by manipulating the topic focus and thus leading people to encode pictures in the passive rather than active voice. Clark and Chase (1972) were able to do the same thing with *above* and *below* by telling people to attend to either the top or bottom of a picture.

Again we find that the effects of a linguistic factor can be interpreted as a special case of a performance factor. The linguistic variable, whether it be sentence voice or lexical marking, reflects what people usually do when they deal with sentences and words in everyday contexts. When we take pains to systematically manipulate those contexts [as in the studies by Olson and Filby (1972) and Clark and Chase (1972)], we change how people usually process sentences, and then linguistic variables per se lose their effectiveness. The immediate inference is that regularities in language, like the frequent use of the active rather than the passive voice, reflect the way people usually talk. Bever (1970) and Bever and Langendoen (1971) advocate a more general position, namely, that syntactic constructions, such as reversals in the sequential order of agents and patients in actives and passives, limitations on relative clauses and embeddings within sentences, reflect the cognitive processes by which people normally deal with speech.

A syntactic regularity which may be attributable to the ways that people use language to communicate information most effectively is the sequential ordering of adjectives. In English, as in many other languages, the sequential order of adjectives is constrained (Martin, 1969; Danks & Glucksberg, 1971). For example, adjectives referring to size precede adjectives referring to color, which in turn precede those referring to place of origin. Thus, *the large red Turkish truck* sounds right to most people; *the Turkish red large truck* sounds strange. Why should this be so?

One possibility is that it just happened that way, but if that is the case why should so many different languages, including Russian, Japanese, and Indonesian, display the same ordering conventions? Martin (1969) and Danks and Glucksberg (1971) found that adjective order is correlated with certain semantic properties of adjectives. However, the ordering in terms of semantic properties may be a special case, albeit the most typical one, of a more general PRAGMATIC-COMMUNICATION RULE (Danks & Glucksberg, 1971; Danks & Schwenk, 1972, 1974). This rule—that the more informative adjectives generally come first—can be seen most clearly in cases where the usual ordering of adjectives is reversed. Normally, we would say *the large red car*. However, if there are two cars, one large and red and the other large and blue, then we might say *the RED large car* in order to emphasize that the distinguishing property is their color, not their size. When people are asked to describe objects that differ on various dimensions like color and size, they tend to invert the normal adjective order when the normally second adjective is the important one (Oller & Sales, 1969; Danks & Schwenk, 1972). Furthermore, listeners find it easier to understand what a speaker is referring to when adjective orders are varied to suit the situation (Danks & Schwenk, 1974).

The conclusion here parallels our conclusions concerning the differential complexity of active and passive sentences and of marked and unmarked comparatives: when the communicative and linguistic contexts are appropriate, one linguistic construction is no more difficult to deal with than another. When one type of linguistic material is more difficult than another, then the difference may be due to habitual strategies used by people to encode material for comprehension and memory.

What factors influence people's choice of encoding strategy? In the studies of sentence comprehension we could identify two factors—a carry-over from normal everyday practice (for example, using the active voice unless there is a special reason to do otherwise) and specific problem-solving strategies that people develop to deal with the experimental tasks we set for them. Do we find the same variability when we ask people to remember sentences?

MEMORY FOR SENTENCES

We have already seen that sentences can be remembered in two general ways—verbatim or in some interpreted format. VERBATIM MEMORY for sentences corresponds to memory for surface structure, the exact words in the order that they had appeared in. The INTERPRETED FORMAT refers to our memory for a sentence that no longer has the exact words in their original order, and this corresponds to a generalized "deep-structure" format. We obviously remember something other than the verbatim record of what we hear or read. How shall we characterize this "something other"?

Three classes of "something other" have been proposed recently. The first was derived from Chomsky's (1957) theory, which drew a distinction between the surface and deep structures of sentences. The abstracted form of a sentence was likened to the deep structures of transformational-generative grammar. A second form that this "something other" might take is imagery, primarily visual imagery. Finally, this "something other" may be in abstract conceptual form, for example, propositions, semantic relations, and other forms of knowledge. What do these three concepts have in common? Ultimately, they refer to the form and structure of human knowledge. When we go beyond the verbatim memory for the words of a sentence, we begin to deal with the form and structure of what we know. The problem can be put succinctly. I know that John's parents live in Toronto. One day he utters the following sentence to me:

(29a)   I'm going to visit my Mom and Dad
         this weekend.

The following week I utter the following sentence to someone else:

(29b)   John went to Canada last week.

How did I represent the information from sentence (29a) and then use that information to generate sentence (29b)? Was the information held in some form of linguistic deep structure, in some form of imagery, or in some abstract conceptual form?

Linguistic Deep Structures

When Chomsky (1957) developed his arguments for a transformational-generative grammar, he influenced psychologists as well as linguists. Notably, George Miller (1962) saw the potential relevance of Chomsky's work for the study of language behavior, and began, along with others, to use linguistic concepts to characterize the ways in which people dealt with speech. One of Miller's earlier proposals was that sentences were remembered in ways that were analogous to Chomsky's formal grammar. The grammar characterized any given sentence in terms of a surface structure that is derivable from an underlying kernel or deep structure:

> To understand a sentence it is necessary (though not of course sufficient) to reconstruct its representation on each level, including the transformational level where the kernel sentences underlying a

given sentence can be thought of, in a sense, as the 'elementary content elements' out of which this sentence is constructed [Chomsky, 1957, pp. 107–108].

Miller translated this concept into the proposal that people comprehend sentences by "transforming" the surface structure back into its kernel, and then storing two aspects of a sentence in memory. One aspect is the kernel or deep-structure representation; the other is a list of transformations that would be needed to reconstruct the original surface structure. Among the transformations that could be so stored are the ACTIVE (A), PASSIVE (P), NEGATION (N), and QUESTION (Q). The active transformation was considered to be relatively simple; the others were considered to be more complex. The sentences listed below represent transforms of the same underlying deep structure:

Sentence	Transformations
The boy hit the ball.	A
The ball was hit by the boy.	P
The boy did not hit the ball.	N
Did the boy hit the ball?	Q
The ball was not hit by the boy.	PN
Was the ball hit by the boy?	PQ
Did the boy not hit the ball?	QN
Was the ball not hit by the boy?	PQN

Miller made two assumptions about learning and remembering sentences: (a) each additional transformation created additional difficulty in processing, and (b) the kernel and each transformational tag were stored independently in memory. Both of these assumptions were tested in an experiment by Jacques Mehler (1963). He found first that people learned the active sentences faster than any of the other types. Second, when errors were made, they tended to be in the direction of simpler forms as if transformational tags were "lost." Hence, if a PQN sentence is stored as [*the boy hit the ball* + P + Q + N] and the P and Q tags were forgotten, the resulting recall would be *the boy did not hit the ball,* that is, [*the boy hit the ball* + N].

These results are consistent with Miller's extensions of transformational-generative grammar, as were the results of an ingenious experiment by Savin and Perchonock (1965). They took advantage of the fact that immediate memory is limited. For example, when we hear a list of unrelated words and are asked to repeat them, we can usually handle no more than seven or eight at a time (Miller, 1956). If a sentence takes up some of the space in immediate memory, then the space left over would determine how much additional material can be remembered. The more space taken up by the sentence, the less space there is available for other material. If sentences are stored as [kernel + transformational tags], then complex sentences should take up more space than simple sentences because complex sentences need more tags and so should leave less space in memory than simple sentences.

The experiment was designed to reflect this logic. People were given a sentence to remember, followed by eight unrelated nouns (the additional material). The sentence had to be recalled along with as many of the other nouns that could be remembered. The number of nouns recalled with each sentence type was taken as an estimate of the space left over after the sentence had been stored. This experiment and two interpretations of it are illustrated in Figure 4.9. Memory representation A reflects a transformational complexity interpretation; B reflects a simpler interpretation based on the approximate number of words in each sentence type. Savin and Perchonock's results could support either interpretation. Either the number of transformations or the length of a sentence affected the number of words that could be recalled.

The same problem can be raised with respect to Mehler's memory experiment: either transformational complexity or sentence length or relative frequency of the various types of sentences could account for the results. Indeed, a number of replications of the Savin and Perchonock experiment have identified nonlinguistic "performance" factors that account for their results: sentence length (Matthews, 1968), the time delays between the end of the word list and the beginning of word recall (Glucksberg & Danks, 1969), and other purely performance factors (Boakes & Lodwick, 1971).

These alternatives to the early deep-structure hypotheses were compelling, but were hardly definitive. They simply pointed out that the particular experiments had not adequately tested the transformational-generative model. Among other things, one could argue that, when people try to remember isolated sentences, they need not deal with them as they would when talking and listening to one another. In some memory tasks, we can recall sentences or word lists verbatim. In others, we may have to remember the meaning of what we hear or read several hours or days later. One would hardly expect people to use the same learning or encoding strategies in both cases. The obvious solution to the problem was to design more appropriate laboratory tasks.

Unfortunately, a second major problem arose. As syntactic theory developed, it became evident that one had a wide choice of "deep structures." Even within transformational-generative grammar, one had a choice of Chomsky's 1957 model, in which active sentences were considered to be

INPUT

Sentence Type	Sentence	Unrelated Words To be Recalled
A	The boy hit the ball.	bush, horse, car, day, bed, rain, hat, green
P	The ball was hit by the boy.	bush, horse, car, day, bed, rain, hat, green
PQN	Was the ball not hit by the boy?	bush, horse, car, day, bed, rain, hat, green

MEMORY REPRESENTATION A

Sentence Type	Representation: KERNEL	TAG/WORD	TAG/WORD	TAG/WORD	WORD	WORD	WORD	Hypothetical Number of Words Recalled
A	The boy hit the ball	bush	horse	car	day	rain	green	6
P	The boy hit the ball	P	bush	car	bed	hat	rain	5
PQN	The boy hit the ball	P	Q	N	horse	bed	green	3

MEMORY REPRESENTATION B

<table>
<tr><th>Sentence Type</th><th>Representation: SENTENCE PLUS</th><th>WORD</th><th>WORD</th><th>WORD</th><th>WORD</th><th>WORD</th><th>WORD</th><th>Hypothetical Number of Words Recalled</th></tr>
<tr><td>A</td><td>The boy hit the ball</td><td>bush</td><td>horse</td><td>car</td><td>day</td><td>rain</td><td>green</td><td>6</td></tr>
<tr><td>P</td><td colspan="3">The ball was hit by the boy</td><td>car</td><td>bed</td><td>hat</td><td>rain</td><td>4</td></tr>
<tr><td>PQN</td><td colspan="4">Was the ball not hit by the boy?</td><td>horse</td><td>bed</td><td>green</td><td>3</td></tr>
</table>

FIGURE 4.9 Examples of the sets of stimulus items used by Savin and Perchonock (1965). The lower half shows two hypothetical organizations of the material in memory, and corresponding expected recall performance.

"simpler" than passive sentences, and his 1965 model, in which active and passive sentences were equally "complex." Which should one choose, and on what basis? Should one opt for Fillmore's (1968) case grammar relations as "deep structures," or Schank's (1972) conceptual dependencies? It is important to remember that no adequate linguistic theory has yet been formulated. Each of those mentioned is important as a proposal for a type of theory which, in principle (and in the future), might be developed into an adequate grammar.

Given this state of affairs it seems fruitless to argue that our knowledge of sentences and what sentences represent must be in any given linguistic deep-structure format. It seems more useful to explore the possible ways that people remember sentential information. Two general classes of representation other than verbal have been explored recently—imagery and abstract conceptual representation.

Imagery

When people are asked to remember lists of unrelated items, performance is far better with lists of pictures than with lists of words (Paivio & Csapo, 1973). If the words refer to concrete, easily visualized things, they are easier to remember than words that refer to abstract concepts. If people are asked to visualize the referents of words, they remember them better than when they are not asked to do so. These, as well as many other findings of the effectiveness of visual imagery for memory, suggest that the information expressed by sentences might also be represented in memory in the form of images.

Can we represent sentences in the form of images, and if so, when do we do so? One way to find out how people represent material in memory is to ask them to memorize sentences, and then use two or more types of hints or prompts. If one type of prompt is more effective in aiding recall than another, then the memory format is probably similar in certain respects to that more effective prompt. Blumenthal (1967) used this logic to argue that people store "deep-structure" information when they memorize sentences. He used sentences like

(30a)   The gloves were made by tailors.

(30b)   The gloves were made by hand.

If only the verbatim record of the sentences had been retained, then *tailors* and *hand* should be equally effective as prompts for remembering the sentences. *Tailors* was a more effective prompt for later recall, presumably because information about how things are made is not as central to the meaning of a sentence as who made things (the agent of a sentence).

Another possibility is that it is easier to visualize the phrase *by tailors* than it is to visualize the phrase *by hand*. If imagery is the favored way to represent sentential information, then high-imagery material would be remembered better and would also be more effective prompts for remembering.

Consistent with our expectations that people can and do use many forms of representation, it turns out that both imagery value and the "centrality" of the prompt are important. If we use high-imagery sentences like

(31a)   The grades were issued
            by professors.

(31b)   The grades were issued by letter.

and compare the effectiveness of agent prompts (like *professors*) and non-agent prompts (like *letter*), we get no difference. It seems that the type of prompt is not critical if both types are visualized easily. However, when we use low-imagery sentences like

(32a)   The game was played by substitutes.

(32b)   The game was played by permission.

then agent prompts (*substitutes*) work better than nonagent prompts (*permission*). Indeed, the low-imagery agent prompt in sentence (32a) is just as effective as the high-imagery prompts for sentences (31a) and (31b) (Danks & Sorce, 1973).

Whether we use imagery apparently depends on the type of material we are dealing with. If the material cannot be easily imaged, then we can rely on linguistic or on abstract conceptual forms of representation. Indeed, the "image" itself may be more like knowledge about relations among items than like a "mental picture." Sentences that produce vivid picture-like images can be compared with sentences which produce unclear images, at best. Compare sentence (33a) with sentence (33b):

(33a)   A harp is sitting on top of the torch
            held up by the Statue of Liberty.

(33b)   A harp is hidden inside the torch
            held up by the Statue of Liberty.

The first sentence is rated as very high in vividness, the second as low, yet they are recalled equally well. They are also recalled much better than sentences that do not describe a relationship between two items, like sentence (33c):

(33c)   Looking from one window, you see
            the Statue of Liberty; from a

window in the other wall, you see
a harp.

Imagery seems less like a two-dimensional picture and more like a "mental layout" (Neisser & Kerr, 1973). It should not be too much of a step to go beyond mental layouts to abstract conceptual knowledge.

Abstract Conceptual Representation

People seem to remember the meanings of sentences, even when those sentences have virtually no imagery value. When imagery is not appropriate, we use other devices to comprehend and remember them. We can understand and remember sentences like

(34)   Philosophers are concerned with
          epistemological issues.

With sentences like this one (Franks & Bransford, 1972), and with high-imagery sentences as well, we remember the gist and often forget the specific words and sentences themselves. This was neatly demonstrated in an experiment performed by Jacqueline Sachs (1967). Sachs read stories like this to people:

There is an interesting story about the telescope. In Holland, a man named Lippershey was an eye-glass maker. One day his children were playing with some lenses. They discovered that things seemed very close if two lenses were held about a foot apart. Lippershey began experimenting and his "spyglass" attracted much attention. *He sent a letter about it to Galileo, the great Italian scientist.* [zero syllables] Galileo at once realized the importance of the discovery and set about to build an instrument of his own. He used an old organ pipe with one lense curved out and the other in. On the first clear night he pointed the glass toward the sky. He was amazed to find the empty dark spaces filled with brightly gleaming stars! [80 syllables] Night after night Galileo climbed to a high tower, sweeping the sky with his telescope. One night he saw Jupiter, and to his great surprise discovered near it three bright stars, two to the east and one to the west. On the next night, however, all were to the west. A few nights later there were four little stars. [160 syllables] [Sachs, 1967, pp. 438–439]

The italicized sentence *He sent a letter about it to Galileo, the great Italian scientist* is the critical sentence, although people did not know it while hearing the story. After zero, 80, or 160 syllables, the story was interrupted and a test sentence was presented. People were to respond "yes" if that test sentence had occurred verbatim, and "no" if it differed in any way from the critical sentence. A test sentence could be any one of these four types:

IDENTICAL: He sent a letter about it to Galileo, the great Italian scientist. (no change)

SEMANTIC: Galileo, the great Italian scientist, sent him a letter about it. (change in word order and meaning)

PASSIVE: A letter about it was sent to Galileo, the great Italian scientist. (no change in meaning, change in sentence voice)

FORMAL: He sent Galileo, the great Italian scientist, a letter about it. (no change in meaning, change in order of phrases)

Only the first type, identical, should get a "yes" response. How well did people do? If the test comes immediately after the critical sentence, performance is quite good for all test sentence types (see Figure 4.10). After only 80 syllables (about 27 seconds), performance is close to chance level unless the test sentence changed the meaning of the critical sentence. If it did, then people would notice the difference, and say "no." Otherwise,

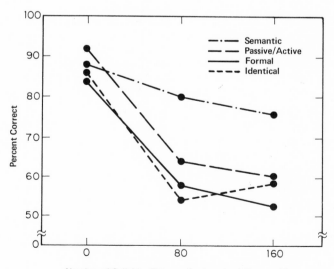

FIGURE 4.10   People remember the meaning of a sentence and very little else about it. (After Sachs, 1967.)

they could hardly detect any changes at all. We store information about the meaning or idea of a sentence and little if anything is remembered about surface details a mere 27 seconds after hearing the sentence. Test yourself. Did this sentence occur a few lines back? *Four types of test sentences were used.*

Sach's results clearly demonstrate that people can remember meaning and little else about the messages they hear. Do people also remember more than they actually hear? Bransford and Franks (1971) maintain that we do. They envision comprehension as a constructive process. As information is received, it is integrated with other information to form a single new "understanding." Bransford and Franks presented four unrelated complex ideas, each of which was composed of four simple ideas. In Table 4.2 the FOUR is an example of one of the complex ideas and the ONES are the four simple components. Listeners heard 24 sentences, 6 from each unrelated set (indicated by an "a" for acquisition in Table 4.2), but were not told to remember them. They only had to answer a simple question immediately following each sentence. Sentences from the four different complex ideas were interspersed, so that listeners might have difficulty connecting up the four complex ideas. Following presentation of the sentences, the listeners were given a recognition test of 28 sentences, most of which had not been presented during acquisition (indicated by a "t" for test in

TABLE 4.2
Sentences Comprising a Complex Idea[a,b]

FOUR:	(t)	The ants in the kitchen ate the sweet jelly which was on the table.
THREEs:	(a)	The ants ate the sweet jelly which was on the table.
	(a)	The ants in the kitchen ate the jelly which was on the table.
	(t)	The ants in the kitchen ate the sweet jelly.
TWOs:	(a)	The ants in the kitchen ate the jelly.
	(a & t)	The ants ate the sweet jelly.
	(t)	The sweet jelly was on the table.
	(t)	The ants ate the jelly which was on the table.
ONEs:	(a)	The ants were in the kitchen.
	(a)	The jelly was on the table.
	(t)	The jelly was sweet.
	(t)	The ants ate the jelly.
Other FOURs:	(t)	The warm breeze blowing from the sea stirred the heavy evening air.
	(t)	The rock which rolled down the mountain crushed the tiny hut at the edge of the woods.
	(t)	The old man resting on the couch read the story in the newspaper.

[a] From Bransford and Franks (1971).

[b] a, acquisition; t, test.

Table 4.2). People recognized both old (marked with "a" and "t") and new (marked with only a "t") sentences as having occurred previously, even though this was correct only of the "olds." In addition, the more complex the test sentence was, the more confident they were that they had heard it previously. This result is most striking for the FOURS, because people never heard any FOURS at all during the acquisition phase, nor did they hear any sentence that was as long or as complex. Yet they were more certain that they had heard the FOURS than any other sentence type. The comprehension process appears to involve more than simply encoding what is presented: it is constructive in integrating information into a single coherent schema. Constructive comprehension of this kind is not dependent on imagery, for low-imagery sentences like

(35)   The intense desire to be successful
        can determine all personal action.

work just as well in constructive memory tasks as do high-imagery sentences (Franks & Bransford, 1972).

In these experiments people evidently constructed a single representation or schema for the information involved in each complex idea. Is all the information equally accessible or was the recognition memory test too insensitive to detect differences? Read these two paragraphs and answer the question that follows.

A: The council of elders in the land of Syndra meets whenever a stranger arrives. If the council meets and if the stranger presents the proper gifts to the council, he is not molested by the natives. The explorer Portmanteau came to Syndra without any valuable gifts.

B: The arrival of strangers in the land of Syndra, like the explorer Portmanteau, who did not bring valuable gifts, always resulted in a meeting of the council of elders, which insured that the stranger was not molested by the natives upon receipt of the proper gifts.

Q: Was Portmanteau molested by the natives? [From Kintsch & Monk, 1972, p. 27]

If you are like most of us, it took you longer to read paragraph B than paragraph A, even though both present identical information. Paragraph A was written using simple sentences that straightforwardly expose the underlying logic. Paragraph B was written as a single complex sentence. Kintsch and Monk (1972) constructed many paragraphs like these and found that reading times for complex paragraphs were longer than for simple ones. However, the time for readers to answer the question was the same. Once the information was registered and organized in memory, it was equally accessible for further use regardless of how it got there.

Now we are more confident in concluding that people can construct complex schemata to store information in memory. We can apparently use many representational formats—verbatim, various linguistic structures, abstract conceptual, visual and acoustic imagery—to code and store information. The particular mode or modes used on any given occasion depends on the kind of information involved and the characteristics of the task.

COMPREHENSION AND KNOWLEDGE OF
THE WORLD

Comprehension, broadly conceived, is an active process that uses prior knowledge to interpret and organize the meanings of utterances. Bransford and Franks' and Kintsch and Monk's experiments required people to integrate only knowledge from the experimental materials alone. We must also be able to integrate what we hear with what we already know. If we hear the sentence

(36)   John remembered to let the dog out.,

we know that the dog is out. We also know that the dog is supposed to be out. However, there is a qualitative difference between these two items of information. That the dog is out can be logically inferred from sentence (36), and is, therefore, called an INFERENCE. The latter information, that the dog is supposed to be out, is a PRESUPPOSITION. When comprehending the sentence, we assume that the presupposition is true, even though it is not necessarily true. One way to show the difference is to negate the sentence, as in either (37a) or (37b):

(37a)   John did not remember to let the
         dog out.

(37b)   John forgot to let the dog out.

Both mean the same except that in sentence (37a) the negation is explicit and in (37b) it is implicit. That the dog is not out cannot be inferred from either sentence (37a) or (37b): someone else may have let the dog out or the dog may still be in. However, the presuppositions of sentences (36), (37a), and (37b) remain the same. Even if John did forget to let the dog out, we still assume that he was supposed to do so. Just and Clark (1973) examined the difference between inference and presupposition in a sentence-verification task. After reading either (36) or (37b), the reader responded to tests of the inference, *the dog is out* versus *the dog is in,* or to tests of the presupposition, *the dog is supposed to be out* versus *the dog is supposed to be in.* The latencies to answer "true" or "false" were measured. No differences were found for the presupposition, but it took longer to decide about the inference for sentence (37b). Hence, we are able to use the explicit information, and we can also use our knowledge of interpersonal expectations and sociocultural restrictions on utterances to arrive at interpretations of the situations described by sentences.

We also make inferences about necessary spatiotemporal relations among the referents of a sentence. Say we hear the following description:

(38)   The river was narrow. A beaver hit
         the log that a turtle was sitting on
         and the log flipped over from the
         shock. The turtle was very surprised
         by the event [Johnson, Bransford,
         & Solomon, 1973, p. 204].

We organize what we have heard into a coherent structure. On the basis of that construction people would probably respond "yes" to a recognition item like sentence (39) because we know that, if the log flipped over, the turtle was very likely knocked into the water:

(39)   A beaver hit the log and knocked
         the turtle into the water.

However, had we substituted *beside* for *on* in the second sentence of the description in (38), people would have probably not made the same inference because, when the turtle is sitting *beside* the log rather than *on* it, we would not infer that the turtle had fallen into the water. Johnson *et al.* (1973) found that, when people hear descriptions like (38) with *on,* they inferred subsequent events like (39) over 60% of the time. If the description is changed by substituting *beside* for *on,* they made the inference less than 25% of the time.

This experiment demonstrated the construction of spatial schemata (see also Bransford, Barclay, & Franks, 1972). Harris and Brewer (1973) showed a somewhat similar phenomenon for the temporal dimension. Memory for verb tenses was strongly dependent on time cues that provided a temporal context. When we hear sentences and passages, we do more than simply assign meanings to them in isolation. We relate them to what we know is possible and likely in the real world, constructing a whole happening, not just a single event (Bartlett, 1932).

In other cases, our knowledge of the world is required to help us comprehend and interpret what we hear. Read the following paragraph carefully:

With hocked gems financing him, our hero bravely defied all scorn-
ful laughter that tried to prevent his scheme. "Your eyes deceive,"
he had said. "An egg, not a table, correctly typifies this unexplored
planet." Now three sturdy sisters sought proof. Forging along, sometimes through calm vastness, yet more often over turbulent peaks and
valleys, days became weeks as many doubters spread fearful rumors
about the edge. At last, from nowhere welcome winged creatures appeared signifying momentous success [adapted from Dooling & Lachman, 1971, p. 217].

Now turn the book over and write down as much as you can remember.
It was probably fairly difficult to understand or remember much of the
passage. If you had known that the paragraph was about "Christopher
Columbus Discovering America," your task would have been much easier.
Now have someone else read and recall the same passage, but provide
the title in advance. He will probably do much better than you did because
he can use what he knows about Columbus to interpret the material (Dooling & Lachman, 1971). As you have probably realized already, it does
not help much to have the title after you have read the paragraph; you
need to have it beforehand (Dooling & Mullet, 1973). The knowledge
about Columbus is used during the original comprehension activity, not
just at the time of recall to reconstruct the passage.

Bransford and Johnson (1972) have obtained similar results using a
picture to facilitate construction of the schema. They used material like
the following paragraph:

If the balloons popped, the sound wouldn't be able to carry since
everything would be too far away from the correct floor. A closed
window would also prevent the sound from carrying, since most build-
ings tend to be well insulated. Since the whole operation depends on
a steady flow of electricity, a break in the middle of the wire would
also cause problems. Of course, the fellow could shout, but the human
voice is not loud enough to carry that far. An additional problem
is that a string could break on the instrument. Then there would be
no accompaniment to the message. It is clear that the best situation
would involve less distance. Then there would be fewer potential
problems. With face to face contact, the least number of things could
go wrong [Bransford & Johnson, 1972, p. 719].

Like the paragraph from Dooling and Lachman (1971), this one is difficult
to integrate without some interpretable context, although the individual
sentences are all perfectly grammatical and meaningful. Now look at the
pictures in Figure 4.11. The one on the left provides a complete context

FIGURE 4.11   Which picture helps you interpret the paragraph (see text)? (After Bransford & Johnson, 1972.)

for understanding the paragraph. The one on the right does not help much, even though it contains the same materials. The trouble is that the materials are not in the appropriate relationships with one another to help interpret the paragraph. Only the picture on the left improved recall for the paragraph and then only when it was viewed before hearing the passage.

All of this suggests that neither sentences nor longer utterances are comprehended in isolation. If a semantically rich grammar is necessary for dealing with sentences, an equally rich "grammar" would be needed for dealing with discourse in general. This conclusion sets the stage for questions about language acquisition. When children begin to acquire their native language, what must they know and learn before they can begin to acquire the sounds, words, and syntactic structures of their language?

SUGGESTED READINGS

For a general introduction to Noam Chomsky's linguistic theory, see J. Lyons, *Noam Chomsky* (New York: Viking, 1970). J. Greene, *Psycholinguistics* (Baltimore, Maryland: Penguin, 1972), provides an overview of generative-transformation grammar and a summary of the psycholinguistic experiments derived from that orientation. Good reviews of syntactic structure as a psychological variable can be found in N. F. Johnson, "Sequential verbal behavior" and M. Garrett and J. Fodor, "Psychological theories and linguistic constructs," both in T. R. Dixon and D. L. Horton (Eds.), *Verbal behavior and general behavior theory* (Englewood Cliffs, New Jersey: Prentice-Hall, 1968). For an excellent review of most of the topics covered in this chapter, see P. N. Johnson-Laird, "Experimental psycholinguistics," *Annual Review of Psychology,* 1974, **25,** 135–160. The report of a conference by J. B. Carroll and R. O. Freedle (Eds.), *Language comprehension and the acquisition of knowledge* (Washington, D.C.: Winston, 1972), provides several perspectives on the comprehension of sentences and connected discourse. For a thorough discussion of the relations between formal theory and the study of language behavior see W. J. M. Levelt, *Formal grammars in linguistics and psycholinguistics,* Volumes I, II, and III (The Hague: Mouton, 1974).

5
Learning Our First Language

Without formal instruction all healthy children acquire a reasonable command of their native language or languages. What do children learn as they do so, and how do they do it? Children acquire their language on the basis of their experience—the speech they hear and what happens when people talk. From this complex of experience children acquire the rules and mechanisms for understanding and producing interpretable speech. During the progression from babbling to adult speech, children develop increasingly complex grammars. This notion represents a departure from the view that children speak a garbled and error-ridden version of adult language. Instead, children's speech can be characterized at any given level of language development as a rule-governed system. The rules children use at one stage differ systematically from the rules at other stages, and they differ systematically from the rules adults use. Even when children use the rules of adult language, their "mistakes" are not mistakes in the usual sense. For example, when a child says "I goed" instead of "I went," he is displaying the use of a past-tense rule. The trouble is, of course, that the rule is applied inappropriately. It is overextended to an irregular verb, but it is certainly not applied randomly or nonsystematically.

This is the central feature of children's speech: it is systematic and rule governed almost from the very first words. The two major objectives of research on language development are (a) to discover and describe the various rule systems underlying children's speech, and (b) to discover how children learn those rules.

119

Whatever the rules are, they are not taught explicitly. First, the rules children use in the early stages are not the same rules that adults use. Second, it is doubtful that rules could be taught explicitly with much success. What would it mean to a two-year-old child to be told that we form the past tense of regular verbs by adding the suffix -ed? Rules like this must somehow be inferred or discovered by everyone who learns to speak English as a first language. For lack of an adequate understanding of how language might be learned, a mechanism for language acquisition has been postulated. This is the LANGUAGE ACQUISITION DEVICE (or LAD).

The language acquisition device may consist of a unique capacity or ability that is specialized for language acquisition (Chomsky, 1968; McNeill, 1966a). Alternatively, it may consist of a concatenation of general cognitive abilities, including sensory, perceptual, conceptual, and social mechanisms (Slobin, 1971b). Whichever it may be, the language acquisition device is that subsystem of our cognitive apparatus which develops a series of grammars as the child matures. These grammars successively tend to approximate adult grammar until the final target is reached—adult language. The role of the language acquisition device in language acquisition is schematically represented in Figure 5.1, along with the potential relations among (a) the hypothetical language acquisition device; (b) the grammar; (c) external inputs (experience); and (d) various internal states.

Input 1 is the perception of the physical and social world, and input 2 represents the speech of people in that world. Input 3 represents the child's developing conceptual system. The language acquisition device itself may be regarded as an integral part of that conceptual–cognitive system, or as a separate mechanism which can draw information from "cognition" and transmit information back. In either case, the language acquisition device constructs the grammar, using all the available information. The grammar itself has two separable components: a COMPREHENSION COMPONENT

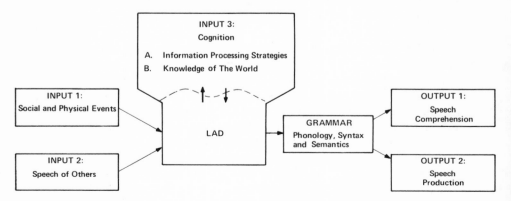

FIGURE 5.1   The components involved in language acquisition.

and a PRODUCTION COMPONENT. The comprehension component includes the mechanisms for speech perception and for semantic and syntactic analyses. The production component applies the rules of the grammar to meanings that a child intends to express and realizes these meanings in overt speech.

This description cannot be taken literally. Its only purpose is to highlight the kinds of interactions and relations involved in learning to understand and speak a language. It leads us to ask specific kinds of questions about various aspects of the language acquisition process. First, when language is acquired, what specifically is acquired? What shall we put into the box labeled "grammar"? Chomsky (1968) proposed an innate universal grammar as one answer to this question:

> Suppose that we assign to the mind, as an innate property, the general theory of language that we have called "universal grammar." This theory . . . specifies a certain subsystem of rules that provides a skeletal structure for any language and a variety of conditions, formal and substantive, that any further elaboration of the grammar must meet. The theory of universal grammar, then, provides a schema to which any particular grammar must conform. Suppose, furthermore, that we can make this schema sufficiently restrictive so that very few possible grammars conforming to the schema will be consistent with the *meager and degenerate data actually available to the language learner* [italics added]. His [the child's] task, then, is to search among the possible grammars and select one that is not definitely rejected by the data available to him. What faces the language learner, under these assumptions, is not the impossible task of inventing a highly abstract and intricately structured theory on the basis of degenerate data, but rather the much more manageable task of determining whether these data belong to one or another of a fairly restricted set of potential languages [p. 76].

According to this view, the language acquisition device starts with a fundamental knowledge of any of the languages that a child might possibly encounter. A language is not so much learned as it is "selected" from among a set of innately given structures. This proposal assumes, among other things, that the "data" available to a child are "degenerate." What are these data? Chomsky restricts these data to input 2 in our diagram (the speech a child hears), and to the syntactic aspects of input 2, at that. This assumption raises a second set of questions. What are the necessary and sufficient inputs to the language acquisition device? What do inputs 1 and 2 actually consist of, and what are the relations between inputs 1 and 2? Until quite recently, very little was known about the kind and amount of speech children are exposed to, and how the speech they hear and speak is related to the things and events in the world about them. Some recent observations suggest that the data available to children are neither meager nor degenerate (Shatz & Gelman, 1973; Snow, 1972), and that the relations between speech and other experience may be critical (Bloom, 1970). We return to this issue later.

Next, what is involved in input 3—what must a child know in order to construct a grammar? For example, when a child learns the word *table,* it would be useful (and perhaps necessary) to have some concept of what a table is. It would also be useful to know that in general things have names.[1] Finally, what are the important characteristics of the feedback children receive about their speech? Do parents correct children's syntax? Should they do so?

Before we can come to any decisions about the nature of the language acquisition device, each of these questions must be answered in some detail. We begin by considering what children learn when they acquire their native language.

WHAT IS ACQUIRED AND WHEN?

What Is Learned First?

If we observe children carefully, we are tempted to believe that they seem to understand much of what people say long before they themselves say anything at all. How much children can comprehend and what they do comprehend are difficult to specify. Can preverbal children comprehend more speech than a family's Irish setter? The answer, most likely, is yes, but the necessary detailed observations have yet to be made (Nelson, 1973). When children do begin to talk, our intuition tells us that they first learn speech sounds, then words, then sentences. If children were to follow this sequence of sounds to words to sentences, then language acquisition might be impossible. How could children learn what a word means

---

[1] The most dramatic illustration of how the concept of naming can be crucial to language learning is how Helen Keller learned her first "word" (Keller, 1903). Helen Keller became deaf and blind before she had learned to talk. All efforts to teach her touch signs for things had seemed doomed to failure. One day, in a flash of insight, Ms. Keller grasped the relation between a touch sign on her hand and the feel of water trickling on her other hand. The pattern of touch on one hand meant "water." This incident released, as it were, a flood of new learning. Once the concept of a naming relation between signs and referents had been communicated, learning proceeded fluently and easily. As is well known, Ms. Keller became a prominent citizen and author.

unless they could first understand the intended meaning of the utterance? Macnamara (1972) has astutely noted that a child must first "know" what someone is saying before he can figure out what the words mean. Unless one knows what someone is saying, there is no way to relate the sounds to the concepts expressed by those sounds. The first step toward acquiring a language is thus the ability to understand or infer what a speaker is talking about. Until a child can do that, language learning cannot proceed.

A similar argument applies to the acquisition of phonology. At an early stage, children may be able to imitate speech sounds without systematically organizing those sounds. Before a child can begin to acquire a phonemic system, however, he must first learn a minimal set of words. He must learn words before he can learn phonemes because phonemes are defined in terms of the differences they make in word meanings.

We have been treating language in terms of its components—sounds, words, and sentences. This classification is useful for analytic purposes, and we will continue to use it here. Still, we cannot emphasize too strongly that this classification is artificial—it is a convenient fiction. In acquisition and usage the components are inseparable. Consider the interactions involved in learning speech sounds and learning word meanings. Phonemic distinctions can be identified and learned only in the context of semantic distinctions. As described in Chapter 2, the phonemes /p/ and /b/ are different only because they make a semantic difference: *pit* versus *bit*, *pat* versus *bat*, and so on. If each of these pairs of words had the same meaning, then the sounds [p] and [b] would be allophones of the same phoneme. Children must be able to discriminate among words before they can infer that, say, /p/ and /b/ are two different phonemes. In this case, voicing is recognized as a distinctive feature because it makes a difference in the meanings of words.[2]

If the components of language are inextricably interrelated, how shall we characterize the sequences of learning those components? Beyond the very first stages, the components are learned together and interactively. At the very beginning, language does not start with sounds and then move to words and then to sentences. It starts with meanings. First, some understanding of what people are saying is necessary. Once children begin to understand what people are saying, they can begin to decode the meanings of some words. When some minimal set of words can be comprehended, then work can begin on the phonological system. During this period children must rely on a phonetic, rather than phonemic, system for speech

[2] It is possible that the child has a head start for recognizing critical differences among some speech sounds. As reported in Chapter 2 (page 42) four-week-old infants discriminated categorically between [bæ] and [pæ] (Eimas, Siqueland, Jusczyk, & Vigorito, 1971). Whether this early categorical perception occurs with other speech sounds has yet to be determined.

production—imitative production of individual speech sounds.[3] The acquisition of syntax, including knowledge of the structural meanings of sentences, develops concurrently, again with comprehension leading production. For convenience, we start with the acquisition of the sounds of a language.

Learning the Sound System of a Language

Babbling.   During the latter part of the first year of life infants begin to vocalize incessantly. They produce a wide variety of speech-like sounds, and some of these sounds resemble the sounds of the parents' language. Others are not found in the native language, and some are not speech sounds in any language (coughs, gurgles, and what have you). Out of this universe of sounds infants gradually select out the particular sounds of their native language. One mechanism that may operate to facilitate this selection is the differential rewards children get for making various sounds. Once in a while a child will utter a sound that resembles a real word. For example, an eight-month-old child may frequently say "Hi." Adults react to this utterance with smiles and they say "Hi" right back. This kind of social interchange should reinforce the response of saying "Hi," and the child should say "Hi" more often. Should not the child soon develop the sounds /h/ and /ai/ as a result of this selective reinforcement?

Some utterances may enter a child's repertoire in this way, but selective reinforcement cannot be the only mechanism involved in phonological development. First, the sequence in which speech sounds appear at different periods of development is fairly regular. During the babbling stage of the first year, consonants appear in an orderly sequence, from back to front. For example, /k/ occurs before /p/. For vowels, the order is just the opposite. A front vowel like /i/ (as in *beet*) is usually produced before a back vowel like /a/ (as in *mama*). It is highly unlikely that parents selectively reinforce their children to do this, either intentionally or accidentally. During the second year, when a child's first words normally appear, the order of speech sound production is the reverse of the first year's babbling sequence. The first words usually include a front consonant like /p/ or /m/ and a back vowel like /a/. Here too, it is unlikely that parents

---

[3] Even imitation is no simple matter, because it presupposes a knowledge of how the vocal tract can be used. How does a child know how to produce any particular speech sound he hears? This question is not unique to speech imitation. How does a child know how to imitate a parent's smile, or the movement of hands and fingers? How do children learn the correspondences between other people's limbs, fingers, lips, eyelids, and the like, and his own limbs, fingers, and so forth? If language learning seems mysterious to us, the development of the accurate self-image that is necessary for imitative behavior is no less so.

now reverse their pattern of reinforcement to lead their children through a new sequence of sound production. They, of course, will reinforce utterances like *mama* and *papa*, which are likely to occur during this period.

Between the babbling and first-word stages we find a period of relative silence. For about a month or so, children say very little. The first words have yet to be produced, and little or no babbling can be observed. This too restricts the role that reinforcement might play. If parents have been effectively reinforcing speech production, why should children stop vocalizing for a while? The babbling should not stop but, instead, change gradually into real speech.

Finally, the babbling behavior itself seems to be resistant to parental reactions. Much of this behavior looks more like solitary play than speech intentionally directed toward other people. Children often discover that they can make funny sounds, like a cough or a loud, high-pitched squeal. Parents seldom if ever reward this behavior. Indeed, many parents do their best to suppress it, usually to no avail. A child may go on and on, varying pitch, loudness, and stress patterns as if he were practicing how to control his vocal apparatus. How parents respond to this behavior could not seem to matter less.

Our suspicion that babbling provides the infant with vocal practice is strengthened somewhat by one peculiar characteristic of babbling behavior. Toward the end of the babbling period a child's vocalizations begin to take on the intonation patterns of the parents' speech. A Japanese babble sounds like adult Japanese speech; an English babble sounds like adult English speech. Not a single bit of these babbled utterances is interpretable, even though it may sound as if the child is uttering complete and quite complicated sentences. Parents who notice this are often delighted but, despite expressions of parental joy, children soon stop babbling altogether. Shortly thereafter, one–word utterances appear, and the child begins to show some evidence of acquiring the individual speech sounds of his language.

Beyond Babbling.   What goes on during the relatively silent period between babbling and the first words? We can only speculate. One possibility is that the child is attending to the individual words he hears rather than to the sounds people make when they speak. If he can learn to hear and understand words, then he can begin to discover the rudiments of the phonemic system. As the child acquires words, he can begin to learn which speech–sound differences are important (phonemic) and which are not. There are two aspects to this learning, PERCEPTION and PRODUCTION, and they progress at different rates. It is quite common for children to hear important differences before they are able to produce them. Parents and linguists delight in anecdotes about children like Erika. When Erika was three, she pronounced her name "Ewika." If someone repeated "Ewika?," she would protest, "No, Ewika!" "Is it Erika, then?" "Yes, you siwwy, Ewika!"

Is this kind of mispronunciation the result of an inability to articulate the sounds [r] and [l]? Not at all. Erika had no difficulty with [r] or [l] sounds in certain other contexts. For example, she pronounced the word *late* perfectly. Only when [r] or [l] followed a vowel were they pronounced as [w]. Neal Smith (1973), a linguist who systematically observed his own child, found the emergent sound system highly systematic. "Mispronunciations" were consistent and regular, and, as the child developed, the kinds of mispronunciations changed systematically. When changes occurred, they did so abruptly, and always involved a set of speech sounds rather than just one sound. Smith also observed that as soon as the child shifted his pronunciation patterns, he could no longer recognize a word if it were pronounced in accordance with his previous pattern. For example, at one time he had pronounced the consonant cluster [kw] as [k], and he pronounced [n] as [m]. Hence, the word *queen* was pronounced *keem*. After he had shifted to adult pronunciation, he was unable to understand what "keem" meant.

These observations are consistent with the notion that children learn systems of sounds, not just how to articulate individual sounds. If children learned nothing more than individual sounds, then bilingual children should make the same pronunciation mistakes in each of their two languages. If a child does not contrast /r/ and /l/ in English, then he should make the same mistake in a second language such as Spanish. Mazeika (1971) observed the phonological development of a child in a Spanish–English home. The errors made in English were not the same as the ones made in Spanish. Sounds that the child apparently could not make when he spoke English were correctly produced when he spoke Spanish, and vice versa. Therefore, it must be the case that the child is able to produce the sounds, but has not yet learned when to say what. It is as if the child is figuring out the system of sounds used in each language separately. The bilingual case presumably mirrors the monolingual case. Whatever language a child learns, he must discover the relevant distinctive features for the sound system of that language. In English, for example, children must learn that voicing is phonemic, and that aspiration is not. In Hindi, aspiration is phonemic, and, if a child grows up in an English–Hindi environment, he must learn both patterns, and must keep them separate. Learning to produce individual speech sounds is not enough.

The notion that children acquire distinctive feature systems instead of individual sounds was first advanced by Roman Jakobson (1941). Jakobson further claimed that all children, regardless of the language involved, acquired phonemic contrasts in the same sequence. The first contrast learned is between consonants and vowels, and this would usually involve two maximally different sounds, such as a front consonant /p/ and a back vowel /a/. These two classes then would be differentiated further by adding various features until all the distinctive features of the language had been acquired.

Is the order of acquiring distinctive features invariant? This is difficult to test because we cannot find out whether a child knows a distinctive feature contrast unless he knows pairs of words that depend upon that contrast.[4] The evidence we do have suggests that there is far more variability than would be expected if all children acquired distinctive features in the same sequence (Garnica, 1973). This is not inconsistent with the notion that distinctive feature systems are acquired, but it does suggest that the order of feature learning depends upon at least two factors. One is the factor suggested by Jakobson—the relative discriminability of feature contrasts. The second factor involves the role of word meanings. Unless at least two words known by the child are differentiated by a given feature contrast, that contrast cannot be discovered. Hence, the particular sets of words a child learns should influence the order in which feature contrasts are acquired.

Children thus are faced with "two different tasks which have previously been lumped under the title of 'phonology acquisition' . . . while the child is learning pronunciation, or phonetic representation, he is also learning the system, or phonological [phonemic] representation" (Moskowitz, 1970, p. 440). The appearance of a phonemic system seems to coincide with the "appearance of a need for naming" (Shvachkin, 1973, p. 104). The development of a sound system, then, involves two sequences. The order in which phonetic representations are acquired depends primarily on the sounds a child hears and imitates. The order of acquiring phonemic contrasts, on the other hand, depends on the feature contrasts that differentiate the words a child learns and uses.

Syntax and Semantics

The First Utterances.   By the time a child has uttered his first words (between 10 and 18 months of age) a massive amount of conceptual learning already has occurred. The child has learned to differentiate himself from others, and is learning to interpret the world he lives in (Sinclair-de Zwart, 1969). The first utterances are single words, but these single words can represent much information. An adult rarely uses a single word to express

[4] This inferential problem is not unique to phonemics. When can we confidently infer that a child has acquired some abstract knowledge, be it phonemic, semantic, or syntactic? Usually, we look for effective use of the knowledge, as in the differentiation of two words to demonstrate knowledge of a phonemic contrast, or the production and comprehension of a class of sentences to demonstrate syntactic competence.

a full message; very young children often do. An adult might say "the dog is eating"; a very young child might say "doggie" to represent the same meaning. These one-word utterances are called HOLOPHRASTIC speech to convey the notion that a single word can represent a whole message.

Adults usually can interpret what a child means from the social and physical context of his utterances. Depending upon what is happening at the moment, a child might use the utterance *milk* to express any one of the following meanings:

(1a)   I want some milk.

(1b)   I want more milk.

(1c)   The milk is gone.

(1d)   Where is the milk?

(1e)   That is milk.

(1f)   Daddy is drinking milk.

(1g)   Mommy, drink the milk.

(1h)   Doggie spilled the milk.

(1i)   I'm thirsty.

And so on. At this point a child's conceptual capacity is not fully reflected in his speech. He may think of any of the ideas or concepts expressed by sentences (1a–i), yet lack the linguistic competence to express those ideas.

During this period of language development children acquire new words at a rapidly accelerating rate. Katherine Nelson (1973) observed 18 children as they uttered their first 50 words. These words appeared, on the average, in about seven months, with the sharpest spurt in the last two months (average age for Nelson's sample was 19.6 months). By 24 months the average production vocabulary was 186 words, and the rate of acquisition was accelerating rapidly.

What do children talk about at this age? In some theories of language development it is suggested that children first talk about concrete objects and events, and later acquire more abstract words. Brown (1958) offers an alternative viewpoint: "It is not invariably true that vocabulary builds from concrete to abstract. *Fish* is likely to be learned before *perch* and *bass; house* before *bungalow* and *mansion* [p. 18]." Instead of a uniform progression from concrete to abstract or vice versa, Brown (1958) suggests that ". . . the sequence in which words are acquired is not determined by the cognitive preferences of children so much as by the naming practices of adults [p. 20]."

Brown's suggestion may characterize vocabulary growth later in childhood, but not the very first words children use. In Nelson's (1973) study, children consistently talked about some things and never about other things, regardless of what their mothers talked about. Animals, food, and toys were among the first ten words of every child. Notably missing from the first 50 words were *diaper, pants, overalls, jacket, sweater,* and *mittens,* even though parents must have used these words quite often in the child's presence. The clothing words that children did tend to use referred to items that they could easily manipulate, like shoes and socks. Nelson (1973) characterizes the early referential behavior of children:

> They do not learn the names of things in the house or outside that are simply "there" whether these are tables, plates, towels, grass, or stores. With very few exceptions all the words listed are terms applying to manipulable or movable objects.
>
> The most common attribute of all of the most frequent early referents is that they have salient properties of change—that is, they do things (roll, run, bark, meow, go *r-r-r* and drive away). . . . The omissions are in general, of things that—however obvious and important—just sit there: sofas, tables, chests, . . . trees, grass. The words that are learned [uttered] are not only the ones the child acts upon in some way (shoes, bottle, ball) but also ones that do something themselves . . . —trucks, clocks, buses, and all the animals [pp. 31–33].

Children seem to name what interests them, and what interests them are things that do something. They notice changes and differences, and this tendency should be useful to them in their search for phonemic patterns because such patterns can only be discovered by noticing differences among words. This interest in things that do something is also consistent with the general notion that children initially learn about the world by interacting actively with it, not by passive observation (Nelson, 1974).

What are parents doing as children learn to talk? Among other things, parents frequently expand short utterances. If a child says "bottle," a parent might say "Do you want your bottle?" This reply is really the parent's guess about what the child intends to communicate, and sometimes parents make mistakes. These mistakes are a potential source of information for the child, pressuring him toward speech elaboration. Single words, no matter how aptly chosen, are too ambiguous to represent the many possible meanings children need to express.

The First Sentences.   The first step toward syntactic competence is putting two words together. Two-word utterances start about the middle of the second year. In some respects, they resemble TELEGRAPHIC SPEECH (Brown & Fraser, 1963). When we write a telegram, we make it as short as possible because every word costs money. We often leave out function words like *to, from,* and *the,* and try to communicate with content words alone. If we wanted to tell someone that we planned to leave Chicago on Wednesday to arrive in New York on Friday, we might write: *Leaving Chicago Wednesday Arrive New York Friday.* Young children's two-word utterances are analogous to telegrams. They are short, omit function words, and represent meanings that adults would express with longer and more complex sentences.

The cost of each word in a telegram is in money. The "cost" of each word a child utters is in cognitive processing capacity and memory. There are limits to the amount of information anyone can process in a given unit of time. Young children have yet to learn how to construct complex sentences, but more critically they lack the memory capacity for storing the elements they need to produce a long sentence. When we produce a sentence, we must have an abstract representation of it "all there" before we begin to utter the first word (Lashley, 1951). We need to know what we are going to say before we say it. If only two-word utterances can be generated, then those two words had better be important ones.

How should we characterize such utterances beyond noting that they are all two-word combinations? Two levels of analysis are involved—the surface-structure syntax and the semantic relations represented by these surface structures. The surface-structure syntax conforms to a pivot grammar (Braine, 1963a, 1963b). A PIVOT GRAMMAR is a system of syntactic rules that specify whether a word may occur alone or must occur with another word in a particular order. All words in the lexicon belong to one of two grammatical classes, pivot or open. The PIVOT CLASS contains a relatively small number of words, and these words are used quite frequently. Pivots are usually used with an OPEN-CLASS word in either first or second position. Words like *allgone, hi, bye-bye* and *it* are pivot-class words. Words like *shoe, vitamins,* and *mommy* are open-class words (see Table 5.1).

A pivot grammar contains only two major types of sentences. One type consists of a pivot word plus an open word, for example, *allgone milk, allgone juice, do it, push it, buzz it.* The other type consists of two open words, like *Mommy milk.* This permits only three surface structures: pivot + open, open + pivot, and open + open.[5] These three surface structures,

---

[5] The pivot + open and open + pivot constructions represent a single generic sentence type, contrasting with the open + open construction. When a child first enters the two-word stage, he probably will have only one pivot class and produce either pivot + open or open + pivot utterances, but not both. He soon develops a second distinct pivot class, and the remaining pattern emerges.

TABLE 5.1
Some of the First Sentences in Child Speech[a]

I. Operations of reference (pivot word + open word)	
NOMINATION:	*That* (or *It* or *There*) + *book, hat, clown, hot, big,* etc.
NOTICE:	*Hi* + *Mommy, cat, belt,* etc.
RECURRENCE:	*More* + *milk, cereal, nut, read, swing, green,* etc.
NONEXISTENCE:	*Allgone* + *rattle, juice, dog, green,* etc.
II. Relational operations (open word + open word)	
ATTRIBUTIVE:	*Big train, Red book,* etc.
POSSESSIVE:	*Adam checker, Mommy lunch,* etc.
LOCATIVE:	*Sweater chair, Book table, Walk street, Go store,* etc.
AGENT–ACTION:	*Adam put, Eve read,* etc.
AGENT–OBJECT:	*Mommy sock, Mommy lunch,* etc.
ACTION–OBJECT:	*Put book, Hit ball,* etc.

[a] From Brown (1970, p. 220). Copyright © 1970 by The Free Press, a division of the Macmillan Company.

however, can represent much more than just three types of sentences. The structural meanings expressed by children using two-word utterances are far more numerous and complex than a pivot grammar implies.

Two-word utterances can represent a number of different semantic relations. Brown (1970, 1973) has classified the most common types of two-word utterances into two major categories—reference operations and relation operations (see Table 5.1). When we use a REFERENCE OPERATION, we say something about an object or event. Nomination is one type of reference operation—we name the object. When a child says *that book,* he may be expressing the message *that thing over there is a book.* This operation is different from telling someone that he has just noticed something (*hi book*) or that something that was here is now gone (*allgone juice*). Within the same class of surface structures (pivot + open) we find at least four types of semantic relations.

When we examine the open + open surface structure, we find at least seven types of RELATIONAL OPERATIONS—utterances that describe relations among two objects, events, or characteristics. *Big train* specifies an attribute of a train. The possessive (*Adam checker*) specifies that something belongs to someone. The locative specifies where something is (*Book table*). As with the pivot + open construction, one surface structure can be used to represent many semantic relations.

If this characterization of children's two-word utterances is accurate, then a pivot grammar is, at best, a partial description of children's language behavior. Lois Bloom (1971) argues that pivot grammars are not only incomplete descriptors, but inaccurate as well. She studied three children extensively and found that only one of them used "a preponderance of utterances" that conformed to a pivot grammar. Even then, the two-word utterances could be classified into several grammatical categories. For example, one child used the utterance *Mommy sock* in two different contexts. In one instance, the child was picking up her mother's sock. In a second, mother was putting the child's sock on the child. The semantic interpretations of the two "identical" utterances are different, as are the grammatical relations between the words *mommy* and *sock*. In the first case, there is a possessive relation, and in the second, an agent–object relation.

Just as in adult grammar, identical surface structures may represent several different grammatical and semantic relations. If an adult were to say

(2a)   They are flying planes.,

we would probably know which of the following alternatives was intended from the context of the conversation:

(2b)   They are piloting airplanes.

(2c)   They are passengers in airplanes.

(2d)   Those things are planes that fly.

(2e)   Those people are transporting
          woodworking tools by air freight.

(2f)   Those woodworking tools actually
          fly through the air.

If we cannot interpret sentence (2a), we could ask the speaker what he means. We can rarely ask young children to explain what they mean. Since their utterances are syntactically ambiguous, the only way we can interpret an utterance like *Mommy sock* is to know the context of that utterance. We have to know where the child is, where he just was, what he is doing, what other people are doing, and whom he is talking to. The speech alone is not enough.

Bloom (1970) used contextual information to analyze the range of semantic and syntactic relations expressed by young children (19 to 27 months). Even a simple two-word negation, like *no truck*, could represent three distinct categories of negation. If a child said *no truck* when she looked into a box and did not find a truck there, then this utterance represented the concept of nonexistence. Something was not there. When this same utterance was produced when the child refused an offer of a truck, then it represented the concept of rejection—she did not want the truck. When an adult pointed to a car and said "truck," the utterance *no truck* represented the concept of denial—that is not a truck.

Similarly, concepts of relations among people and things, like agent–action, action–object, and agent–object can also be inferred from children's two-word utterances. The range and variety of ideas and concepts a child has can clearly exceed her ability to express them unambiguously. This is most apparent when a child is acquiring two languages, for she may often be able to express a concept in one language before she can do so in another. Slobin (1971a) describes two girls who were bilingual in Hungarian and Serbo-Croatian. In Hungarian, locative relations are expressed relatively simply by individual suffixes, each of which specifies a locative relation like *in, on, from, to,* and so on. In Serbo-Croatian, the situation is far more complex. Locative positions (like *on*) are referred to by prepositions (as they are in English), but locative directions (like *from*) require a system of noun inflections that vary as a function of the interaction between position and direction, the gender of the noun, and the final sound of the noun. As each of these girls grew up, they began to specify locative relations explicitly in Hungarian before they could do so in Serbo-Croatian. It would be absurd to conclude that these children did not know certain concepts of temporal–spatial relations when they spoke Serbo-Croatian, but did have those same concepts when they spoke Hungarian. Conceptual competence cannot be inferred from linguistic competence alone.

Young children frequently cannot be understood without reference to the immediate context. If children are to talk about things that are not in the here and now and still be understood, then they must acquire the syntactic and semantic devices appropriate for such communication. Utterances like *Mommy sock* cannot be interpreted unless we know what Mommy and sock are doing. Is Mommy putting a sock on her own foot or on the child's? Is she mending it, holding it, is she present at all? *Mommy sock* is inadequate because it is too ambiguous. Where does the child go from here?

The next step involves longer utterances. One useful measure of a child's language development is the average length of his utterances, measured in morphemes. This measure is commonly referred to as the MEAN LENGTH OF UTTERANCE (MLU). If two children have about the same mean length of utterance, then they are quite likely to have attained the same level of syntactic development (Brown, 1973). Syntactic development involves the acquisition of surface structures beyond the two-word utterances illustrated in Table 5.1. At first, three-term relations like agent–action–object (for example, *Mommy drink milk*) are expressed as two-term relations: agent–action, action–object, or agent–object (for example, *Mommy drink, drink milk,* or *Mommy milk,* respectively). The next step combines these relations, so that *Mommy drink* might be combined with *drink milk* to yield a three-word utterance, *Mommy drink milk.*

Next, children learn to specify other semantic properties by additional syntactic devices, such as inflections. For example, it is obligatory in English to specify whether an object is singular or plural. At first, children refer to a single book or to several books by the word *book*. Sooner or later, children add the plural morpheme (-s) to *book* to make *books,* and to all other plural references as well. Children also have to learn to specify various properties of actions. *Mommy read book* could mean that mother is reading a book, or that mother should read a book, or that the child is curious and wants to know if mother will read a book later. Semantic modulations, such as number and tense, usually develop after children learn to express the semantic relations that can be generated by combining the two-part structures of early speech.

Semantic Development: Differentiation and Generalization

There are at least two aspects to semantic development. The first is relatively straightforward. As the child grows, his vocabulary increases immensely—from the production vocabulary of 50 words at about 17 months to many thousands by adolescence. As the vocabulary grows, word meanings also grow and change.

How do word meanings grow? When a child learns to utter a new word, like *flower,* the development task is just beginning. The concept represented by that word must be differentiated from related concepts, it must be generalized appropriately to all members of the category that adults call *flowers,* and it must be related to superordinate and subordinate categories like *plants* and *roses.* We can emphasize one or another of these developmental progressions. From the differentiation viewpoint, children initially group things into broad categories and gradually subdivide these into smaller categories (McNeill, 1970). A broad categorization of the world might include animals, plants, people, machines, and natural objects like rocks, rivers, and mountains. Gradually, each of these broad categories is subdivided. Animals are classified as mammals, fishes, insects, or birds. Classification ends when it is no longer communicatively useful to make finer distinctions. Children who live in urban North America rarely subcategorize the category of horses—except perhaps to discriminate between ponies and horses. Children who live on a ranch will learn various names for the different kinds of horses they talk about—mares, stallions, foals, quarter horses, and so on.

One result of a differentiation progression like this is overgeneralization. When children first acquire a name for something, they often apply that name too widely. All four-legged furry animals might be called *bow-wows* or *doggies,* and the mailman might be called *Daddy.* The word *flower* may be used to refer to all plants, later only to small plants, and still later to flowers only. McNeill (1970) describes this progression as a process of adding semantic features to a word until its full denotative meaning is acquired. At first, a child might classify a flower as a physical object, then as a living thing, then as a relatively small living thing, and then as a plant. Finally, word-selection restrictions are added which distinguish flowers from other plants. For example, one can arrange flowers, but one usually does not arrange watermelons. Though one can arrange fruits, one does not eat flowers. A typical progression of feature addition is illustrated in Figure 5.2. The order in which features are added may vary across children and words, and two or more features may be added at any given time.

If the order of features can vary, then word meanings need not always grow from the general to the specific. When children are acquiring their first 50 words, we find very few category names or superordinate terms. Most of the early vocabulary consists of highly specific names for things (Nelson, 1973). In many cases, children name individual objects without indicating that they notice similarities among members of the same category (Anglin, 1970). A tulip may not be called a *flower* because it is a tulip. Another child's father may not be called a *Daddy* because he's not "my Daddy." This is the opposite of overgeneralization—it is overdifferentiation. Children as old as four or five years may still insist that they are not *daughters,* they are *little girls.*

Generalization and differentiation of word meanings co-occur as children learn adult systems of classifications. Adults typically use words at some intermediate level of generality when they talk to children. If a father and daughter are looking at a picture of a collie, the most likely name he will use would be *dog* rather than *collie* or *animal.* If he were to use *collie,* the child would have to progress from the specific to the general; if he were to use *animal,* she would have to progress from the general to the specific. In either case, the child will eventually learn that the word *collie* refers to a subset of the category *dog* (DIFFERENTIATION) and that *collie* also refers to a member of the superset *animal* (GENERALIZATION). As Brown (1958) has pointed out, the naming practices of adults will have much to do with the kinds of words children learn, and with their later generalizations and differentiations.

FIGURE 5.2 How word meaning may grow. Hypothetical features are added from most general to specific. (After Mc-Neill, 1970.)

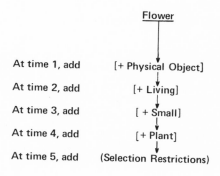

	Flower
At time 1, add	[+ Physical Object]
At time 2, add	[+ Living]
At time 3, add	[+ Small]
At time 4, add	[+ Plant]
At time 5, add	(Selection Restrictions)

When Is Language Development Completed?

The rationalist-innate view of language acquisition expressed by theorists like Chomsky (1968) and McNeill (1966a, 1970) was based in part upon the assumption that children had acquired the essentials of their native language by the time they were four or five years old. Beyond this time, further language development supposedly involved mainly further vocabulary growth and sharpening of communication skills. It seemed inconceivable that children could learn so much in so short a time, and hence the appeal to the language acquisition device—an innate language structure.

Recently, this conclusion has been challenged. Carol Chomsky (1969) found that some major syntactic structures are acquired between the ages of five and ten. These are, as one might expect, relatively complex, but they are not uncommon in ordinary speech. Among these are pairs of sentences that have the same surface structure but different deep structures, for example, *John is easy to see* versus *John is eager to see*. Children were shown a doll named John with a blindfold over its eyes. They were then asked whether John was easy to see. Up to about nine years of age, children incorrectly answer "no." Apparently, the younger children interpret the question as whether the doll can see rather than whether someone can see the doll. Children up to nine also have difficulty with constructions like *John promised Bill to go* versus *John told Bill to go*. The person who "goes" is different: John in the first sentence and Bill in the second, yet younger children interpret both sentences to mean that Bill goes. In addition to syntactic development, phonological and semantic development also proceed through childhood into adolescence (Palermo & Molfese, 1972). What goes on during this relatively long period of time, especially during the early years? How do we learn our native language?

HOW IS LANGUAGE ACQUIRED?

Now that we have some notion of the kinds of things that are involved in language development and the time course for that process, we are faced with the question of how children go about learning their native language. Given the complexity and variety of abilities and knowledge involved in language acquisition, it is likely that every form of learning contributes in one way or another. As in every other developmental process, physiological–maturational processes must also play a central role.

Biological Factors

Whatever the specific biological and social factors may be, human beings seem to be particularly well designed for language learning. All human languages share common features, and only humans seem to master the complex communication system we call language, despite the impressive performances of chimpanzees like Washoe. Furthermore, all children seem to acquire language equally well and at about the same rate, assuming normal health. Even children classified as retardates and confined to institutions display adequate linguistic competence, although gross differences in vocabulary size and language styles do exist.

The biological components of language acquisition are reflected in the importance of maturation. Children do not talk at birth and cannot make certain kinds of speech sounds because their neurological and anatomical equipment is not yet ready. Neither the brain, nor the shape of the mouth and throat, nor the position of the larynx is ready for speech production. The particular level of neural development is particularly critical for language acquisition. Normally, language processing involves neural activity in the dominant hemisphere of the brain (for right-handed people, this would be the left hemisphere). If this part of the brain is damaged in adulthood, there is severe impairment in language behavior, and chances for recovery are relatively poor. If the injury occurs before puberty, then chances for recovery are much better. The younger the person, the greater is the possibility that other parts of the brain can take over the functions that would have been performed by damaged areas. Normally, the two cerebral hemispheres of the brain are connected by the corpus callosum. What goes on in one hemisphere can be communicated to the other. Some people are born without a normally functioning connection, and these "split-brain" people cannot transfer information from one hemisphere to another. In these cases, language functioning develops in both hemispheres rather than just one, helping to compensate for the lack of communication between the two halves of the brain.

If the corpus callosum is damaged or cut in adulthood, only the dominant hemisphere can "speak." Information that is channeled exclusively to the "speaking" left hemisphere can be perceived, understood, and described by a split-brain patient. Information channeled exclusively to the right hemisphere can also be "understood," but cannot be described verbally. The patient behaves appropriately, but acts as though he is completely unaware of what information he received and what he did about it. For example, if a split-brain adult is shown a pair of scissors in his left visual field (which is channeled exclusively to the right side of the brain), he says that he sees nothing (see Figure 5.3). Nevertheless, he can pick out a pair of scissors from among other objects, all of which are hidden from view behind a screen, but only with his left hand (the right side of the brain controls the left hand). His right hand is controlled by the left side of the brain, and since this side of the brain receives no information directly from the other, he cannot select the correct object with his right hand. For the same reasons, he cannot talk about what he

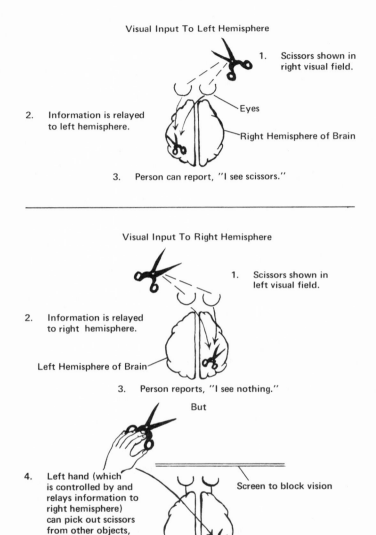

Visual Input To Left Hemisphere

1. Scissors shown in right visual field.

Eyes

2. Information is relayed to left hemisphere.

Right Hemisphere of Brain

3. Person can report, "I see scissors."

Visual Input To Right Hemisphere

1. Scissors shown in left visual field.

2. Information is relayed to right hemisphere.

Left Hemisphere of Brain

3. Person reports, "I see nothing."

But

4. Left hand (which is controlled by and relays information to right hemisphere) can pick out scissors from other objects, when person is asked to pick out what was shown before.

Screen to block vision

5. Right hand cannot do it.

FIGURE 5.3 How a person with a split brain may see something yet not be able to say what he has seen.

has seen or about what he is doing with his left hand. The speech apparatus in the left hemisphere has no access to information in the right hemisphere (Gazzaniga, 1970). Thus far, no split-brain adults have developed compensatory language functioning in the nondominant hemisphere, just as few adults with brain damage in the dominant hemisphere fully recover lost speech functioning.

These observations suggest that the brain is particularly well suited for language acquisition between birth and puberty, and that it loses some of this capability after puberty. Before puberty, a child may learn several languages and speak them each with no trace of a foreign accent. When languages are learned after puberty, they are almost invariably spoken with an accent derived from the native language. Lenneberg (1967) has summarized many of the known relations among language development, central nervous system maturation, and the effects of brain damage upon speech functioning. His summary is shown in Table 5.2. Despite some questionable assertions,[6] Lenneberg clearly demonstrates the importance of physical maturation. Unfortunately, we cannot specify the relations between maturation and language development. According to Lenneberg (1967), "the specific neurophysiological correlates of . . . the capacity for language acquisition cannot be attributed directly to any one maturational process studied so far [p. 179]." The same statement could be made today.

Learning and Experience

Some aspects of language may be acquired via the relatively simple learning mechanisms of classical and operant conditioning. Staats and Staats (1957), among others, have shown that affective meanings, as measured by the semantic differential, can be classically conditioned. If a word (or a nonsense syllable) is repeatedly paired with an unpleasant event, then that word acquires negative qualities of its own. If we pair a word with a moderately painful electric shock, the word acquires a negative connotation. If a word were to be paired with positive events, then it would take on favorable connotations. We do not even need to use real events to get these shifts in affective meaning. If a neutral word is repeatedly paired with negatively loaded words, then that neutral word gradually acquires negative connotations, and is rated negatively on the semantic differential evaluation scales. Guilt (or innocence) by association can, apparently, be acquired quite readily.

---

[6] First, language development is not confined to the ages between 21 and 36 months (see page 136 in this chapter). Second, the possibility of learning a foreign language in adulthood without an accent is categorically denied. This is open to some question, considering the reputed success of military and diplomatic training programs, especially during times of war.

TABLE 5.2
Summary of the Biological and Maturational Factors
in Language Acquisition[a]

Age	Usual language development	Effects of acquired, lateralized lesions	Physical maturation of central nervous system	Lateralization of function	Developmental potential	Explanation
0–3 months	Emergence of cooing.	No effect on onset of language in half of all cases; other half has delayed onset but normal development.	About 60–70% of developmental course accomplished.	None: symptoms and prognosis identical for either hemisphere.	Perfect equipotentiality.	Neuroanatomical and physiological prerequisites become established.
4–20 months	From babbling to words.					
21–36 months	Acquisition of language.	All language accomplishments disappear; language is reacquired with repetition of all stages.	Rate of maturation slowed down.	Hand preference emerges.	Right hemisphere can easily adopt sole responsibility for language.	Language appears to involve entire brain; little cortical specialization with regard to language though left hemisphere beginning to become dominant towards end of this period.
3–10 years	Some grammatical refinement; expansion of vocabulary.	Emergence of aphasic symptoms; disorders tend to recover without residual language deficits (except in reading or writing). During re-	Very slow completion of maturational processes.	Cerebral dominance established between 3 and 5 years but evidence that right hemisphere may often still be involved in speech and lan-	In cases where language is already predominantly localized in left hemisphere and aphasia ensues with left lesion, it is possible to re-	A process of physiological organization takes place in which functional lateralization of language to left is prominent. "Physiological redundancy" is gradually reduced and polarization of activities

		covery period, two processes active: diminishing aphasic interference and further acquisition of language.		guage functions. About one-fourth of early childhood aphasias due to right hemisphere lesions.	establish language presumably by reactivating language functions in right hemisphere.	between right and left hemisphere is established. As long as maturational processes have not stopped, reorganization is still possible.
11–14 years	Foreign accents emerge.	Some aphasic symptoms become irreversible (particularly when acquired lesion was traumatic).	An asymptote is reached on almost all parameters. Exceptions are myelinization and electroencephalogram spectrum.	Apparently firmly established but definitive statistics not available.	Marked signs of reduction in equipotentiality.	Language markedly lateralized and internal organization established irreversibly for life. Language-free parts of brain cannot take over except where lateralization is incomplete or had been blocked by pathology during childhood.
Midteens to old age	Acquisition of second language becomes increasingly difficult.	Symptoms present after 3–5 months after injury are irreversible.	None.	In about 97% of the entire population language is definitely lateralized to the left.	None for language.	

[a] After Lenneberg (1967).

Referential properties of words also may be acquired by conditioning procedures. Operant conditioning techniques have been used with some success to teach referential word meanings to mentally retarded and other institutionalized patients (Krasner, 1958). By positively reinforcing a child when he makes appropriate sounds (for example, whenever he says the word *truck* in the presence of a toy truck or a picture of a truck), the child could gradually learn to associate the word and its referent. Some early word learning might follow this paradigm.

There are a number of reasons for believing that mechanisms other than association and reinforcement must be involved in semantic and syntactic development, however. First, children learn new words too quickly to depend upon conditioning mechanisms alone. Beyond the very first stages of word acquisition, we do not need to pair a word repeatedly with its referent and provide appropriate reinforcement. A child can ask, "what that?," we tell him, and that's that. Second, we rarely observe parents of young children providing either positive or negative reinforcement for correct syntactic usage. Brown and Hanlon (1970) carefully examined their longitudinal data on three children to see whether parental approval or disapproval might be an important factor in their children's speech behavior. There seemed to be no discernible relations between the syntactic correctness of what children said and parental approval. What parents did respond to was the truth value of what was said, not how it was said. The utterance *that a dog* would only be corrected if the child seemed to be talking about a cat. The syntax would not be "corrected." Approval in the early stages thus may be a factor in correct referential usage, but not in syntactic usage. In later childhood, particularly beyond the first school years, parents and teachers do correct children's syntax.

Finally, the meanings and syntactic rules acquired by all children are far too abstract to be identified overtly by either the child or his parents. Only in the laboratory might the appropriate contingencies be arranged explicitly and systematically, and even there, behavior modification and operant conditioning techniques have met with limited success. Either we have not yet learned how to apply operant conditioning techniques appropriately, or we need other forms of learning and experience for language development. Very likely, both of these alternatives are true.

Outside the clinic or laboratory, the learning situation for a child must be analogous to our own situation when we listen to very young children. We assume that a child intends to talk about something, and we use our knowledge of the situation and of the child to help us interpret his speech. One of our children used the utterance *dadong* to refer to a finger or fingers when he was about 14 months old. How could we know this? He said *dadong* when he held up his own fingers, when we pointed to a picture of fingers, and when we waggled our own fingers. The only way we could map the novel and arbitrary sound sequence onto its referent was by first knowing what the referent was. We engage in the same kind of guessing game when we are first exposed to a completely foreign language in a natural setting. At first, we try to figure out what people are saying, and we use all the clues we can. Later, after we have learned some of the new words, we might be able to learn more about the language by using a dictionary or by asking people what this or that means. Our initial learning, however, relies entirely on the referential context. Imagine someone trying to learn a completely new language by listening to the radio. Unless a translation is available, the task is hopeless. We could not even begin to discover the phonemic system, and we might not even be able to segment the stream of speech into words. Once language learning is underway, then we can learn more just by listening.

Young children must go through the same sequence—first understanding what people are saying, and then mapping the sounds onto the meanings. Macnamara (1972) makes this point clearly and forcefully:

> Infants learn their language by first determining, independent of language, the meaning which a speaker intends to convey to them, and by then working out the relationship between the meaning and the language. To put it another way, the infant uses meaning as a clue to language, rather than language as a clue to meaning [p. 1].

"Meaning," in this context, refers to the message intended by a speaker. "Language" refers to phonology, semantics, and syntax. If this is the strategy adults would follow if they were to be suddenly placed in a foreign-language context, then

> . . . it is not too fanciful to think of the infant as treating the sentences he hears as glosses on [descriptions of] the events that occur about him. The grammar he writes is not in Latin or any other language, but in some neurological code of which as yet not a single letter has been deciphered [Macnamara, 1972, p. 12].

How does a child "write the grammar"? Because the rules are not given explicitly, children must infer or derive them from the samples of speech they hear and their interpretations of the meanings of those samples. They must engage in RULE-INDUCTION procedures. The acquisition sequences for noun pluralization rules and for past tense inflections provide clear examples of rule-induction behavior. We form the past tense for verbs in two ways, regular and irregular. The regular form adds the morpheme -*d* or -*ed* to the verb, for example, *learn–learned, acquire–acquired,* and *type–typed.* There is another class of verbs that indicate the past in irregular ways, for example, *teach–taught, get–got,* and *write–wrote.* It so happens that some of the irregular verbs are among the most frequently used in the language, so words like *run, ran, do, did, make,* and *made* are learned quite early in both present and past tense forms. Young children use both tenses correctly before they learn the inflectional method to indicate past tense. When they do learn the inflectional rule, they overgeneralize and apply that rule to those irregular forms that they had been using correctly. A child who had been saying *ran, did,* and *made* now says *runned, doed,* and *maked.* It takes some time before the child learns the correct forms for verbs like these—often well into the second or third grade. This learning sequence can be mimicked in experiments with adults. If adults learn an artificial rule system that contains infrequent regular and frequent irregular forms, they first learn the frequent irregular forms. They then learn the rule and make mistakes on those irregular forms, and then finally learn the exceptions to the rule (Palermo & Eberhart, 1968).

What learning strategies do children follow to acquire rules like these? One possible strategy involves IMITATION, but not imitation in the usual sense of the word. What is a child imitating when he says something like *Daddy runned* or *This is my bestest color?* He can't be imitating the words *runned* or *bestest* because he has never heard those words spoken, at least by adults. He is really imitating a "rule"—a method for producing novel utterances. He is not imitating the sounds or the surface characteristics of what he hears in cases like these. The limitations of overt, echoic imitation have been pointed out by McNeill (1966a, 1970). Children often have great difficulty in imitating what they hear if the speech to be imitated does not conform to the child's current grammar. McNeill illustrates this with an example of what can happen when a parent tries to teach correct usage by asking for correct imitations:

> CHILD: Nobody don't like me.
> MOTHER: No, say "nobody like*s* me."
> CHILD: Nobody don't like me.
>
> .
> .
> .
>
> (eight repetitions of this dialogue ensued)
>
> .
> .
> .
>
> MOTHER: No, now listen carefully. Say *"nobody likes me."*
> CHILD: Oh! Nobody don't like*s* me [McNeill, 1966a, p. 69].

Trying to correct a child's speech by asking for corrected imitations may be unproductive, to say the least. If imitation is to be used as a teaching strategy, then parents should tailor the speech to be imitated to each child's current state of language development. A clue as to how this might be done is provided by what children themselves do when they use imitation as a learning strategy.

When children imitate spontaneously, they seem to do so as a strategy for learning new syntactic constructions. Lois Bloom and her colleagues (Bloom, Hood, & Lightbown, 1974) systematically observed 19- to 26-month-old children's speech in naturalistic settings over a period of several months. The parents seldom asked their children to imitate, nor did they try to correct syntactic errors by asking for a corrected imitation. Some children never spontaneously imitated what others said, but others consistently did so. Those children who did imitate consistently did so systematically. They rarely if ever imitated a construction that they were already using by themselves. They also never imitated a construction that was clearly well beyond their own level of syntactic development. They did imitate only those constructions that they could understand and that they seemed about ready to acquire themselves. Typically, when a child imitated a particular construction, he would soon begin to use that construction himself (usually within several weeks of the first imitation), and thereafter never spontaneously imitated that construction again.

Imitative behavior seems to be useful for language learning, but it is clearly not necessary. Some children never seem to imitate at all, yet develop normally anyway. Overt spontaneous imitation seems to be one of several strategies children may use to acquire their language.

What other learning strategies can we find? Some parents habitually expand their children's utterances (Brown & Bellugi, 1964). If a child says *Eve lunch,* mother might say *Eve is having lunch?*; if a child says *throw Daddy,* the expansion might be *Throw it to Daddy.* These kinds of EXPANSIONS can have two quite different effects. If the expansion reflects a correct interpretation of what the child intended to say, then it provides an exemplar of the adult version of the child's sentence. When this happens, the child has received some information that might be useful for later learning. If the expansion represents a misinterpretation of what was intended, then this too can be valuable. Misinterpretations inform a child that his utterances are ambiguous, providing motivation for further language elaboration.

Another way to provide information for children is to speak normally, responding to their speech as if they were speaking as adults. do. This is called MODELING—behaving in ways that we want children to behave. When Eve says *Eve lunch,* her mother might say *I'm eating lunch too,* or *Is it good?* Here too, correct interpretations as well as misinterpretations of what Eve intended to say can provide her with valuable information about the language.

The relative effectiveness of modeling versus expansion as parental techniques is difficult to evaluate. In one study, Courtney Cazden (1965) worked with three groups of 30-month-old children for three months, spending a half-hour a day, five days a week, looking through picture books. In one group, the adult expanded everything the child said, as "correctly" as possible. In a second group, the adult always responded with adult-model sentences. A third group of children went through the same picture books while the adult said as little as possible. After three months, the expansion and modeling groups had improved more than the minimal interaction group, and the modeling group was slightly better than the expansion group. In a similar study conducted some years later, expansion was more effective than modeling (Nelson, Carskaddon, & Bonvillian, 1973). The most reasonable conclusion is that both modeling and expansion can facilitate language development, but that neither need be superior to the other. To our knowledge, no experiments have directly evaluated the potential utility of expansions or modelings which are based on misinterpretations of what children say, and so we do not know about the value of showing children that we may not understand what they say.

The one major factor coming out of the many studies of language development is the sheer amount of linguistic interaction available to children. The more adult speech a child hears, the faster will he develop in language skills. Sheer exposure to language itself, however varied or optimized, is patently insufficient. It must be language in an interpretable context. The speech a child hears must refer to events, things, and people in his immediate world if he is to figure out the speech code. Initially, word meanings and sentence meanings can only be learned by some variant of a naming and pointing procedure. The word *table* must be learned in the context of real tables. The structural meaning of a sentence like *Throw it to Daddy* can only be learned in the context of a palpable thing to throw and a real Daddy. Consistent with these notions, Nelson's (1973) study of children's language development in the first 30 months revealed two major correlates of early learning rates. The more often a child was taken on outings, the faster was his or her language development. The more time spent watching television, the slower was his or her language development. Though not necessarily true for every child, it does seem that active interaction with people and the world facilitates early language development.

WHAT DOES THE LANGUAGE
ACQUISITION DEVICE DO?

We have been able to discuss the acquisition of vocabulary and the concommitant acquisition of the sound system without invoking a "special" language acquisition mechanism. The only "special" factor we have had to deal with is the apparent decrease in the brain's ability to mediate new language functions beyond the age of puberty (see Table 5.2). Why do we need an innate structure like the language acquisition device?

The language acquisition device was invoked specifically to account for the acquisition of syntactic competence. It seemed relatively easy to understand how children might learn a vocabulary and the sound system of their language. Syntax, however, involves the acquisition of complex and abstract rules, and these rules are not explicit in the speech children hear. Furthermore, because syntax was treated as independent of semantics in formal linguistic theory, syntax acquisition was considered to be independent of learning anything else (Chomsky, 1965, 1968). The samples of speech that could provide the information for rule induction were considered to be the only experience relevant to syntactic development, and the syntactic characteristics of that speech were considered to be the only relevant characteristics. What people talked about, and the related social and physical events, were considered to be irrelevant.

These assumptions led to the proposal that we are born with a model of universal grammar prewired in the brain. This conclusion seemed inescapable, especially in view of the difficulty adults had in trying to learn miniature artificial languages. Only the simplest sorts of syntactic rules could be learned in a laboratory context in which the only input was an abstract artificial language. It seemed that people could not learn semantically empty grammars (Miller, 1967; Segal & Halwes, 1965, 1966; Smith, 1966). This was so discouraging to scientists who had been trying to discover how syntax was learned that they began to doubt that it could be learned at all. George Miller, one of the pioneers of the new psycholinguistics, once commented that there were only two tenable theories of syntax acquisition—the impossible theory or the miracle theory (Miller, personal communication). Given a choice between the impossible (learning) and the miraculous (an innate language acquisition device), theorists like McNeill (1970) chose the latter.

Recently, three lines of research have developed that provide interesting clues about how children might acquire syntax, and that, in turn, challenge the major assumptions underlying the appeal to an innate language acquisition device. These three assumptions were:

1. Speech is the only relevant input and that this speech is not only complex but meager and degenerate as well.

2. Adults cannot learn the syntactic rules of miniature artificial languages.

3. Children everywhere seem to develop language in the same ways, despite wide variations in cultures and in languages.

First, what kind of speech do children hear? Is it as complex, meager, and degenerate as Chomsky (1968) suggested? It is unlikely that adults speak to young children as they do to one another. We normally "tailor" our speech to suit our listeners and the context of what we are talking about (see Glucksberg, Krauss, & Higgins, 1975; see also Chapter 7, pages 198–203). Do parents and older children simplify their speech to young children? If they do, young children might be able to infer syntactic rules from appropriately simplified and interpretable speech. It turns out that young children do hear simplified speech. Catherine Snow (1972) compared the speech of adult women to two-year-old children versus ten-year-old children. The speech to two-year-olds was consistently simpler than speech to ten-year-olds, whether the adults were experienced mothers or not. For example, sentences like *Bill who is the son of the woman who lives next door* would be uttered to older children, but rarely to younger children. Typical speech to two-year-olds is: "That's a lion. And the lion's name is Leo. Leo lives in a BIG house. Leo goes for a walk every morning. And he always takes his cane along" (Snow, 1972, p. 562). These ideas would never be expressed to a two-year-old by saying, "That's a lion named Leo who lives in a big house and goes for a walk every morning invariably taking his cane along." Snow concluded that children do not hear a language full of mistakes, complex sentences, and semisentences. What they hear is "relatively consistent, organized, simplified and redundant . . . [a] set of utterances which in many ways seems quite well designed as a set of 'language lessons' " (Snow, 1972, p. 561). Four-year-old brothers and sisters also use simpler and more redundant speech when talking to younger children than when talking to peers or to adults (Shatz & Gelman, 1973). The speech children hear need be neither degenerate nor meager, nor need it be as complex as had been assumed. Instead, the speech children hear is well suited for the communication needs of both parents and children, and for language learning as well.

A second reason for assuming an innate language acquisition device was the difficulty adults had in learning the syntactic rules of miniature artificial languages. Surely the difference between children (who can and do acquire syntactic rules) and adults (who apparently could not do so) must be attributable to something like a language acquisition device? The language acquisition device is presumably operative during a critical period for language acquisition that lasts until puberty. This conclusion might be warranted if adults really could not learn new syntactic rules. Fortunately, adults can do so, both in the real world and in the laboratory. In the real world, adults readily learn foreign languages when they need to do so (albeit with an accent). In the laboratory, adults can learn rules when the "sentences" of the language are "meaningful" (see Figure 5.4). The "sentences" of those artificial languages that adults could not learn made no

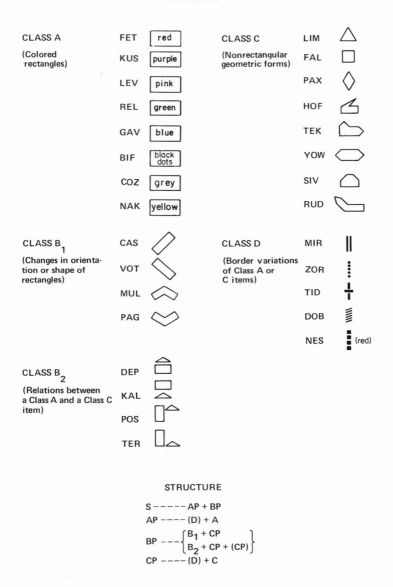

CLASS A (Colored rectangles)	FET	red
	KUS	purple
	LEV	pink
	REL	green
	GAV	blue
	BIF	black dots
	COZ	grey
	NAK	yellow

CLASS B₁
(Changes in orientation or shape of rectangles)

CAS, VOT, MUL, PAG

CLASS B₂
(Relations between a Class A and a Class C item)

DEP, KAL, POS, TER

CLASS C
(Nonrectangular geometric forms)

LIM, FAL, PAX, HOF, TEK, YOW, SIV, RUD

CLASS D
(Border variations of Class A or C items)

MIR, ZOR, TID, DOB, NES (red)

STRUCTURE

$$S ----- AP + BP$$
$$AP ---- (D) + A$$
$$BP --- \begin{cases} B_1 + CP \\ B_2 + CP + (CP) \end{cases}$$
$$CP ---- (D) + C$$

FIGURE 5.4 An artificial language: referents and structure. (After Moeser & Bregman, 1973.)

149

TABLE 5.3
Two-Word Sentences in Child Speech from
Several Languages[a,e]

Function of utterance	Language					
	English	German	Russian	Finnish	Luo	Samoan
Locate, name	there book that car see doggie	buch da (book there) gukuk wauwau (see doggie)	Tosya tam (Tosya there)	tuossa Rina (there Rina) vettä siinä (water there)	en saa (it clock) ma wendo (this visitor)	Keith lea (Keith there)
Demand, desire	more milk give candy want gum	mehr milch (more milk) bitte apfel (please apple)	yeshche moloko (more milk) day chasy (give watch)	anna Rina (give Rina)	miya tamtam (give-me candy) adway cham (I-want food)	mai pepe (give doll) fia moe (want sleep)
Negate[b]	no wet no wash not hungry allgone milk	nicht blasen (not blow) kaffee nein (coffee no)	vody net (water no) gus' tyu-tyu (goose allgone)	ei susi (not wolf) enää pipi (anymore sore)	beda onge (my-slasher absent)	le 'ai (not cat) uma mea (allgone thing)
Describe event or situation[c]	Bambi go mail come hit ball block fall baby highchair	puppe kommt (doll comes) tiktak hängt (clock hangs) sofa sitzen (sofa sit) messer schneiden (cut knife)	mama prua (mama walk) papa bay-bay (papa sleep) korka upala (crust fell) nashla yaichko (found egg) baba kreslo (grandma armchair)	takki pois (cat away) Seppo putoo (Seppo fall) talli 'bm bm' (garage 'car')	chungu biro (European comes) odhi skul (he-want school) omoyo oduma (she-dries maize)	pa'u pepe (fall doll) tapale 'oe (hit you) tu'u lalo (put down)

	English	German	Russian	Finnish	Luo	Samoan
Indicate possession	*my shoe* *mama dress*	*mein ball* (my ball) *mamas hut* (mama's hat)	*mami chashka* (mama's cup) *pup moya* (navel my)	*täti auto* (aunt car)	*kom baba* (chair father)	*lole a'u* (candy my) *polo 'oe* (ball your) *paluni mama* (baloon mama)
Modify, qualify	*pretty dress* *big boat*	*milch heiss* (milk hot) *armer wauwau* (poor doggie)	*mama khoroshaya* (mama good) *papa bol'shoy* (papa big)	*rikki auto* (broken car) *torni iso* (tower big)	*piypiy kech* (pepper hot) *gwen madichol* (chicken black)	*fa'ali'i pepe* (headstrong baby)
Question[d]	*where ball*	*wo ball* (where ball)	*gde papa* (where papa)	*missä pallo* (where ball)		*fea Punafu* (where Punafu)

[a] The examples come from a variety of studies, published and unpublished. Data from the three non-Indo-European languages are drawn from the recent doctoral dissertations of Bowerman (Harvard, 1973: Finnish), Blount (Berkeley, 1969: Luo), Kernan (Berkeley, 1969: Samoan). The examples given here are representative of many more utterances of the same type in each language. The order of the two words in the utterance is generally fixed in all of the languages except Finnish, where both orders can be used freely for some children.

[b] Bloom (1970) has noted three different sorts of negation: (1) nonexistence (e.g., *no wet*, meaning "dry"), (2) rejection (e.g., *no wash*, meaning "don't wash me"), and (3) denial (e.g., *no girl*, denying a preceding assertion that a boy was a girl).

[c] Descriptions are of several types: (1) agent + action (e.g., *Bambi go*), (2) action + object (e.g., *hit ball*), (3) agent + object (e.g., *mama bread*, meaning "mama is cutting bread"), (4) locative (e.g., *baby highchair*, meaning "baby is in the highchair"), (5) instrumental (e.g., *cut knife*), (6) dative (e.g., *throw daddy*, meaning "throw it to daddy"). (The use of the terminology of grammatical case is suggestive here; see Fillmore's discussion of deep cases as underlying linguistic universals.)

[d] In addition to why-questions, yes-no questions can be made by pronouncing any two-word utterance with rising intonation, with the exception of Finnish. (Melissa Bowerman reports that the emergence of yes-no questions is, accordingly, exceptionally late in Finnish child language.)

[e] From Slobin (1970).

reference to anything at all. They represented a semantically empty syntax. As we emphasized earlier, natural language learning starts with interpretable meanings. Could it be that artificial language learning also requires interpretable meanings?

Moeser and Bregman (1972, 1973) constructed a miniature artificial language and a set of objects to which the words of that language referred. The elements of the language and their pictorial referents are shown in Figure 5.4. This language was presented either with or without the pictures. In principle, the syntactic rules of the language could be learned in either condition. Six people tried to learn the language, three with the pictures, and three with the language alone. The three people who had the pictures with the samples of the language readily learned the syntax. No one who tried to learn the language without the pictures picked up any of the syntax at all, despite extensive experience (3,200 trials). Referential relations seem to be critical for the initial learning of syntactic relations. After the syntax and semantics have been learned, new material (for example, more complex rules and additions to the vocabulary) can be learned without further reference to pictures. Moeser and Bregman (1973) concluded that ". . . much of early sentence learning must be mediated through an understanding of the reference field that the speech is about while later learning may be built directly upon the early syntactic framework [p. 91]."

If language is learned in the ordinary sense of the term, then how can we explain the apparent universality of developing language structures? We find the same progression from one-word utterances to two-word utterances, and the two-word utterances all seem to represent the same set of semantic relations. The parallels among children from widely different language communities are illustrated in Table 5.3. These parallels may be characterized as semantic rather than purely syntactic. Given that all children at one point in their development use two-word utterances, the formal similarity of their sentences is automatically predetermined. That the same semantic relations (the functions of the utterances) are also found everywhere may reflect the fact that young children the world over talk about the same sorts of things—objects, events, people, and the relations among these. The similarities in children's speech arise from the inevitable constraints of being human and living in the same world. For example, Slobin (1972) listed a typical set of semantic relations expressed in the speech of English, German, Russian, Finnish, Turkish, Samoan, and Luo children. He comments that "the entire list could probably be made up of examples from two-year-old speech in any language" (Slobin, 1972, p. 199).

Why do children talk about the same things the world over? Brown (1970) suggests that "the meanings expressed . . . seem to be an extension of the kind of intelligence that has been called 'sensory motor' by . . . Jean Piaget. . . . If the meanings of the first sentences are an extension [or expression] of sensory–motor intelligence, then they are probably universal in mankind [p. 223]." In other words, all people are human and live in the same world. What may be innate is not linguistic capacity per se but a nervous system that predisposes humans to develop conceptions of the world in particular ways, given the world we have. Language acquisition need be no more innate than the knowledge that objects still exist when they disappear from view. Very young children (about six months or younger) act as if an object no longer exists when it is removed from view. By the age of eight months or thereabouts, children learn that, when, for example, a ball rolls behind a chair, the ball still exists. They will look for it at the other side, waiting for it to roll out (Piaget, 1954). All children learn this, just as all children learn their first language in about the same way.

We are just beginning to find out what children and parents do during the language-learning years, and to understand how children acquire their knowledge of the world and of their language. To argue at this point that language is innate or that language is learned in one way rather than another is profitless. Let the language acquisition device remain as a label for our ignorance until we can describe its content, structure, and functioning, or until we can dispense with it entirely.

SUGGESTED READINGS

Two collections of papers provide a variety of perspectives on language development. One, edited by C. A. Ferguson and D. I. Slobin, *Studies of child language development* (New York: Holt, Rinehart and Winston, 1973), includes reprints of work on language acquisition across the world, including Russian, Japanese, and English contributions. *Cognitive development and the acquisition of language,* edited by T. E. Moore (New York: Academic Press, 1973), contains recent papers about the relations between cognition and speech development.

Roger Brown's long-term study of syntactic development is continuing, and the first detailed report of this work appears in *A first language: The early stages* (Cambridge, Massachusetts: Harvard University Press, 1973). More limited in overall scope, but none the less valuable, is Katherine Nelson's monograph, *Structure and strategy in learning to talk* (*Monographs of the Society for Research in Child Development,* 1973, Serial No. 149). Nelson traces the semantic and syntactic development of children from their first words to the beginnings of syntax (about 30 months), and provides a wealth of important information on what children talk about and how different mothers' interactive styles may affect what and how children learn.

For a broader survey of language development, see P. S. Dale's book, *Language development* (Hinsdale, Illinois: Dryden, 1972). Finally, Lois Bloom's review of theory and data in language development research provides an insightful overview of developments in the field ("Language development review," in F. D. Horowitz (Ed.), *Review of child development research,* Volume 4. Chicago: University of Chicago Press, 1975).

6
Dialects and Schooling

When we compare people's speech, we often find differences in vocabulary, in pronunciation, and in "grammar," as well as differences in style and communicative clarity. Do these differences in linguistic performance reflect differences in linguistic competence? Differences in linguistic competence, that is, a speaker's "knowledge" of the grammatical rules of a language, could come about in two ways. First, people could differ in terms of how well they had acquired the "correct" rules of their language. Second, people could differ with respect to the particular rules their particular languages have. But, as we noted in Chapter 5, we have not yet been able to specify fully the linguistic competence of young children, let alone that of adults. Our best guess, given what we know about language, is that differences among people in their levels of linguistic competence are either trivial or nonexistent. This conclusion applies to differences among people who speak the same language, as well as to differences among people who speak different languages. Hundreds of languages have been studied, yet no one has found a "primitive" language or a language that could be regarded as less complex or less effective than any other.

Languages, of course, do differ from one another. Different languages accomplish the same communicative objectives in quite different ways. For

154

example, Russian has no articles. If we translate the English sentence

(1a)   The book is on the table.

into Russian, it would be, in literal form

(1b)   Book on table.

In French and in German the gender of a noun is always specified. *La plûme* (feminine) is *the pen* (gender unspecified); *le livre* (masculine) is *the book* (gender unspecified). We cannot refer to any object in French or German without specifying gender. It is an obligatory syntactic marking. In English, we do not specify gender unless we use such pronouns as *him, her,* or *it,* but we must normally specify number—singular or plural. In some languages there is no obligatory singular–plural distinction for any words, just as in English there are some words, like *sheep,* that are not marked for number. In still other languages, distinctions may be even finer, with different forms for singular (one), dual (two), and plural (three or more). These syntactic differences among languages do not reflect differential complexities of the various languages. There is no basis for judging any one system better or worse than any other: All languages are adequate for communication.

Grammatical rules may, and often do, vary within languages as well. Sometimes these differences within a language are so small that they have no effect on communication, but sometimes the rules differ enough to cause real difficulties. British and American English differ in a number of ways. There are obvious differences in pronunciation. As Cole Porter tunefully pointed out, "we say tomayto, they say tomahto." There are also differences in the lexicon. If you ask for a napkin in an English restaurant you might be advised to go to the loo. *Napkin* (or *nappy*) in British English means diaper, and *loo* refers to the toilet. The two English languages differ syntactically as well. In American English, one would say

(2a)   Harvard *plays* Yale; U.S. Steel
        announces a price cut.

In Britain, it would be

(2b)   Harvard *play* Yale; U.S. Steel *announce*
        a price cut.

British treat the collective nouns *Harvard* and *U.S. Steel* as plural nouns. Americans treat them as singular nouns. The languages also differ in their use of articles. Americans would say

(3a)   I went to the hospital.

British would delete the article *the* and say

(3b)   I went to hospital.

Which way of speaking is better? Which is more complex or more efficient?

The differences between British and American English might be a result of their geographical separation. Because of the distance involved, interaction between the two linguistic communities has been limited. Geographical distance often determines the extent of social and linguistic interaction. It is said that, as one travels along the Rhine River, people in adjacent communities can understand one another all along the way, but as the distance between communities increases, mutual intelligibility decreases until people cannot understand one another at all, even though they all speak "German." Within North America such differences are much smaller, but still exist. Most of us recognize differences between Canadian and American pronunciations of certain words, such as *about* (/æbut/ and /æbawt/, respectively). People who live in the North pronounce the word *greasy* so that it rhymes with *fleecy,* whereas the usual Southern pronunciation rhymes with *easy.* Lexical differences are also common. A flat cooking pan is usually called a *frying pan* in the North and a *skillet* in the South.

We can talk about another kind of distance, social distance. In Britain, the variety of accents can be overwhelming to Americans, and some are virtually unintelligible to them. The "standard" pronunciation in England is referred to as R.P., which stands for RECEIVED PRONUNCIATION. This is the Queen's English, and refers to the pattern and style of speech one is expected to use when one is received at the Royal Court. This is also the dialect of English used by the upper classes, and until recently the only acceptable dialect in radio and television broadcasting. In the United States, as in other countries, different dialects of English are identified with different ethnic and social groups within the same geographical regions. William Labov (1966) even found dialect differences within the same department store in New York City, depending upon the expected social class of the customers in various departments. In departments where luxury items were sold, salespeople rarely dropped the /r/ in words like *car* and *park,* and tended to pronounce the last syllable in words like *ringing* as /ɪŋ/ rather than /ɪn/. In other departments, such as bargain housewares, the opposite was true.

In most societies there is wide dialectical variation among geographical regions and among social classes. When people refer to the "standard" dialect, they usually mean the one that approximates the dialect of the most prestigious group in a society, and it is usually an idealization of that dialect. In a large country like the United States, "Standard English" is an idealized dialect that does not reveal either the region or the social class of the speaker. It is most prevalent among television and radio announcers and newscasters, particularly in the Northeast. It is not necessarily an indicator of social status—after all, President John F. Kennedy had a noticeable regional dialect, as did President Lyndon B. Johnson.

American English, like British English, is represented by a variety of dialects. Some of them are considered "standard"; others are considered nonstandard. Not surprisingly, the dialects spoken by the upper and middle classes are among the standard, and those spoken by the poor are among the nonstandard.

The distinction between "standard" and "nonstandard" was inevitably applied to the differences between Black and White speakers of English. We focus on these differences and their social implications for the remainder of this chapter, but our conclusions are not limited to Black–White differences. Societies in which dialectal variations have had profound social consequences are not unique in the history of man, and the contrast between Black and White dialects of English in the United States is but one of many examples.

BLACK AND WHITE DIALECTS OF ENGLISH

Americans speak one or another dialect of the same language, English. Many Blacks speak a dialect of English that is perceptibly different from the dialects most Whites use. Black dialects are commonly referred to as Black English, and White dialects as Standard English. We refer to these two classes of dialects as Black dialects and White dialects, respectively, to avoid the misleading implications that anything other than Standard English is substandard, and that White people speak a uniform dialect across the various regions of the United States and Canada. "Standard" English can best be identified with formal written English.

The intuitive assumption many people make is that the differences between Black and White speech represent errors or mistakes (poor speech) by Blacks. Is this assumption justified? When an Englishman says *I am going to hospital,* he is not making a mistake. He is speaking in accordance with a set of grammatical rules that differ systematically from an American's. Similarly, Black English dialects differ systematically from White English dialects. The differences are not in complexity or efficiency, but in the kinds of rules used in the dialects. For example, in Black dialects the sentences

(4a)   George he working in surgery.

(4b)   George he be working in surgery.

are not garbled versions of White dialects. Each is a perfectly correct grammatical construction, and the two sentence meanings are somewhat different. Sentence (4a) would be used to tell someone that George is at work in surgery at that moment. Sentence (4b) means that George has a job in surgery, but implies nothing about where George is at that moment. If someone were to say

(4c)   George he be working in surgery
        right now.,

this would be taken to mean that George's job is temporary or in danger of being lost.

In White dialects the meaning of sentence (4a) would be expressed by saying

(4d)   George is at work in surgery
        (right now).

and the meaning of (4b) by saying

(4e)   George works in surgery (or,
        George has a job in surgery).

These distinctions are obligatory in Black dialects. One must distinguish between simple present tense (4a) and DURATIVE *be* (4b). This distinction is optional in White dialects. One can say

(4f)   George is working in surgery.

and leave it up to the listener to decide whether one means that George is there right now or George has a job there. Usually, the context of a conversation allows one to interpret the utterance appropriately.

Analyses of sentence forms like these have led linguists to conclude that Black dialects of English are systematically different from White, and furthermore that the Black dialects are as rich, as complex, and as internally consistent as any other dialects of English. How and why did Black dialects arise?

Some linguists argue that Black English "probably derived from a creolized form of English, once spoken on American plantations by Negro slaves and seemingly related to creolized forms of English which are still spoken by Negroes in Jamaica and other parts of the Caribbean" (Stewart, 1970, p. 351). Others suggest that the initial contact between English and the various languages spoken by African tribesmen occurred in Africa during the course of the slave trade. In either case, people's native African languages could not be used to communicate with Westerners nor could they be used to communicate among Africans who spoke different languages. As a result, African people probably developed a pidgin English, both in Africa and in North America. A PIDGIN is an amalgam of two languages—the native language and the new one (in this case, English).

The pidgin borrows heavily from the new lexicon, but retains some of the phonological and syntactic structures of the original language. When a pidgin language becomes a stabilized and functional medium of communication for a community, it is called a CREOLE language. The creole language becomes the native (and perhaps the only) language acquired by the children of the community. With each succeeding generation, the language becomes more and more stable. A common African source for both North American and Caribbean Black dialects is usually cited to account for their similarity of grammatical structures.

Whatever the details of the historical development, Black English dialects are now recognized as full-fledged dialects of English. Black and White dialects differ systematically in several ways. The most obvious difference is phonological. In Black dialects, final consonant clusters are often reduced or deleted, so that the word *test* is pronounced /tɛs/, *best* is pronounced /bɛs/, and *rest* is pronounced /rɛs/ (all rhyme with *Tess*). The difference between the vowels /ɪ/ and /e/ may not be maintained before nasal consonants; hence, the words *pin* and *pen* become homonyms (they both rhyme approximately with the word *tin* as pronounced in White dialects). When these observations were first made, some investigators thought that Black people had impaired auditory abilities, presumably because of impoverished environments (Deutsch, 1964). What they failed to understand was the very nature of speech perception. Do English speakers fail to hear the difference between the two Arabic words /kalb/ and /qalb/ because their hearing is impaired? Do both White and Black middle-class people in Texas and Kansas pronounce *pin* and *pen* alike because "they can't tell the difference"? A systematic examination of the sound system of Black dialects indicates that it is as consistent and rule-governed as any other linguistic sound system (Labov, 1970).

Black and White American dialects also differ syntactically. Table 6.1 lists several differences between Black and White syntactic structures (Baratz, 1969). In Black dialect, a linking verb or copula may be deleted. In White dialect, it may not be deleted. For example, in White dialect we would say *He is going;* in Black dialect we could say *He goin'*. In Black dialect, we can indicate possession without using the possessive suffix. *John cousin* translates as *John's cousin*. Similarly, if we have a number before a noun, Black dialect permits deletion of the plural marker. Hence, *five cents* may be pronounced as *five cent*. Similarly, Black dialects do not require that verb inflections be added in some circumstances, as in *He run home* or *She have a bicycle*. In each case, an obligatory syntactic marker in White dialect may be deleted, but in each case the deletion does not make the meaning ambiguous. In White dialects, these syntactic markers are redundant—we do not really need them to interpret the messages. Much of any language is, of course, redundant, and a certain degree

TABLE 6.1
Examples of Grammatical Differences between White
and Black English Dialects[a]

Variable	White	Black
Linking verb	He *is* going	He . . . goin'
Possessive marker	John*'s* cousin	John . . . cousin
Plural marker	I have five cent*s*	I got five cent . . .
Subject expression	John . . . lives in New York	John *he* live in New York
Verb form	I *drank* the milk	I *drunk* the milk
Past marker	Yesterday he walk*ed* home	Yesterday he walk . . . home
Verb agreement	He run*s* home	He run . . . home
	She *has* a bicycle	She *have* a bicycle
Future form	I *will* go home	I *'ma* go home
"If" construction	I asked *if he did it*	I ask *did he do it*
Negation	I *don't* have *any*	I *don't* got *none*
	He *didn't* go	He *ain't* go
Indefinite article	I want *an* apple	I want *a* apple
Pronoun form	*We* have to do it	*Us* got to do it
	His book	*He* book
Preposition	He is over *at* his friend's house	He over *to* his friend house
	He teaches *at* Francis Pool	He teach . . . Francis Pool
Be	Statement: He *is here all the time*	Statement: *He be* here
Do	Contradiction: No, *he isn't*	Contradiction: No, he *don't*

[a] From Baratz (1969).

of redundancy is necessary if we are to minimize errors of interpretation. Any dialect, including the Black American dialects, will retain those redundancies that are useful, and selectively omit many that are not.

Another syntactic device used in Black dialects but not in White is NEGATIVE CONCORD. For example, *He don't got none* is perfectly acceptable, even though traditional teachers of rhetoric might deplore the double negative. If interpreted in White dialect, the double negative signifies an affirmative. In Black dialect, the double negative reinforces or emphasizes the negation (just as, in White dialect, adding the plural marker -*s* to the noun in *five cents* reinforces the plurality already indicated by the number). One might object and argue that the logic of the situation demands that double negatives be interpreted as affirmatives. If we apply strict logical criteria to language usage, however, we raise more problems than we settle. Suppose someone asks

(5a)   Do you want to go to the movies?

You don't want to go, so you answer, "no." Suppose now that you had been asked (5b) and you still don't want to go:

(5b)   Don't you want to go to the movies?

You would still answer "no." English-speaking people respond to questions on the basis of the logic of the situation, not the logic of the sentence. Japanese-speaking people do the reverse. Japanese speakers would answer "no" to the first question and "yes" to the second if, in fact, they did not want to go to the movies. Is English superior to Japanese? Are Black dialects superior to White, or vice versa, because each dialect handles some communicative problems in different ways? As far as we are able to judge, all languages and all dialects are qualitatively equivalent in terms of their functional utility.

This conclusion has not prevented people from attributing deficits in conceptual ability to people who speak low-status dialects. As recently as ten years ago, aspiring teachers in the New York City school system had to pass a speech test and would fail that test if they spoke in a New York City accent. Every undergraduate in the City College of New York had to take and pass four semesters of speech, which included debating, rhetoric, and "proper" pronunciation. Needless to say, "proper" did not include either the Black or White New York City accent. You might dentalize your *T*'s and say "toity-toid" out in the world, but not in that speech class. One reason for the emphasis on form and pronunciation is the general belief that people who do not speak high-status dialects cannot think or argue logically. One result of this myth is our tendency to embellish our language with unnecessary verbiage (note the phraseology we are endeavoring to employ at this point in time).

Labov (1970) illustrates quite clearly that fancy talk and reasoned argument do not depend on one another. He compares the speech of two Black men. One of them uses a New York City Black dialect. The other speaks in a White dialect.

The Logic of Nonstandard English:
WILLIAM LABOV

The first is Larry H., a fifteen-year-old core member of the Jets [a street gang in New York City], being interviewed by John Lewis [JL]. Larry is one of the loudest and roughest members of the Jets, one who gives the least recognition to the conventional rules of politeness. For most readers . . . , first contact with Larry would produce some fairly negative reactions on both sides. It is probable that you would not like him any more than his teachers do. Larry causes trouble in and out of school. He was put back from the eleventh grade to the ninth, and has been threatened with further action by the school authorities.

JL: What happens to you after you die? Do you know?
LARRY: Yeah, I know. (What?) After they put you in the ground, your body turns into—ah—bones, an' shit.

JL: What happens to your spirit?

LARRY: Your spirit—soon as you die, your spirit leaves you. (And where does the spirit go?) Well, it all depends . . . (On what?) You know, like some people say if you're good an' shit, your spirit goin' t'heaven—'n' if you bad, your spirit goin' to hell. Well, bullshit! Your spirit goin' to hell anyway, good or bad.

JL: Why?

LARRY: Why? I'll tell you why. 'Cause, you see, doesn' nobody really know that it's a God, y'know, 'cause I mean I have seen black gods, pink gods, white gods, all color gods, and don't nobody know it's really a God. An' when they be sayin' if you good, you goin' t'heaven, tha's bullshit, 'cause you ain't goin' to no heaven, 'cause it ain't no heaven for you to go to.

JL: Well, if there's no heaven, how could there be a hell?

LARRY: I mean—ye-eah. Well, let me tell you, it ain't no hell, 'cause this is hell right here, y'know! (This is hell?) Yeah, this is hell right here!

JL: . . . but, just say that there is a God, what color is he? White or black?

LARRY: Well, if it is a God . . . I wouldn't know what color, I couldn' say,—couldn' nobody say what color he is or really *would* be.

JL: But now, jus' suppose there was a God—

LARRY: Unless'n they say . . .

JL: No, I was jus' sayin' jus' suppose there is a God, would he be white or black?

LARRY: He'd be white, man.

JL: Why?

LARRY: Why? I'll tell you why. 'Cause the average whitey out here got everything, you dig? And the nigger ain't got shit, y'know? Y'unnerstan'? So—um—for—in order for *that* to happen, you know it ain't no black God that's doin' that bullshit.

Let us now turn to the second speaker, an upper-middle-class, college educated Negro man (Charles M.) being interviewed by Clarence Robins [CR] in [a] survey of adults in Central Harlem:

CR: Do you know of anything that someone can do, to have someone who has passed on visit him in a dream?

CHARLES: Well, I even heard my parents say that there is such a thing as something in dreams some things like that, and sometimes dreams do come true. I personally have never had a dream come true. I've never dreamt that somebody was dying and they actually died (Mhm) or that I was going to have ten dollars the next day and somehow I got ten dollars in my pocket. (Mhm). I don't particularly believe in that, I don't think it's true. I do feel, though, that there is such a thing as—ah—witchcraft. I do feel that in certain cultures there is such a thing as witchcraft, or some sort of *science* of witchcraft; I don't think that it's just a matter of believing hard enough that there is such a thing as witchcraft. I do believe that there is such a thing that a person can put himself in a state of *mind* (Mhm), or that—er—something could be given them to intoxicate them in a certain—to a certain frame of mind—that—that could actually be considered witchcraft [Labov, 1970, pp. 164–168].

Larry speaks a Black dialect and uses the grammatical rules of that dialect. He uses negative concord (*You ain't goin' to no heaven*), the durative *be* (*when they be sayin'*) and deletes the linking verb (*if you bad*). He also uses the rhetorical style of his society. If we outline his statements as he interacts with the interviewer, we find a well-developed argument. The argument is direct and convincing. He does not cloud the issues with superfluous speech that softens and obscures the impact of what he is saying. Larry can think logically and deal with abstract concepts. Charles M., in contrast, uses the upper- and middle-class conventions of discussion. He uses the grammar of a White dialect in a way that would please the most pendantic. He also follows the subtle sociolinguistic rules of middle-class culture—he is fluent, he uses abstract words, and he routinely qualifies what he says (*I don't particularly believe in . . . ; I do feel that in certain cultures . . . ; I personally have never had . . .*). We tend to assume immediately that Charles is an educated man and that Larry is not. Can we also conclude that one of them is more intelligent or can think more logically than the other?

DEFICIT OR DIFFERENCE?

The Poverty Cycle

Differences among dialects do not necessarily reflect deficits in one or another dialect-speaking group. Nevertheless, the traditional interpretation of anyone who speaks anything other than "good" English (or good French, or German, or any other language) is that he or she is not very well educated, and therefore is likely to be not quite as bright as someone who speaks "properly." A corollary of this notion is that nonstandard speech results from a deficit of some sort. People who speak Black dialects (or poor-White dialects) do so because they were somehow unable to learn the "standard" dialect—presumably because of their impoverished developmental environments. This viewpoint is illustrated by the concept of the poverty cycle in Figure 6.1. We can start anywhere in the cycle. Poor people have an economic disadvantage (they don't have enough money). Why don't they have enough money? Because they tend to have no jobs at all or low-paying jobs, and have little opportunity for getting and keeping better jobs (last hired, first fired). Such a situation is called an employment disadvantage. This, in turn, may result from inferior schooling (an educational disadvantage), which in turn is the result of poor early environments for social, physical, and intellectual development. Why the developmental disadvantage? Because the parents are poor. Why are they poor? Because . . . and so on.

Notice that it does not follow that speaking one dialect or another results from any kind of disadvantage whatever, other than belonging to a group that is disadvantaged in the first place. Nevertheless, social scientists on both sides of the Atlantic Ocean have been quick to point out the linguistic disadvantages of belonging to the lower classes. Studying a different social context than the Black–White dialectal differences in the United States, Basil Bernstein (1958, 1959, 1960, 1970), a British sociologist, has compared middle- and lower-class dialects in England. He has ignored the formal phonological and syntactic differences, presumably because little can

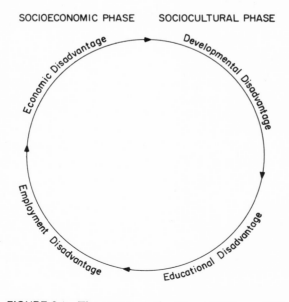

FIGURE 6.1   The poverty cycle. (From Williams, 1970.)

be made of them. Instead, he has postulated that the different social classes use different language "codes." One, a restricted code, is attributed to lower-class speech. Middle-class people are said to use both a restricted code and an elaborated code. The criteria for deciding whether a sample of speech represents a restricted or an elaborated code have never been clearly specified. Most recently, Bernstein (1970) has emphasized the social contexts in which each code is developed and used. The restricted code is presumed to be more context-bound than the elaborated code. The restricted code relies on the immediate context of a conversation to disambiguate statements. Precise meanings are not always carefully stated, and an in-group solidarity between speakers and listeners is essential for communication. All people use restricted codes at one time or another, but only some people (not the lower class) use an elaborated code when it is appropriate to do so. Elaborated codes are not restricted to particular situations and to particular listeners. They are "designed" to communicate a message to anyone, regardless of context. Bernstein (1970) bases his arguments upon his own observations and examples like

> . . . analyses [Hawkins, 1969] of the speech of middle-class (story A) and working-class, (B), five-year-old children in London. The children were given a series of four pictures which portrayed the sequence of a story and they were invited to tell this story. The first picture shows some boys playing football near a house; the second shows the ball breaking a window; the third shows a man making a threatening gesture; in the fourth, the children are moving away, while watched by a woman peering out of the window.
>
> (A) Three boys are playing football and one boy kicks the ball—and it goes through the window—the ball breaks the window—and the boys are looking at it—and a man comes out and shouts at them—because they've broken the window—so they ran away—and then that lady looks out of her window—and she tells the boys off.
>
> (B) They're playing football—and he kicks it and it goes through there—it breaks the window and they're looking at it—and he comes out and shouts at them—because they've broken it—so they run away—and then she looks out and she tells them off [p. 26].

Story A is considered superior to Story B. The grounds for this judgment are that Story A is elaborated. If the person listening to the story did not have the appropriate pictures in front of him, he would understand Story A but would not understand Story B. Can we be sure of this? First, we could argue that Story B is in fact the more appropriate one. The child knows that the person who is listening to the story is also looking at the pictures. Why elaborate when one does not have to? Second, is it perfectly obvious that Story B could not be understood without the pictures? What would have happened had the children been asked to tell the story to someone who did not know what was in the pictures? Would the implied social class differences still have emerged if actual communication performance had been assessed? We do not really know the answer to this question, but a recent survey of the published literature on this issue found no consistent differences in communicative skills associated with either race or social class (Glucksberg, Krauss, & Higgins, 1975).

Finally, we should clarify the source of Bernstein's Stories A and B. Hawkins (1969) constructed them as exaggerated exemplars of elaborated and restricted speech. Contrary to Bernstein's implications, they were not produced by either working-class or middle-class children, and they were not "based upon" analyses of any children. They were carefully written to illustrate what Hawkins understood to be elaborated and restricted codes. What Hawkins actually did was to count the relative frequency of pronominal usages in stories told by working-class and middle-class children, and he found that the former tended to use more pronouns than did the latter. The inference that a "restricted" code was being used by working-class children and an "elaborated" code by middle-class children is hardly justified by the actual data. After all, appropriate use of pronouns is considered to be a rather high-level linguistic skill.

Despite the appalling lack of evidence, some American investigators have seized on Bernstein's distinction between restricted and elaborated codes to explain the difficulties that "disadvantaged" children have in communicating in school. These children are considered to be nonverbal, and this, in turn, results in low IQ scores and poor school performance (Hess & Shipman, 1965). As Labov (1970) has pointed out, such data are highly suspect. The very fact that a child speaks a low-status dialect and belongs to a low–status social group can affect other people's assessments of his knowledge and abilities.

Dialects and Test Performance

The deficit assumption accepted by most of us is neither new nor unique to American society. In the musical play *My Fair Lady* based on Shaw's *Pygmalion,* Eliza Doolittle, a bedraggled Cockney flower girl on the streets of London, is transformed into an upper-class lady. Henry Higgins, a linguistics professor, bets a colleague that by teaching Eliza to speak properly, he can change her entire way of life. Under his tutelage, she acquires the dialect of the English upper classes of the time, and is integrated into that class. As Professor Higgins pointed out, "The way an Englishman speaks absolutely classifies him; the moment he opens his mouth he makes another Englishman despise him."

Most of us are no different. We tend to scorn people who do not speak as we do. One of the most common forms of derision is to mimic the accent, dialect, or speech mannerisms of others. All foreigners are fair game, as well as groups within one's own country. In various sections of the United States, the speech of Italians, Puerto Ricans, Chicanos, Jews, Irish, Blacks, Easterners, Northerners, Southerners, Brooklynites, and Texans are targets of derision. The list is endless, and includes our family and friends when we become angry with them.

Small wonder that we attribute deficiencies of intellect and character to people who speak dialects other than our own, and that the targets of our derision often fail to perform well in testing situations. Labov (1970) describes how performance can change dramatically when a testing situation changes. In the first of three testing situations a young Black boy was brought into a room where a friendly White interviewer showed him a toy and said, "Tell me everything you can about this." The boy said very little, uttering ten phrases separated by long periods of silence. This is a typical result in this kind of testing situation and has led to the conclusion that lower-class Black children are relatively nonverbal. The obvious remedy is to concentrate on verbal skills (Bereiter & Engelmann, 1966; Deutsch, 1967). But what if such children are as verbal as any? Would a change in the testing situation change our diagnosis?

In a second interview situation, a skilled Black interviewer was substituted for the White one. He posed several questions to an eight-year-old Black boy named Leon. Leon looked as though he were, indeed, "nonverbal." He responded with one-word answers or with hesitant "ummmms" or "ahmmms." Either Leon was truly nonverbal or there was something about the situation which did not reveal the verbal abilities he might have. To test this last possibility, a third interviewing situation was arranged. This time the same Black interviewer brought along Leon's best friend, sat on the floor with the children, and passed around a bag of potato chips. The interviewer started things rolling by using natural street conversation in the local dialect. These seemingly minor changes in the situation produced dramatic changes in Leon's speech behavior. What was a semimute monosyllabic boy was now a verbal geyser. The two boys carried on a lively animated conversation, punctuated with argument, accusations, and denials. Gone were the monosyllabic utterances and long periods of silence. By any evaluative criteria, Leon was as verbal as one could imagine.

If standard testing situations are anything like the first two interviews described by Labov, then it is not surprising that many children are described as nonverbal (see Hess & Shipman, 1965). Leon's interviewer had been specifically trained to elicit verbal material. He was a Black man who grew up in Leon's neighborhood, and knew the boys quite well. Yet, in his first interview with Leon, Leon remained "nonverbal." Is it any wonder that a white stranger in a classroom may not be able to get children like Leon to reveal the verbal abilities they may have?

Aside from the difficulties posed by dialect differences between teachers and children, the social power differences between dominant adults and children can be extremely difficult to overcome. Labov (1970) concludes: "The social situation is the most powerful determinant of verbal behavior and . . . an adult must enter into the right social relation with a child if he wants to find out what a child can do. This is just what many teachers cannot do [p. 163]." This conclusion applies to all children, regardless of dialect. Recently, a toy company ran a television commercial to convince people that their toys were sturdy and long lasting. As part of the commercial, one saw a series of incidents where a parent points to a smashed toy and asks the child, "what happened?" The routine response in this situation was "nothing."

If these observations are relevant to testing situations, then evaluations of language performance should depend heavily upon the social context and the kind of dialect used in the tests. White children should do better than Black children when a White dialect is used, and Black children should do better than White when a Black dialect is used. As Slobin and Welsh (1973) have pointed out, children's imitations of sentences tend to conform to their own grammatical knowledge. They do not behave like little tape recorders, but instead transform what they hear into what they know about the language. If the Black dialect were to be unsystematic and simply a degraded form of White dialects, then both Black and White children should have difficulty with Black-dialect sentences. Furthermore, both Black and White children should do better with the White dialect sentences,

TABLE 6.2
Some Examples of White and Black English[a,b]

White English	Black English
1. My aunt who lives in Baltimore used to come to visit us on Sunday afternoons.	1. My aunt, she live in Baltimore, and she used to come visit us Sunday afternoon.
2. Gloria's friend is working as a waitress in the Hot Shoppes on Connecticut Avenue.	2. Gloria friend she a waitress, she be working the Hot Shoppes on Connecticut Avenue.
3. Patricia sits in the front row so that she can hear everything the teacher says.	3. Patricia all the time be sitting in the front row so she can hear everything the teacher say.
4. Does Deborah like to play with the girl that sits next to her in school?	4. Do Deborah like to play with the girl that sit next to her at school?

a Pronunciations have been rendered in standard written form.
b From Baratz (1969).

and we might expect that White children would outperform Black children as well.

Joan Baratz (1969) gave White and Black children a sentence-imitation task. Some of the sentences conformed to the phonological and grammatical rules of White dialects, and others to the rules of Black dialects. Examples of both types of sentences are shown in Table 6.2. Each child heard each sentence one at a time on a tape recorder and then tried to repeat it word for word. The results were quite clear. Black and White children performed equally well overall, with Black children making more errors on the White dialect sentences, and White children making more errors on the Black dialect sentences. Furthermore, errors were not random. When a White child heard a Black-dialect sentence, he would tend to repeat it back in White-dialect form. For example, if he heard *He be working at the factory*, then he would be likely to repeat it as *He is working at the factory*. Black children tended to do the opposite. Both groups erred in the direction of their own language systems, translating the unfamiliar forms into their own dialects.

On the basis of results like these, we suspect very strongly that it would be impossible to devise "culture fair" tests—that is, a single set of tests that would be appropriate for anyone. We can only hope to devise CULTURE–APPROPRIATE tests, with different tests and test forms for various cultural and linguistic groups. Only then can we diagnose educational problems accurately and then take appropriate action.

DIALECTS AND READING

What should teachers and educational systems do if the children in a school system speak several dialects of English? Before we can begin to answer this kind of question we must answer at least two logically prior questions:

1. What is the relationship between written language and spoken language?

If the written language were to be completely phonic, with one-to-one correspondences between graphic symbols and speech sounds, this question would be easy to answer. English is certainly not completely phonic, so a second question becomes relevant:

2. Is the written language closer—phonically, semantically, and syntactically—to one dialect than it is to another? Are White dialects more closely attuned to standard reading material than are Black dialects, especially in the early grades?

The programs that have been suggested to deal with the problems of dialectical variation in our school systems are based on the assumption that a child's "deviant" dialect is a major source of reading difficulties. This assumption is common to both "deficit" and "difference" viewpoints. The deficit position holds that Black dialects reflect a developmental and educational disadvantage (see Figure 6.1, page 164). The difference position is that all dialects are equally effective, but that there is a mismatch between Black children's language and the language used in the schools. Both positions attribute school difficulties to the particular dialects spoken by children. Therefore, both positions lead to proposals and programs focused on language and verbal behavior. The deficit position concentrates on "improving" children's language skills; the difference position concentrates on tailoring the language of the schools and the reading materials to the dialects of the children. In both cases, one or the other dialect is the target of change.

Two programs emerge from these two positions. From the deficit viewpoint, Black children require language remediation. They should learn to speak Standard English and to suppress their own dialect. One problem arises immediately—what is Standard English? Should Black children (or White children) in Boston be taught to speak the dialect spoken in Boston, or the dialect spoken in Texas, Kansas, or Brooklyn? A second problem with such a remediation approach is that children would be required to relinquish an important aspect of their social and cultural identity, perhaps with little prospect for full acceptance into the majority culture. Giving up one's own social identity can leave one with none at all. These are long-range considerations, but there are immediate consequences as well. Every child is highly sensitive to the evaluations of his or her peer group. Very few children are willing to be obviously different—in dress, manner, or speech—from their friends. Add to these issues the simple fact that trying to change how people talk rarely succeeds (remember speech class?) and does not demonstrably result in intellectual gains.

The opposite approach stems from those who hold that dialects differ but do not necessarily reflect intellectual deficits. The target of change here is the language of instruction. Teachers should speak in the children's dialect, and all reading materials should be written in that dialect. This approach poses at least two formidable problems. First, there are the practical problems of producing textbooks and reading materials, and finding teachers and administrators who are both qualified and willing. Second, and far more important, most societies are unwilling to accept without prejudice people who do not speak the dominant dialects. As a case in point, consider the French-speaking Canadians. They have their own schools, but are still at a severe social and economic disadvantage in English-speaking Canada, even within the Province of Quebec, where the French-speaking population is in the majority. Furthermore, the segregated, "separate-but-equal" schools of our own recent past in the United States were hardly exemplars of a novel and promising approach.

One compromise between these two extreme positions is represented by a variety of bidialectal approaches. Three variants of this position can be identified. The first two are based on the same assumption made by the two extreme positions just reviewed—that there is a mismatch between the written language and the spoken language of Black children.

One type of program would have a White dialect taught in school as a second language, as if the white dialect were a foreign language (see Stewart, 1964). Presumably, speaking one dialect of English should make it easier to learn another. One problem is this: what dialect of English do we pick as the standard? A down-East Maine twang or a Texas drawl? Second, this task may not be as easy as one might think within the school context. Would it be easy to teach American children to speak in a Scottish dialect of English? People can and do become bidialectal, but it usually takes time and a personally-relevant reason to do so. In Washington, D.C., Black dialects vary widely in terms of their similarity to White dialects (Stewart, 1964). The dialects most similar to White dialects are called ACROLECTS; those most different are BASILECTS. Young children are most likely to use basilect, whereas older children and adults tend to use the acrolect. Among adults, women are more likely to use the acrolect than men, and higher-status people are more likely to do so than lower-status people. Use of the acrolect or White dialects seems to be related to the motivation to be in contact with the mainstream of social, economic, and political life, as well as the need to communicate effectively with a wide spectrum of people. For social, economic, and political reasons, it is important to speak a "standard" dialect. There are a variety of other reasons why it may not be feasible to teach dialects as "second languages." Not the least of these reasons is the relative ineffectiveness of our second-language teaching in the first place. How many of us can speak the foreign languages we were exposed to in school?

The second bidialectal approach would begin reading instruction with primers written in the child's own dialect. As children progress with their so-called dialect readers, "standard" English would be introduced gradually. This approach differs from the first in that it involves a gradual transition from one dialect to another in reading materials. The first introduces the "standard" immediately as if it were a foreign language.

Both of these approaches are based on assumptions we feel are wrong. The first assumption is that written English is, in fact, peculiarly well suited to a standard White dialect. The second is that we can prepare reading material that is just as well suited to any other dialect, including Black English. If the first assumption is correct, then the "standard" must be quite variable. Black and White children often speak different dialects, but so do children from Maine, Texas, Louisiana, Kansas, and many other regions of the country. Are all the regional dialects of White children equally well suited to the standard written language? Are the various Black dialects found in the United States equally ill suited to that standard written language?

The syntactic forms of standard written English may be more appropriate for White dialects, but this is relatively trivial for beginning primers with their vocabulary lists and very short, simple sentences. The lexical differences between White and Black dialects are also minimal at this early stage of reading. The major differences between White and Black dialects when children first begin to read are phonological. Is standard written English phonically closer to White dialects than to Black dialects? If it were, then we might be able to develop a writing system that would be phonetically more appropriate to Black dialects.

The problem, of course, is that written English is not perfectly phonic for either class of dialects. *Threw* and *through* are pronounced alike in both dialects, yet they are spelled differently. *Enough* and *though* do not rhyme in either dialect, yet they are spelled similarly. The word *basically* is spelled as if it had four syllables, yet in neither dialect do we pronounce it as if it had four syllables—*basically* has three syllables.

People who speak White dialects do not pronounce everything they read, but they can transform what they read aloud into their own spoken dialect. When they do this, and the teacher recognizes that the words are pronounced correctly, no problems arise. A child in Maine and a child in Texas may pronounce the word *chair* in two quite different ways, and their respective teachers will accept their pronunciations as correct. Imagine now that the teachers are switched. Unless teachers know how the word should be pronounced in the respective regional dialects, they might mistakenly think that the children were reading incorrectly.

To return to the real world, we already have seen that the words *pin* and *pen* in most White dialects are pronounced differently. In most Black dialects, *pin* and *pen* sound identical. This poses no problems when the pronunciation is characteristic of a regional dialect (as it is in Kansas and Texas), but it can be a critical problem elsewhere if a teacher corrects a child's reading when the child sees *pen* and the teacher hears him pronouncing *pin*. From the child's viewpoint, he has read the word correctly, but the teacher says he is wrong. In this situation, the child is being punished for doing exactly what he should be doing. He is decoding a written symbol into speech. The teacher, not knowing the child's dialect, cannot discriminate between reading errors and dialectal pronunciations. If a child says [pɪn] when he reads the word *pen,* he is reading incorrectly only if he normally pronounces the word that refers to a writing instrument as [pɛn]. If he normally pronounces that word so that it rhymes with *tin*, then he is reading correctly. In other words, teachers should know what they are correcting—reading or pronunciation. It can only confuse a beginning reader to be punished for reading correctly, and progress can be retarded severely. How can anyone possibly learn to read when perfectly appropriate reading performance is "corrected," and corrected inconsistently at that?

The case is presented well by Ralph Fasold (1969) in a discussion of the relation between spelling and pronunciation:

> The problem for the Black English speaking child . . . [and others with systematic phonological differences] . . . is that the corrections he receives are *not* consistent. When he reads *basically* as [beysɪkliy], his reading is acceptable, reinforcing . . . [a] . . . correct principle of reading. But when he is told that [tɛst] rather than [tɛs] is the correct way to read *test*, . . . [a] . . . spurious principle of oral reading is reinforced. Not being a speaker of standard English, he has no way of knowing why some words are to be read according to one principle and others according to another. As a result, the child is likely to conclude that there is actually no principle at all. Since there is no way to determine the relationship between written symbols and their pronunciation, wild guessing is the only way to seek the teacher's approval. Since wild guessing so rarely produces the desired approval, complete despair may well be the next step.
>
> This difficulty can be overcome by training teachers in Black English pronunciations so that they will consistently accept words that are correctly read according to the rules of Black English phonology. This means that [wɪf] is a correct reading for *with*, [bɪ:t] is the right way to read *bid* and that *test* is properly read as [tɛs] [p. 88].

None of these bidialectal approaches has been extensively tested to date. However well or poorly they might work if tried, teaching children to read will not solve the overriding problems of racial and ethnic discrimination. At the very least, we should be absolutely clear about the import of dialect differences. They signify nothing about the capacities or abilities of speakers of those dialects. To believe or act otherwise is to reveal our own ethnocentrism.

SUGGESTED READINGS

For an extensive discussion of Black English, see J. L. Dillard, *Black English: Its history and usage in the United States* (New York: Random House, 1972). The deficit-difference issue is considered from a variety of viewpoints in F. Williams (Ed.), *Language and poverty* (Chicago: Markham, 1970). See especially the articles by B. Bernstein, "A sociolinguistic approach to socialization: With some reference to educability"; by W. Labov, "The logic of nonstandard English"; by W. A. Stewart, "Toward a history of American Negro dialect"; and by F. Williams, "Language, attitude, and social change." The problems Black children have with reading and various proposed solutions are developed by several authors in J. C. Baratz and R. W. Shuy (Eds.), *Teaching Black children to read* (Washington, D.C.: Center for Applied Linguistics, 1969). Articles of particular interest are those by R. W. Fasold, "Orthography in reading materials for Black English speaking children"; by J. C. Baratz, "Teaching reading in an urban Negro school system"; and by W. A. Stewart, "On the use of Negro dialect in the teaching of reading."

7
Language, Thought, and Communication

Language and thought interact in various ways. What is the relation between language and thought? This question has engaged philosophers, linguists, and psychologists for centuries. There is, of course, no single answer to the question, just as there are no single definitions of the concepts LANGUAGE and THOUGHT. Depending on our conceptions of language and thinking, we can say that language determines thought, that thought determines language, and that thought and language are independent of one another. Any one or all of the statements may be true. In what senses are they true, and how may thought and language interact with one another?

LANGUAGE AND THOUGHT

Benjamin Lee Whorf, a student of the noted anthropologist and linguist Edward Sapir, was a fire insurance investigator as well as a linguist. He was struck by the way that labels could influence people's behavior. Which is more dangerous, a gasoline drum filled with gasoline or an empty one? A number of spectacular fires convinced Whorf that people thought of empty drums as perfectly safe. They acted as though the word *empty* really meant empty. An "empty" gasoline drum is one which is empty in only one sense: it once held gasoline but now does not. It still contains invisible but highly volatile fumes. "Empty" drums are in fact more likely to explode than filled ones.

From observations like this and from his work with American Indian languages, Whorf became convinced that the language we use influences the way we think and act. He extended this notion to include the syntax of the language itself as a major determiner of our conceptual world. Different languages "talk about" the world in different ways, and so impose different conceptions of reality upon different speakers. This has become known as the LINGUISTIC RELATIVITY HYPOTHESIS. Whorf's teacher Sapir characterized the relationship between language and conceptions of reality as follows:

> Human beings do not live in the objective world alone, nor alone in the world of social activity as ordinarily understood, but are very much at the mercy of the particular language which has become the medium of expression for their society. It is quite an illusion to imagine that one adjusts to reality essentially without the use of language and that language is merely an incidental means of solving specific problems of communication or reflection. The fact of the matter is that the "real world" is to a large extent unconsciously built upon the language habits of the group . . . we see and hear and otherwise experience very largely as we do because the language habits of our community predispose certain choices of interpretation [Sapir, 1968, p. 162].*

If this is "the fact of the matter" and if languages differ from one another in ways that are critical for conceptual development, then at least one form of the linguistic relativity hypothesis would be correct. If people speak different languages, then they will think differently. This hypothesis depends upon the truth of two separate assertions. First, language itself is a critical factor in the development of our conceptions of reality and the maintenance of certain ways of thinking about the world. This is an assertion of LINGUISTIC DETERMINISM, namely that language per se shapes thought. Second, linguistic relativity is a separate assertion. LINGUISTIC RELATIVITY asserts that languages do, in fact, differ in just those ways that produce differences in conceptual development and differences in adult modes of thought. If two people speak different languages, linguistic determinism alone might be operative, and yet the two people could still think in precisely the same ways and have precisely the same conceptions of reality. In contrast, the linguistic relativity hypothesis would assert that because the languages are different, the thought must be different too. To what extent is each of these assertions true? Since linguistic relativity depends upon linguistic determinism, let us consider linguistic determinism first.

* Originally published by the University of California Press; reprinted by permission of The Regents of the University of California.

Linguistic Determinism

In the most extreme form of this hypothesis, there is neither language nor thought, just speech. John B. Watson (1913), one of the founders of radical American behaviorism, simply equated thought with speech: "thought processes are really motor habits in the larynx [p. 174]." Whenever we believe we are thinking, we are really only making implicit speech movements. On the face of it this position seems absurd—and it is. A contemporary analogy would be the assertion that a computer does not really execute any computational operations; only the teletype unit that prints the output does anything. Nevertheless, Watson's position was taken seriously, possibly because we had no mechanical system like a high-speed digital computer to provide an analogy for mental operations.

At least four lines of evidence can be cited to dispose of the thought-is-speech notion rather quickly. First, nonspeaking animals display rather complex thought processes, both in the laboratory and in the wild. Second, nonspeaking humans display relatively normal conceptual development prior to systematic language training (Furth, 1966). Third, adults who lose speech as a result of brain damage, or who temporarily lose speech as a result of temporary paralysis, can still think. They can solve abstract problems, do arithmetic, reason logically, and so on. Finally, thought can be completely nonverbal. Visual thinking is something we are all capable of to some extent. For example, how do you go about answering a question like: What side of the front door was the doorknob on in the house you lived in just before the one before the one you live in now (Lindsay & Norman, 1972)? Can we "think" in visual and action formats? Try this problem:

> Imagine a rectangle three times as tall as it is wide. Now, mentally draw two diagonals, one from each of the top corners. Now draw two horizontal lines parallel to the base that divide the rectangle into three equal parts. How many segments are now in the rectangle?

Is this problem worked out by using implicit speech, or by visual imagery? Most people would answer "both": first they visualize the segmented rectangle, then they verbally count the segments. Other examples of nonverbal thought can be found in Ghiselin's (1955) book on creative thinking, in which mathematicians, scientists, and artists describe their own thought processes. Clearly, neither speech nor language can be equated with thought.

A more reasonable form of linguistic determinism is that the culture of a community is transmitted to children primarily via the speech of others. A child's conception of the physical and social world develops out of two kinds of experiences, direct and mediated. The direct experience consists of what he perceives as well as what he does. The mediated experience consists of what others tell him about people and the world. From their visual properties he may categorize bananas and carrots into one group and apples in another. From eating experience, all three belong in the category of edible things. Most of us would group bananas and apples together, with carrots belonging to another group of edibles. This particular categorization is mediated through interpersonal experience in the form of language. Bananas and apples are both labeled *fruit*.

That thought is language, or even that language completely controls or determines thought, is too strong to be correct. But a weak form of linguistic determinism probably operates: language influences thought, especially when we do not consciously avoid the restrictiveness of language. Since much of our world is organized as a result of communication from others, and much of that communication is linguistic, language must unavoidably exert some influence on how we conceptualize our experiences. Does linguistic relativity operate in addition to this form of linguistic determinism? Different languages may differ in ways which lead to different organizations of the experiential world. Do people who speak different languages think differently?

Linguistic Relativity

We start with an assumption of weak linguistic determinism. Much of what we know, and how we think about what we know, has been acquired through interpersonal experience, namely, what others have told us about the world. Languages can and do differ from one another in at least two ways—lexically and grammatically.

Lexical differences involve the ways in which things are labeled, and this can include the number of labels or words for things, the ways in which concepts are categorized, and the presence or absence of superordinate categories. An oft-quoted example of lexical differences between languages is the number of words for snow. The Eskimos have many words for the different varieties of snow; we have only one. Similarly, Arabs have more than 20 words for camel; we have just one. Even something as physically real as the color spectrum can be lexically categorized in quite different ways. Gleason (1961) shows that not only the number of categories, but also the locations of the boundaries between labeled color regions, can vary considerably across languages (see Figure 7.1). Even something as universal as the rainbow can be divided up in more or less arbitrary fashion.

Does this mean that one or more of the following differs among speakers of different languages: (*a*) ease of talking about colors, (*b*) recognition memory for colors, (*c*) perception of colors, and (*d*) subjective organization of the color space. Which of the above kinds of differences (*a, b, c,* or *d*) should we take as evidence of differences in thought or conceptualization? Most of us would agree that differences in (*a*), ease of talking about colors, need not reflect important differences in conceptual organization or structure. Differences in (*c*) and (*d*) would, by definition, reflect differences in world view and conceptualization. Differences in ability to remember colors (*b*) is an intermediate case.

The ways in which people who speak different languages deal with colors has been studied fairly intensively. Ease of talking about or communicating about something should be influenced by the availability of an adequate vocabulary. People do have trouble talking about things for which they have no words. Within any language, colors differ with respect to CODABILITY, the extent to which any particular color has an agreed-upon, short name (Brown & Lenneberg, 1954). In English, the word *red* would refer to a highly codable color, the phrase *the color of a sunset over the Rockies on a hazy December day* would refer to a low-codable color. Both within and between languages, communication accuracy—the ability of a speaker to tell a listener which color to select from an array of colors—depends to some extent on the codability of the target color. Colors that have short, agreed-upon names (like *red, green,* or *blue*) are easy to identify on the basis of verbal descriptions. Colors that have longer or less agreed-upon names, or both, like *passion pink* or *magenta,* are not as easy to identify (Lantz & Stefflre, 1964; Stefflre, Castillo Vales, & Morley, 1966). This is not surprising, and does not necessarily imply that people who speak different languages conceptualize colors in different ways.

Memory for colors is less directly tied to linguistic processes. Just like ease of communication, recognition memory for colors and some other stimuli can be affected by codability (Brown & Lenneberg, 1954). If I showed you a colored chip that you would call *bluish-green* and then some time later show you that chip along with two others that are also called *bluish-green,* you might have some trouble remembering just which one of the three you had seen before. If the three colored chips had quite different names, you would have very little trouble, even though the three differently named chips do not differ physically any more widely than the other three. You could remember the name and that would help you pick out

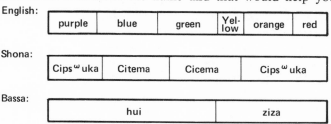

FIGURE 7.1 Three ways to categorize the rainbow. Shona and Bassa are African languages. (After Gleason, 1961.)

the correct color. To the extent that naming can be used to aid memory, the codability of colors could influence your ability to remember which colors you had seen before. Because memory is not what we usually mean by thinking or conceptualization, these findings are merely suggestive of more important differences among people. Furthermore, this sort of influence of naming might be specific to certain classes of perceptual events. Our ability to recognize faces or real-world scenes is quite independent of the codability of those stimuli. We sometimes forget or remember names and faces independently, often to our embarrassment.

Perception of objects and events and our subjective organization of those experiences come somewhat closer to what we usually mean by thought and conceptions of reality. Here the effects of codability seem to be minimal. The codability of a color has no effect on our ability to judge whether two colors are the same or different so long as we can view them simultaneously. To this extent, people who speak different languages perceive colors in the same way. Similarly, the laws of color mixture work equally well across linguistic boundaries: red and yellow make orange, and yellow and blue make green when the appropriate pigments are mixed.

What about the structure or subjective organization of the color space? The structure of the subjective color space for American English-speaking people is well known. One way to represent this structure is illustrated in Figure 3.9 (Chapter 3, page 75). That particular "map" of subjective organization of colors was constructed from similarity judgments of color names. A virtually identical map can be constructed from similarity judgments of the colors themselves. In this case, the subjective organization of the words referring to colors and the subjective organization of the colors themselves are isomorphic with one another. Would people with a markedly different set of color names have a different subjective map of the color space? If they did, then we would be justified in concluding that they think about colors in a different way than Americans do.

In West New Guinea there is a group of people called the Dani. Their color terminology differs markedly from English. They have only two color names, *mili* and *mola*. *Mili* refers to dark and "cold" colors; *mola* refers to light and "warm" colors (Heider & Olivier, 1972). They are therefore an ideal group of people to compare with Americans, who have many more color names. Both Dani and Americans were given a memory task involving an array of 40 color chips. The array was used as a multiple-choice test. Each chip was shown, one at a time, for 5 seconds. Thirty seconds later the entire 40-color array was shown, and the person had to pick out the chip he had seen 30 seconds before. This procedure provides two kinds of information. First, we can estimate the accuracy of recognition memory, which indicates how well people can remember colors for which they do or do not have names. Second, we can derive estimates of the similarities among the 40 colors if we assume that when an error is made a similar, but not identical, color would be picked. The more often color A is picked incorrectly instead of color B (and vice versa), the more similar are colors A and B.

As might be expected, Americans made somewhat fewer errors than did the Dani. Not only did the Americans have far more experience with memory tasks like this one, they also had a more differentiated color vocabularly that could be used as a memory aid. Contrary to expectation, the kinds of errors (confusions) that occurred were very similar in the two groups, yielding virtually identical subjective structures of the color space for the Dani and the Americans. Despite the vastly different naming practices of the two peoples, color similarities, as indexed by confusion errors, were perceived in the same ways. The color "maps" derived from both groups' confusion errors are shown in Figure 7.2. They are far more similar to one another than one would expect on the basis of the differences between the color terminologies. Heider and Olivier (1972) conclude: ". . . although there are linguistic variables which correlate with color memory accuracy under certain conditions, the nature of color memory images themselves and the way in which they structure the color space in memory appear little influenced by language [p. 352]."

We do not yet know whether this conclusion can be generalized to other perceptual domains—geometric forms, real objects, people, and so forth. Perhaps our lexicon does not determine how we conceptualize concrete referents, yet may have profound effects upon how we structure abstract ideas and concepts. The available data, however, deal only with concrete referents like color. These data suggest that differences among the lexicons of languages primarily reflect differences in what people tend to talk about, not what they can think about. The major effect of the availability of a particular set of terms is on communication accuracy, with some effect on recognition memory accuracy. When we need to talk about something for which we have no adequate terminology, we invent one. We do this individually, in small groups, and in society as a whole: witness the continual appearance of new words in our society, for example, *TV, freak-out, hippie, holograph, porno, rip-off, jet set,* and *psycholinguistics.* The lexicon, and perhaps the grammar, follows communication needs.

If differences in the lexicons among languages do not have easily demonstrable effects on thinking, how about differences in syntax? Do German and French speakers conceptualize interpersonal relations differently than English speakers do simply because they must specify their relation to the people they talk to by choosing the "familiar" *du* or *tu,* or the "polite" *Sie* or *vous.* English speakers are not forced to make such choices, since English has only one form, *you.* But English speakers often have to decide whether to call someone by his or her first or last name. Do Russian speakers think differently about objects because they never have to specify whether something is definite or indefinite? (Russian does not use articles

DANI COLOR MEMORY

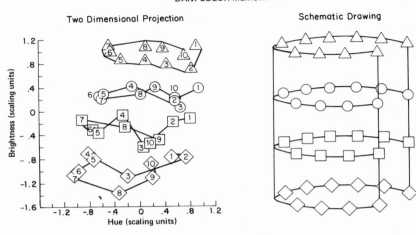

Two Dimensional Projection   Schematic Drawing

U.S. COLOR MEMORY

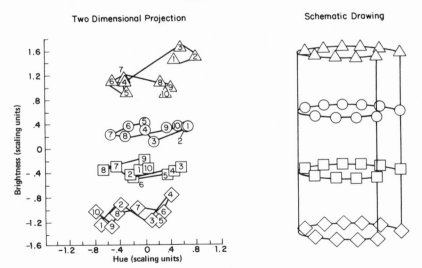

Two Dimensional Projection   Schematic Drawing

FIGURE 7.2 Color memory space for Dani and Americans. (After Heider & Olivier, 1972).

corresponding to *the* and *a.*) Does it make any difference for our concepts of such things as tables, books, windows, and houses, if we have to specify gender or not? Leaving aside the thorny question of causality, are such grammatical differences at least correlated with conceptual differences? When the grammars differ, can we infer that conceptualizations also differ?

We have very little information about syntactic influences on thought. Some comes from an experiment with Navaho children conducted by Joseph Casagrande (reported in Carroll & Casagrande, 1958). Just as English requires that the time of an action be specified by the tense of the verb, the Navaho language has certain verbs that take different forms, depending on the shape of the object one is talking about. Navaho has different verb forms for picking up a ball (round) versus picking up a stick (long and thin) versus picking up a sheet of paper (flat and flexible). Does this characteristic of the language affect the relative saliency of shapes for Navaho speakers? In general, young children tend to group objects by color before they group things by shape (Brian & Goodenough, 1929). Since Navaho children learn to use these shape-specific verbs quite early, will they therefore categorize things by shape rather than color at an earlier age than do English-speaking children? If they do, then perhaps the verb forms have influenced the development of their classification schemes.

Casagrande found that Navaho-speaking children from a reservation classified objects according to shape more than did English-speaking Navaho children from the same reservation. This result is consistent with linguistic relativity. However, English-speaking white children from the Boston area performed more like the Navaho-speaking children from the reservation than like the English-speaking Navaho children. This anomaly was explained by appealing to the possibility that middle-class children from Boston develop faster than do Navaho children. Although this post hoc explanation is consistent with other data that middle-class children do shift from color to form classification earlier than do lower-class children (Honkavaara, 1958), the effects of syntax still seem to be minimal.

In spite of the limited evidence that differences in grammar and thought are correlated, people persist in inferring modes of thought from the syntax of a language. Consider a passage from Whorf (1956):

Languages and Logic:
BENJAMIN LEE WHORF

Our Indian languages show that with a suitable grammar we may have intelligent sentences that cannot be broken into subjects and predicates. Any attempted breakup is a breakup of some English translation or paraphrase of the sentence, not of the Indian sentence itself. . . . When we come to Nootka, the sentence without subject or predicate is the only type. The term "predication" is used, but it means "sentence." Nootka has no parts of speech; the simplest utterance is a sentence, treating of some event or event-complex. Long sentences are sentences of sentences (complex sentences), not just sentences of words. In Fig. [7.3] we have a simple, not a complex, Nootka sentence. The translation, 'he invites people to a feast', splits into subject and predicate. Not so the native sentence. It begins with the event of 'boiling or cooking,' *tl'imsh;* then comes *-ya* ('result') = 'cooked'; then *-'is* 'eating' = 'eating cooked food; then *-ita* ('those who do') = 'eaters of cooked food'; then *-'itl* ('going for'); then *-ma,* sign of third-person indicative, giving *tl'imshya'isita'itlma,* which answers to the crude paraphrase, 'he, or somebody, goes for (invites) eaters of cooked food'.

The English technique of talking depends on the contrast of two artificial classes, substantives and verbs, and on the bipartitioned ideology of nature. . . . Our normal sentence, unless imperative, must have some substantive before its verb, a requirement that corresponds to the philosophical and also naive notion of an actor who

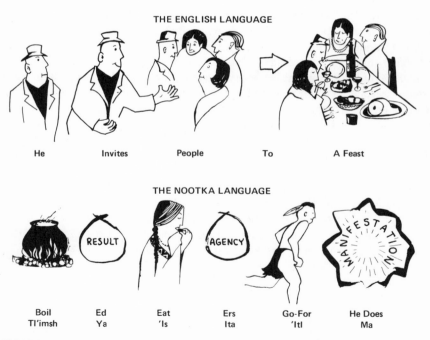

FIGURE 7.3 The different ways in which the same event is literally described in English and Nootka. The English sentence is divisible into subject and predicate. The Nootka sentence is not. Furthermore, the Nootka sentence is just one "word," consisting of the root *tl'imsh* with five suffixes. (After Whorf, 1956, © 1956 by the Massachusetts Institute of Technology.)

produces an action. This last might not have been so if English had
had thousands of verbs like 'hold', denoting positions. But most of
our verbs follow a type of segmentation that isolates from nature what
we call "actions", that is, moving outlines.

Following majority rule, we therefore read action into every sentence, even into 'I hold it'. A moment's reflection will show that 'hold'
is no action but a state of relative positions. Yet we think of it and
even see it as an action because language formulates it in the same
way as it formulates more numerous expressions, like, 'I strike it',
which deal with movements and changes [pp. 242–243].*

Whorf's argument has some rather interesting implications. First, one
must accept literal translation as a correct reflection of the semantic relations expressed by the original utterance. The French phrase *Comment
ça va?* would thus be rendered as *How goes it?* rather than *How are things?*
or *How are you?* Following Whorf's logic, we would have to conclude
that a Frenchman's conception of interpersonal relations is rather different
from an Englishman's. By the same token, the absence of a particular
grammatical form in the surface structure of a language must be taken
as evidence for the absence of the corresponding concept. If, for example,
a language has no grammatical device for expressing time, such as tense
inflections like *-ed* for the past, then we might suspect that the people who
speak that language either do not have a concept of time as do English
speakers, or at the very least do not think about it much. What are the
thought processes of the people described in this passage from a recent
novel?

The speech of the river people posed philosophical as well as linguistic
problems. For example, since they had no regular system of plurals
but only an elaborate system of altered numerals for denoting specific
numbers of given objects, the problem of the particular versus the
universal did not exist and the word 'man' stood for 'all men'. This
had a profound effect on their societisation. . . . The tenses divided
time into two great chunks, a simple past and a continuous present. . . . A future tense was created by adding various suffixes indicating hope, intention and varying degrees of probability and possibility to the present stem [Carter, 1972, p. 91].

If language determines thought, then these people must be quite different
from English speakers. They would have no concept of the future as a
simple counterpart or opposite of the past. But as Harris Savin (personal
communication) has astutely pointed out, neither do speakers of English.
If English grammar reflects our conceptual world, then we are just like
the river people. We, like them, have no future tense per se. We create

* © 1956 by the Massachusetts Institute of Technology.

it by using modal auxiliaries "indicating hope, intention and varying degrees of probability and possibility": I *might* go, I *shall* go, I *will* go, I *should* go, I *would* go, I *could* go. A strict application of linguistic relativity leads us to conclude that our concept of time is quite different from that of the French, who do have a "proper" future tense. We may, in fact, have different concepts of time, but whatever difference there may be is not the simple absence of a concept of future among English-speaking peoples.

The lack of direct evidence and the apparent absurdity of inferring thought from the surface grammatical forms of a language lead us to conclude that differences among languages are in part due to historical accident, and in part due to the communicative needs of particular linguistic communities. Eskimos have many words for snow because they need to talk about various kinds of snow, just as American and Swiss skiers do. If many kinds of snow did not exist and if the differences were not important, then a differentiated vocabulary for talking about snow would never have developed. Similarly, the grammatical devices of any given language are presumably sufficient to express the meanings people need to communicate to one another. Otherwise, new forms develop, such as *finalize,* which appeared in America during the 1950s. In local situations, even the syntax of a language can be drastically altered to suit communicative needs. Under conditions of time and noise pressure, as in communication between a spacecraft crew and ground control, normal English syntax and vocabulary give way to specialized jargon. A more prosaic example can be found at fast-food counters, where it is vitally important to serve as much food to the most people as quickly as possible. Normally, we would say *three hamburgers,* with the number first, the noun second. Routinely, orders in fast-service restaurants are abbreviated and called out in reverse format, *burger three.* Dialects and languages differ, partly for historical reasons and partly for contemporary needs. These differences need not reflect or cause differences in modes or levels of thought.

Bilingualism

When a person is fluent in two different languages, how is his thought integrated with each of his languages? Bilingualism within a community can have profound social consequences, as in Belgium or in French Canada. Are there also intellectual consequences of bilingualism for the individual? Bilingualism offers a unique opportunity for examining the relation between language and thought. Within a single mind we have two languages coexisting. If language determines or even influences thought, then there should also be two conceptual systems, one corresponding to each language. These conceptual systems will be different to the extent that the languages differ and to the extent that language in general influences thought. If, however, language primarily expresses the results of thought processes, then we should find only one conceptual system underlying both languages.

Shared or Separated Conceptual Systems?   A balanced bilingual person is equally fluent in two languages. How does he or she keep the languages separate? How is he able to translate from one to the other? Does he have one set of concepts and ideas that he maps onto each of his languages, or does he have two sets of concepts and meanings, one for each language? The former possibility is called a SHARED system; the latter is called a SEPARATED system (Kolers, 1963). These two types of systems are illustrated in Figure 7.4. The systems must be separable linguistically. When a bilingual person talks he rarely if ever intermixes words from his two languages. People have little difficulty in maintaining at least a temporal separation between their languages. Still, the two language systems are not entirely isolated from one another. Skilled translators, like those who provide simultaneous translations for the United Nations meetings, are able to keep up with a speaker with minimal lag. The two languages within a bilingual's repertoire must be able to interact very quickly and very closely.

One point of contact between the two languages might be at the level of meaning. When the English word *window* and the French word *fenêtre* are decoded by a bilingual, is the final product, the meaning, the same? Paul Kolers (1966a) gave bilinguals lists of words to remember. When the list is all in one language, repeating a word increases the likelihood

SHARED CONCEPTUALIZATION

SEPARATE CONCEPTUALIZATIONS

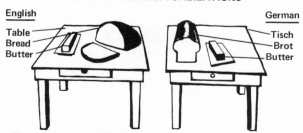

FIGURE 7.4 Shared conceptualization versus separate conceptualizations. Do bilinguals have the same conceptual structure for both languages, or a different one for each language?

that it will be remembered, so Kolers reasoned that, if a word were repeated in translation and if the two languages had different meanings, then repetition in the other language would not really count as a repetition, and so would not facilitate recall. If, however, it makes no difference whether the bilingual heard *window–window* or *window–fenêtre* (that is, if each of these functioned as repetitions of the same "word"), then the two language systems shared a common set of meanings. Kolers presented some of the words to be remembered once in French and once in English, for example, *fold–pli, ten–dix*. Others were repeated in the same language, either in English or in French. It turned out that a translated repetition acted just like a verbatim repetition. Either kind of repetition made it easier to recall the repeated word. At some level of processing the two languages converge upon a common conceptual core.

In Koler's experiment, a connection between two languages facilitated performance. People did better because their two languages were not completely separated from one another. Could people separate their two languages if it would help them to perform better on another kind of task? The Stroop color word test was designed to produce verbal interference. The names of colors like *red, blue,* and *green* were printed in colored inks. The word *red* might be printed in blue ink, *blue* in green ink, and *green* in red ink. The task was to name the color of the ink as quickly as possible, ignoring the words themselves. This is quite difficult because our dominant tendency is to read the words rather than name the color of the ink. Preston and Lambert (1969) reasoned that bilinguals should be able to name the colors very easily if they could only turn off one of their languages. If English words were used, then an English–French bilingual speaker might be able to switch out his English and name the colors in French. If the word *red* were printed in blue ink, he should say *bleu;* for *green* in red ink, he should say *rouge,* and so on. Were bilinguals able to separate their languages in this way? Not at all. The two languages operated as though they represent a common conceptual core, even when it would have been useful to separate them.

A distinction has been proposed between two types of bilingualism: coordinate and compound. If two languages have been acquired in separate and quite distinct contexts, as when a six-year–old German-speaking child moves to the United States and then learns English, separate and parallel language and conceptual systems might result. This would exemplify COORDINATE BILINGUALISM (Ervin & Osgood, 1954). If, on the other hand, a child learns German and English in one place, as when his parents speak both languages at home, then COMPOUND BILINGUALISM should result. In this case, the two languages would represent two alternative ways for expressing the same meanings.

Does a person's acquisition context make a difference? Compound- and coordinate-bilingual speakers typically do not differ from one another in their language usage (Macnamara, 1967), with one minor exception. Coordinate-bilingual speakers seem to have slightly different affective meanings for the words in each language. For example, the word *bread* in English might be thought of as good, weak, and passive on the semantic differential rating scales; the German word for bread, *brot,* might be rated as good, strong, and passive, on the same scales. Compound-bilingual speakers tend to rate the words of their two languages in the same ways: their connotative meanings are the same for the two languages. This difference between coordinate- and compound-bilingual speakers most probably reflects differences in their experiences with the objects that the words refer to. How one feels about *bread* as a concept should depend very much on one's experiences with breads. On this view any fluent bilingual should have the same kind of conceptual system as any other fluent bilingual, whether compound or coordinate. This point is most dramatically illustrated by people's abilities to switch from one language to another.

Switching.   Further evidence for the separability of language systems on the one hand and the unity of the conceptual system on the other comes from studies of language switching. Switching languages apparently takes very little time or effort. Kolers (1966b) tried to measure the time needed for switching by having French–English bilinguals read passages like those shown in Table 7.1. One set of passages (A and B) were printed in French or in English only. Others (C and D) had phrases from both languages intermixed. Both kinds of passages presented precisely the same information. When asked to read silently, bilingual people took no longer to read a mixed passage than a single-language passage. Tests of comprehension revealed no differences in amount of information people acquired from the various types of passages. For comprehension, at least, switching took no time at all or too little time to measure with this technique. When the passages were read aloud, the results changed. It took longer to read a mixed passage aloud than it did to read a single-language passage aloud. Kolers estimated that it took about one-third of a second for each switch from one language to another.

These results, like those obtained from Koler's (1966a) repeated-word memory task and the Stroop color–word task, suggest very strongly that a single conceptual system is common to both languages. The job of a translator is to decode the input in one language, then encode it in another. Simultaneous or running translation can be accomplished rapidly. Surprisingly, the speed of translation is virtually unaffected by the degree of bilingualism (Lambert, Havelka, & Gardner, 1959). What is important is the complexity of the material being translated (Treisman, 1965). The greater the information load, the greater is the lag between input and output. This is not at all surprising because complex ideas take longer to put into words

TABLE 7.1
Examples of Unilingual and Mixed-lingual Passages
Used by Kolers[a]
How fast can you read each passage?

Passage A:

His horse, followed by two hounds, made the earth resound under its even tread. Drops of ice stuck to his cloak. A strong wind was blowing. One side of the horizon lighted up, and in the whiteness of the early morning light, he saw rabbits hopping at the edge of their burrows.

Passage B:

Son cheval, suivi de deux bassets, en marchant d'un pas égal faisait résonner la terre. Des gouttes de verglas se collaient à son manteau. Une-brise violente soufflait. Un côté de l'horizon s'éclaircit; et, dans la blancheur du crépuscule, il aperçut des lapins sautillant au bord de leurs terriers.

Passage C:

His horse, followed de deux bassets, faisait la terre résonner under its even tread. Des gouttes de verglas stuck to his manteau. Une violente brise was blowing. One side de l'horizon lighted up, and dans la blancheur of the early morning light, il aperçut rabbits hopping at the bord de leurs terriers.

Passage D:

Son cheval, suivi by two hounds, en marchant d'un pas égal, made resound the earth. Drops of ice se collaient à son cloak. A wind strong soufflait. Un côté of the horizon s'éclaircit; et, in the whiteness du crépuscule, he saw des lapins sautillant au edge of their burrows.

---

[a] From Kolers (1968).

and also take longer to understand whether we are monolingual or bilingual.

Summarizing the results from the study of bilinguals, there is little support for linguistic relativity. What about linguistic determinism—the notion that language in general influences thought?

SYMBOLIC REPRESENTATION: HOW WE KNOW THE WORLD

Language and Cognitive Development

Within the mainstreams of American and Russian psychology it generally has been assumed that language and conceptual development are inextricably related. Watson's (1913) proposal that thought is speech was foreshadowed by Sechenov's (1863) statement that thought, in children at least, is mediated by speech or whispers. Sechenov's student, Pavlov, considered speech to be the mechanism which makes higher mental functioning possible in humans: "It is nothing other than words which has made us human" (Pavlov, 1941, p. 179). This general viewpoint has continued to this day among the Russians. Following in the tradition of Vygotsky (1920s, 1962 English translation), Luria (1961) views the development of speech as the critical factor in the development of voluntary control of behavior and of higher mental functioning: "[speech is central to] . . . the process in which functions previously *shared between two persons* gradually change into the complicated functional systems in the mind which forms *the essence of human higher mental activity* [p. 18]." In American psychology too, cognitive development is linked to speech development. In particular, the ability of children to perform various conceptual tasks is attributed to their ability to use verbal mediation (see Kendler & Kendler, 1962).

If speech or language is so crucial to thought, or at least to the development of thought, then children who are deprived of speech should be severely retarded. Yet this is by no means the case. Deaf children are often brought up without a formal language system, not even a sign language. They do, of course, have interpersonal contact with others, and presumably communication with others. In general, the cognitive abilities of deaf children and deaf adults are not significantly different from those of normal hearing children and adults (Furth, 1966).

If speech or language per se is not crucial to intellectual development, then what is? We would argue that the most important developmental task for children is the construction of a symbolic representation of the world—people, events, objects, and relationships—and the ability to operate with and upon those representations. In general terms, we call this system of symbolic representation KNOWLEDGE OF THE WORLD. Speech per se is not necessarily crucial to the acquisition or development of symbolic representation, but interpersonal communication is. Whether overt speech or a formal sign language is available to a child or not, he learns about the world partly from his own experiences, and partly from what others tell him about it. Overt speech seems so important because it is so easily noticed and observed. The availability of speech undoubtedly makes the developmental process much easier, but useful as it is, it does not seem to be necessary for the acquisition of knowledge.

Forms of Representation.   Every child develops an internal model or representation of his world. This representation consists of his organized memories of people, things, and events, as well as the capacity to draw inferences, deductions, and predictions from the information stored in memory. The forms of representation can be roughly categorized as enactive, iconic, and symbolic (see, for example, Bruner, Olver, & Greenfield, 1966). En-active and iconic representation are considered to be prior to and simpler than symbolic representation. ENACTIVE REPRESENTATION is knowledge or memory in the form of action. We "know" how to ride a bicycle by knowing how to do so, or remembering what we do when we ride one. We cannot easily put this knowledge into words or draw a picture of it. In the same way, an infant would "know" its mother's breast partly by having an enactive representation of the actions it performs while suckling. A definition given by one child, "a hole is to dig" reveals an enactive component in his knowledge of what a hole is.

ICONIC REPRESENTATION is knowledge or memory of something in one or more sensory-perceptual modalities. Our knowledge of melodies is iconic, particularly if we do not read music. Our memories for people's faces, landscapes, or other things we usually cannot express in words or actions are also iconic. If you can remember which part of the page Pav-lov's name appeared on a few pages ago (upper, middle, or lower third), your memory of that is very likely to be iconic.

The young child's early knowledge of the world consists primarily of enactive and iconic representations of himself and of the world. Piaget (1952) refers to this as the sensory–motor stage, involving the development of sensory–motor intelligence. Whereas some adult knowledge is enactive and iconic, we can also represent experience and knowledge in symbolic form. SYMBOLIC REPRESENTATION provides us with certain important ad-vantages over enactive or iconic representation. For one, enactive and iconic representations are more or less "copies" of experience. They are tied to the specific actions or perceptions involved with the objects and events represented. The concepts of disappearance and recurrence, which are central to the development of object constancy and are expressed by such words as *allgone* and *more,* cannot be easily represented either enac-tively or iconically. They must, by default, be represented symbolically, whether they can be expressed in words or not.

Second, different kinds of representations lend themselves to different kinds of organization. Enactive representation is necessarily sequential, re-flecting the temporal sequence of the actions involved. Iconic representa-tion can be either sequential or spatial, but it cannot be hierarchical. Ab-stract relationships like superordinate–subordinate, class inclusion, or even agent–action–object or possession relations must be symbolic, irrespective of whether or not they are expressed in words. Finally, enactive and iconic representations are not manipulated easily. They usually represent only what was or is, not what could be. They are tied to reality. Symbolic repre-sentation, in contrast, is in principle independent of reality. People can imagine or think or believe almost anything. Normally, symbolic representation frees thought from the here and now, enabling us to think about the consequences of alternative courses of action and to draw inferences from what is known. In short, symbolic representation and symbolic activity serve to make conceptual sense of the world.

Speech is an overt realization of symbolic representation and thought. Vocal speech itself may not be a necessary component of thought, or of the ability to think. As George Miller (1972) has put it,

> Thinking can proceed in terms of relatively specific words *or* in abstract or concrete imagery; thinking is not confined to a realm of general concepts like location, change, causation, and direction. The semantic components and their paraphrase relations comprise *only one of many ways* whereby we can move on in thought to related ideas or related expressions [p. 370, italics added].

How then should we interpret the vast amount of research which demonstrates, in various ways, that language can influence memory and thought? Language can affect thought, but we would argue that in each instance it is a special case of the influence of alternative representations upon thought and action. The fact that language rather than, say, pictures, is used to select or to develop certain representations may be incidental. It is the symbolic character of representation that is critical.

Language as Representation

Representations have three general functions: they are the residue of past experience, they act as a filter or interpreter of the present, and they provide models of potential future states. Alternative representations, whether selected on the basis of words, expectancies, visual contexts, or what have you, can have systematic and profound effects on perception, memory, problem solving, and reasoning.

Perception and Memory.   Perception and memory are closely related. Perception refers to immediate experience; memory refers to past experience. The influence of language on perceptual representation was demonstrated in a classic experiment by Carmichael, Hogan, and Walter (1932). They showed people simple line drawings with alternative labels, as in Figure 7.5. One group was given the original figures, one at a time, with labels from word list 1, another group with labels from word list 2. When asked to draw figures from memory, the drawings tended to look like the objects to which the labels referred. This was interpreted as an effect of language on perception and memory. So it is, but it is more generally an effect of

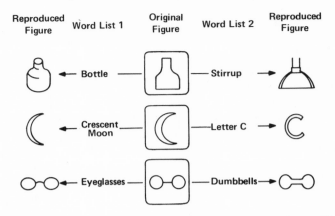

FIGURE 7.5 The Carmichael, Hogan, and Walter (1932) experiment. The original figures were shown to people, along with the labels of word list 1 or word list 2. When the figures were drawn from memory, the reproductions tended to look like the objects named by the labels. (After Carmichael, Hogan, & Walter, 1932, p. 80. Copyright 1932 by the American Psychological Association. Reprinted by permission.)

alternative representations or meanings. The original figures were ambiguous and needed to be interpreted. The same effect could have been produced if unambiguous pictures of bottles or stirrups had been used as contexts for the original figures instead of the words *bottle* or *stirrup*. This experiment demonstrated our capacity for generating alternative representations of external events. It also demonstrated that words, among other things, can influence our choice of representation, and hence our perception of and memory for events.

Words and other symbolic devices that can be deliberately used to help us remember things are called MNEMONICS. One way to improve our memory for unrelated events or items is to reduce the total memory load by grouping or "chunking" the material we want to remember (Miller, 1956). It is easy to remember the digit string

$$1\ 4\ 9\ 2\ 1\ 7\ 7\ 6\ 1\ 0\ 6\ 6$$

if we "chunk" the digits into three groups of four digits each, corresponding to the dates of Columbus discovering America, the signing of the United States Declaration of Independence, and the Battle of Hastings. Few of us could handle the series

$$6\ 6\ 0\ 1\ 6\ 7\ 7\ 1\ 2\ 9\ 4\ 1$$

unless we happen to recognize those same dates in reverse.

The chunking strategy also involves recoding. When material to be remembered is received, it is usually not retained in its original form. Either it is related directly to well-known, easy-to-remember material, or it is translated or recoded into another format. A common recoding device is a poem or rhythmic jingle. Remember "Thirty days hath September, April, June, and November . . ." and "*I* before *E* except after *C* . . ."?

One of the more effective and useful mnemonic devices relies primarily on visual–kinesthetic imagery. It is called the method of loci, and was used extensively by Greek orators to help them remember the succession of topics in a long speech. Assume that you want to remember fifteen items in order. Imagine a house or a large place that you know very well, like a college campus or a section of a city. Starting at a given point, place the items you want to remember in different locations in the order you want to remember them by taking an imaginary stroll through the area. Then, when you want to remember the items, start at the beginning, stroll along the same imaginary path, and "pick up" each of the items in turn. With a little practice this method enables one to memorize a fairly long sequence of words, topics, or pictures relatively quickly and effortlessly.

When using mnemonics like these we actually have to remember more than just the material we want to remember because we also have to remember the mnemonic itself. Despite this extra memory load, the mnemonic strategy eases the memory burden by providing a way to retrieve the material from memory. This retrieval plan is only partly verbal or linguistic. Some of the retrieval cues can be in the form of visual images, like a "picture" of our stroll. The critical factor is not verbal encoding per se, but the construction of meaningful relations among the items to be remembered. These relations can be verbal, but they can also be imaginal.

Problem Solving and Reasoning.   When we have a difficult problem to solve, we often talk to ourselves. How we think about a problem can often be influenced by the words we use to describe it. Consider the problem illustrated in Figure 7.6, which uses an incomplete electrical circuit. You have some clay, some wires, and a screwdriver. How can the circuit be completed if there is not enough wire? One way is to use the metal blade of the screwdriver as a substitute for the missing length of wire. This type of problem, called FUNCTIONAL FIXEDNESS and first studied by Karl Duncker (1945), is surprisingly difficult. Under normal circumstances, less than 20% of bright, well-motivated college students can solve the problem within 20 minutes if the screwdriver had been used to turn screws just prior to working on the problem (Glucksberg & Danks, 1967, 1968). The critical solution object, the screwdriver, is then said to be "functionally fixed" because it was used in a way that was incompatable with its problem-solving function.

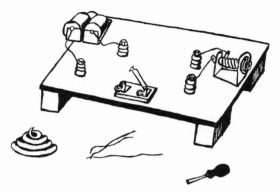

FIGURE 7.6 The circuit problem. How can the circuit be completed if one of the wires is too short? (From Glucksberg & Danks, 1967.)

Among the factors that can influence problem solving in this type of task are the labels or words we use to refer to the critical object. Conceptually isolating the handle and blade of the screwdriver by labeling them separately makes the problem easier. Referring to the screwdriver and the wire with nonsense names, which do not have preestablished reference to particular functions, also helps. When the screwdriver and wire were called JOD and PEEM, for example, people had very little trouble with this problem (Glucksberg & Danks, 1968). It even helps when the name of the tool rhymes with its unusual function. Instead of a screwdriver, people were given a tool that could be called either *wrench* or *pliers*. The problem was easier with the latter name, presumably because the rhyme between *pliers* and *wires* helped to establish a relation between the two objects (Glucksberg & Danks, 1967).

The relative difficulty of deductive reasoning problems also depends on their verbal format. An example we are all familiar with is

> Major premise: All men are mortal.
> Minor premise: Socrates was a man.
> Conclusion: Socrates was mortal.

What kind of mental activity occurs when such problems are solved? Consider the three-term series problem. In its verbal form it goes like this: *If Tom is better than Dick and Dick is better than Harry, then who is the best?* By replacing *better* with *worse* in each proposition and in the question and by alternating the order of the two propositions, we can generate 16 different problems that vary in difficulty.

Clark (1969) has found that the time needed to solve these problems is a function of three principles. First, the principle of PRIMARY FUNCTIONAL RELATIONS states that sentences in general (and these propositions in particular) will be encoded in terms of their underlying functional relations. In our example, one underlying relation is (Tom is good) > (Dick is good). Second, the principle of LEXICAL MARKING holds that for an adjective pair like *good–bad,* one adjective is unmarked, and the other is marked. In this case, *good* is unmarked and *bad* is marked. Marked and unmarked adjectives differ in several important and interesting ways (see our discussion in Chapter 4, pages 101–102), but for our purposes here we can assume that the unmarked adjective is psychologically simpler. Hence, the unmarked forms (like *good, better, best*) should be easier to process than their corresponding marked forms like *bad, worse,* and *worst.* If we measure the time taken to solve problems using these adjectives, marked forms should take longer than unmarked. Finally, the principle of CONGRUITY states that an answer cannot be derived until the form of the question matches the form of the proposition. If the comparative *better* is used in the proposition, then that same comparative should be in the question. If it is not, then the incongruent comparative must be converted, and the problem will take longer to solve.

In an extensive series of experiments by Clark (1969) and his colleagues, the relative difficulty of three-term series problems did vary according to these three principles. Unmarked comparatives (like *good* or *better*) were easier than marked comparatives (like *bad* or *worse*), and problems involving questions congruent with the propositions (both using the same comparatives) were easier than problems involving incongruent questions and propositions.

Clark's linguistic analysis is only one of several alternatives. People can also solve three-term series problems by using visual imagery. Instead of using linguistic representation, they may use spatial paralogic, translating verbal statements into imaginal analogs (DeSoto, London, & Handel, 1965). If *Tom is better than Dick,* and *Dick is better than Harry,* we can imagine placing Tom above Dick, and Dick above Harry. Then, when asked who is worse, Harry or Tom, we can simply note their relative positions in our imaginary array and answer, *Harry,* because Harry is at the bottom.

Huttenlocher (1968) proposed a similar explanation for the relative difficulty of various forms of three-term series problems. She reasoned that if people construct imaginary arrays as analogs of the relations among the objects or people referred to in the problems, then the relative difficulty of problems involving the manipulation of real objects (like placing different colored blocks on a ladder) should parallel the relative difficulty of mental problems. In general, she did find such parallels, suggesting that people can and sometimes do use imagery to solve certain types of problems. The most likely conclusion is that people use both linguistic and imaginal representations, and that the type of problem itself will determine which form of representation will be used. Some problems can be most efficiently solved by using verbal or linguistic representations; others are more easily handled by using imaginal representation.

LANGUAGE AND COMMUNICATION

The task for which verbal representation and language are most suitable is, of course, communication. It is the primary function of language, and languages develop and change in order to serve this function. New words come into a language when we need to talk about new concepts. If we needed to talk about "corpses of dead plants" as a unitary class, we would probably invent a word for the concept. Children learn new words and new ways of constructing sentences to fit their needs to communicate with others. Once phonological, semantic, and syntactic competence has been achieved, the child must learn how to use his linguistic abilities effectively. When a child first learns that things have names, his language resembles a code. He acts as though there were one-to-one correspondences between things and their names. Each thing has only one name, and each name refers to just one thing. For the young child, the name of something seems to be an integral part of the thing itself. If it had a different name, it would be a different thing. Piaget (1926) refers to this as NOMINALISM. The three-year-old child simply cannot imagine that names are arbitrary conventions and can be changed without changing the essence of the object. If he is asked, "Could we call the sun the moon if we all wanted to?," he would reply "No, because it's the sun!"

Adults are usually not quite so rigid about names. There is, of course, no one-to-one correspondence between things and their names. Any thing (object, event, relation) can have many possible names, and every name can refer to a variety of things. I can call the object in Figure 7.7 *animal,*

FIGURE 7.7   What is the "name" for this?

creature, bird, pigeon, pest, pet, ring dove, Streptopelia risoria, or *Charlie.*
The name I use will depend upon whom I am talking to and the particular
context of the conversation. Similarly, any one of the names in the list
could be used to refer to many other things. *Pigeon* can refer to a picture,
a live bird, an item on a menu, a kind of foot, a toe position, a young
girl, or a welcome guest at the poker table.

One result of this flexibility is the development of specific vocabularies
within social groups. Lovers, families, schools, trades, professions all develop specialized vocabularies that outsiders may not understand. Photographers speak of *hypo,* psychologists of *shaping,* skiers of *powder.* In our
family, the word *shade* refers to a foam rubber pad that we used as a
beach bed for our two-year-old daughter. It was called *shade* because it
was covered with the same fabric we had used to make window shades
for her room. Unless you were one of the family, you would probably
mistakenly grab the beach umbrella if, upon leaving for the beach, you
were told, "Don't forget the shade."

These specialized vocabularies or jargons are developed to fit particular
communication needs. Like many words that are used frequently, they tend
to be short and are often abbreviated versions of longer words or phrases.
The photographers' *hypo* is a shortened version of *sodium hyposulfite;* the
psychotherapists' *TLC* is an abbreviation of *tender loving care;* and *nuts
and sluts* is an undergraduate label for *the sociology of deviant behavior.*
In general, the most frequently used words tend to be the shortest (Zipf,
1935), and if a long word comes to be used commonly, it tends to be
shortened. *Automobile* became *auto* or *car* (from *carriage*), *television* became *telly* in Britain and *TV* in the United States, and *telephone* became
phone. This process was demonstrated in several experiments by Krauss
and Weinheimer (1964, 1966). People were asked to talk to one another
about geometric forms like those in Figure 7.8 in the following kind of
task. Two people at a time were seated at a table with a screen between
them (see Figure 7.9). Each of them had a peg and six blocks with holes
drilled through them so that they could be stacked on the pegs. Each block
had one of the geometric forms printed on it. The speaker had his blocks
arranged in a particular order in his dispenser; the listener had the same
set of six blocks arranged randomly on the table. The task was to stack
both sets of blocks on the pegs in the same order. The speaker took a
block from the dispenser and then told his partner which block to stack
first, then second, and so on.

Adults find this task very easy, rarely making any mistakes. The first
time two people go through a set of blocks they use fairly long descriptions.
When they repeat their descriptions on later trials the descriptions become
shorter and shorter until they develop into a private idiosyncratic code.
The participants understand the code, but a newcomer to the situation

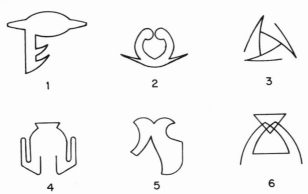

FIGURE 7.8 What names do people use to refer to these shapes? (From Glucksberg, Krauss, & Weisberg, 1966.)

might not. Form 6 (in Figure 7.8) was first described by one pair of subjects as "an upside-down hourglass with legs." Later, this pair referred to it as "hourglass" (see Figure 7.10).

How do children deal with this task? Nursery school children (about three years old) can play the game of "stack the blocks" quite well when

FIGURE 7.9 A communication problem. The speaker and listener have identical sets of blocks, but only the speaker knows which order they should be stacked in. He must tell his listener which blocks to stack so that their two stacks are identical. (From Glucksberg, Krauss, & Weisberg, 1966.)

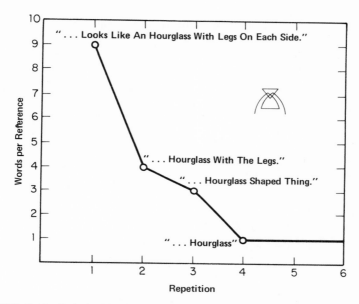

FIGURE 7.10 Relation between repetition and length of reference. The more often a name is used, the shorter it gets. (Courtesy of Robert M. Krauss.)

familiar pictures of circus animals are used (Glucksberg, Krauss, & Weisberg, 1966). When the blocks have pictures that do not have standard familiar names (like the novel geometric forms in Figure 7.8), then the children perform miserably. They do not do better than pure chance in matching the two stacks of blocks. They behave in a way that Piaget (1926) has characterized as EGOCENTRIC rather than SOCIOCENTRIC. Children do not always consider the other person's situation or viewpoint. They often act as if everyone can see and know everything that they see and know. One three-year-old described one of the forms in Figure 7.8 by saying, "the shirt." His partner, who was hidden by a screen, said "Is this it?," holding up a block as if it could be seen by his partner. In reply, the first boy clearly and forcefully said "NO!" Some descriptions given by three- and four-year-olds are shown in Table 7.2. How well do you think you could match these descriptions with the pictures in Figure 7.8? The children who gave these descriptions knew which picture each "name" referred to. Even when they were tested two weeks later, they made no errors. But no one else knew, not even their partners in the game. Each of the descriptions was a private one-person code instead of a publicly comprehensible communication.

TABLE 7.2
Reference Phrases Given by Nursery School Children[a]
Can you match these names with the pictures in
Figure 7.8?

Figure number	Subject 1	Subject 2	Subject 3	Subject 4	Subject 5
1	Man's legs	Airplane	Drape holder	Zebra	Flying saucer
2	Mother's hat	Ring	Keyhole	Lion	Snake
3	Somebody running	Eagle	Throwing sticks	Strip-stripe	Wire
4	Daddy's shirt	Milk jug	Shoe hole	Coffee pot	Dog
5	Another Daddy's shirt	Bird	Dress hole	Dress	Knife
6	Mother's dress	Ideal	Digger hole	Caterpillar	Ghost

[a] From Glucksberg, Krauss, and Weisberg (1966).

When these children were younger, they had learned to produce sentences that unambiguously expressed what they intended to say. Two-word utterances were not enough to enable them to talk about things that were not in the here and now. They learned to say *Mommy, I want lunch* or *Mommy is eating lunch* or *That is Mommy's lunch* instead of the ambiguous utterance, *Mommy lunch.* Now they have to learn still more. They have to learn, for example, that their view of things may not be shared by others. Just because I may know what *Daddy's shirt* refers to does not mean that you will know too.

How long does it take to learn the communication skills needed for the stack-the-blocks game? Kindergarteners do no better than nursery children, and first graders are not much better. As children grow older they improve, but they do not achieve adult levels of performance until the age of eleven or twelve years (Glucksberg & Krauss, 1967). This does not mean that the younger children have no communication skills at all. Even four-year-olds adjust their speech when they talk to adults and to two-year-old children. They use shorter phrases and simpler words when they talk to two-year-olds, just as adults do (Shatz & Gelman, 1973). What they are not able to judge is the specific kind or amount of information another person needs in a particular situation. They also sometimes forget to use the communication skills they do have. A problem like the stack-the-blocks game may be so complicated for a young child that he neglects to take his listener into account simply because he has so many other things to think about.

The communication process is schematically illustrated in Figure 7.11. When we wish to communicate something to someone else, we first generate a trial message. This message then is evaluated for its adequacy. Will it be interpreted correctly by our listener? Various criteria may enter into

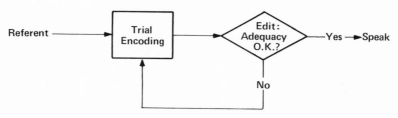

FIGURE 7.11   Some of the steps involved in producing a message.

this evaluation. How old is the listener? What information does he already have, and what information does he lack? Will he be able to hear me clearly? Does he understand my language? Does my message clearly differentiate among potential confusions? If the trial message fails to meet any of these criteria, a different message is generated. If the new message passes the evaluation criteria, it is articulated for the listener. This may seem like an overly complex routine for normal, everyday conversation, but the processes involved are no more complicated than the processes involved in the phonological, semantic, and syntactic aspects of speech production. People tailor their speech to suit the characteristics of the situation and the listener (Glucksberg, Krauss, & Higgins, 1975). Children do so less often and less appropriately, and have particular difficulty with the evaluation stage (Pietrinferno, 1973).

Children take so long to acquire communication skills because so many skills are involved. Vocabulary growth is but one component. Children also have to learn about people and how people differ from one another. We learn how to be sensitive and responsive to people's reactions to us, and to the questions they ask. We have to be able to predict whether one way of saying something will be understood, and be willing and able to rephrase messages. Adults as well as children sometimes fail to communicate appropriately. The foreign tourist who tries to get someone to understand him by talking louder is behaving no differently than some nursery school children. If someone does not speak English, the message "Where is the bathroom?" is hardly improved by shouting louder. The teacher who speaks in a dull monotone while facing his blackboard also is not displaying subtle communication skills.

Style and Metaphor

Using language effectively means communicating what we mean to a listener. The various components of language we have discussed throughout this book—phonology, the lexicon, syntax, social editing, and the like—all contribute to this goal. None is sufficient by itself. While it is true that people differ in each of these language components, differences in pragmatics probably contribute most to differences in communicative ability. The difference between a Shakespeare and one of us is not in our phonology, nor in our vocabulary, nor in our implicit knowledge of syntax. The difference lies in that elusive quality called "style."

Though we are rarely aware of it, much of our communication is nonliteral or metaphorical. We rarely intend what we say to be taken literally. Rather, we expect listeners to make some analogical interpretation of what we say. For example, if you hear someone say

(1)   Dick's half-baked excuses give
       me indigestion.

it is impossible to interpret this sentence in a literal sense. Excuses cannot be baked in an oven nor can they be eaten. Yet the attitude toward Dick's alibis is clearly communicated.

Many metaphors have been used so often that we may not even recognize them as metaphor any longer. For example, a *bottleneck* or *a half-baked idea* does not strike us as metaphorical—and neither does the phrase *strike us*. These are called FROZEN METAPHORS. These examples are so common that the metaphorical interpretations are listed in *Webster's New Collegiate Dictionary* as separate definitions of *neck, half-baked,* and *strike*. In contrast, treating excuses as if they could be eaten is relatively novel, and so this is called a LIVING METAPHOR.

Metaphor is found in a wide variety of linguistic contexts, including everyday interaction. There is far more nonliteral use of language in normal conversation than one might suspect. One reason we do not notice metaphorical language is that it often may be interpreted with no more effort than nonmetaphorical speech. Other than frozen metaphors like *bottleneck,* entire segments of our lexicon consist of metaphor taken from one domain and applied to another. Consider our words for describing time. As Clark (1973) has noted, time is often described in terms of a spatial metaphor. We look *ahead* to the future; the night has been *long; up* to now we have been careless; *between* Monday and Wednesday *comes* Tuesday. These might be called INSTITUTIONALIZED METAPHOR to distinguish them from frozen metaphor, but the principle is the same. Metaphor in literature is, of course, well known and has been extensively described. We will not attempt to detail that taxonomy.

Other areas of metaphorical use have begun to be investigated by Howard Pollio (1974) and his associates at the University of Tennessee. One of the critical components in many theories of psychotherapy is that the patient must gain insight into the core of his particular problem. This insight is often blocked by the patient's resistance to his own problems.

If he can discuss the problem area in figurative language, insight may be facilitated by analogical comparisons because the anxiety surrounding the problem has been avoided. A case described by Goldiamond and Dryud (1968) and discussed by Pollio clearly illustrates this point:

> A suicidal adolescent who is currently under therapy has dropped out of school, and does not work. He watches the late show on TV, and gets up in the morning at 11:00. He can be considered a loser. One of the discussions centered around the fact that there was very little communication between the boy and his father. When either spoke, the other made some comment which terminated the conversation. The therapy had reached the point where it was possible to analyze this transaction and to suggest that the boy might try to respond to his father in some manner which would continue the discussion and perhaps move it in a direction of interest to him. The boy commented that he did not wish his father to control him, but wished to maintain his own autonomy and would not engage in such extended conversation. The metaphor of a tennis game was then brought up by the therapist. If one wished to control the other player in tennis, one had to put oneself under the control of the oncoming ball. Hitting the ball left made the opponent run left. Then hitting it right made him run again, and so on. But, said the young man, I can choose not to hit the ball back. Then you lose, was the answer. You're a loser. This discussion continued with vigor, and the patient raised it several times since [pp. 80–81].

Through the metaphor of a tennis game the boy realized that the failure of communication between him and his father was not one-sided. Pollio has analyzed tape recordings of other therapy sessions and has found that insight and resolution of the patient's conflict often follows the introduction of a key metaphor into the therapy.

We have already suggested that children often use metaphor to communicate concepts for which they do not have a label. Children are frequently more creative with language than adults because they have not yet learned the relevant societal and linguistic constraints. A child can understand more than he can say, which in turn implies that he knows more than he can express. One of the pressures toward acquiring linguistic abilities is his need to express ideas and concepts. What happens when a child has a thought before he has the linguistic ability to express it? Quite often he will invent a metaphor. "Why does Daddy have a hole in his hair?" is a creative if unflattering way of asking about a bald spot. Kornei Chukovsky, a Russian poet, describes the poetic use of language by Russian children. Here is a sample:

Mommie, the [cactus] bites me?
Well, in a way. . .
Then why doesn't it bark too?

.

.

.

The sun sets in the sea. Why is there no vapor?
.

.

.

The ostrich is a giraffe-bird.
.

.

.

A turkey is a duck with a bow around its neck.
.

.

.

What is a knife—the fork's husband?
.

.

.

And here is a reason for the arrival of spring:
The winter got so cold it ran away somewhere [Chukovsky, 1963, pp. 21–23].*

These examples illustrate an aspect of the productivity of language that has scarcely been studied. Metaphoric productivity enables us to talk about things whether or not the language has convenient syntactic and lexical devices. In both individual language behavior and in the historical development of language, metaphorical productivity is the rule rather than the exception. We find productivity at every level of language usage, from phonology through semantics and syntax to pragmatics and style. Language permits a wide choice of expression. If someone spends less money than he might, he may be described as *stingy* or *thrifty*. If someone does not use the "proper" form of English, we may call him *crude and uneducated* or *fresh and realistic*. The same wide choice of adjectives is available to art critics, literary critics, parents, and teachers. If language usage is as creative and flexible as it seems to be, then any strong claims for linguistic relativity seem quite implausible.

* Originally published by the University of California Press; reprinted by permission of the Regents of the University of California.

SUGGESTED READINGS

Many of Whorf's papers were compiled and edited posthumously by John B. Carroll. They are published in B. L. Whorf, *Language, thought, and reality* (Cambridge, Massachusetts: MIT Press, 1956). J. J. Jenkins, "Language and thought," in J. F. Voss (Ed.), *Approaches to thought* (Columbus, Ohio: Merrill, 1969. Pp. 211–237), presents an informal and interesting discussion on the relations between language and thought. A collection of papers on bilingualism may be found in J. Macnamara (Ed.), "Problems of bilingualism," *Journal of Social Issues*, 1967, **23** (Whole No. 2). See especially the articles by J. Macnamara, "The bilingual's linguistic performance . . . A psychological overview," and by W. E. Lambert, "A social psychology of bilingualism." For a collection of papers on coding in memory, see A. W. Melton and E. Martin (Eds.), *Coding processes in human memory* (Washington: Winston, 1972). A selection of papers on the representational functions of language are given in P. Adams (Ed.), *Language in thinking* (Baltimore: Penguin, 1972). See S. Glucksberg, R. M. Krauss, and E. T. Higgins, "The development of referential communication skills," in F. D. Horowitz (Ed.), *Review of child development research*, Volume IV (Chicago: University of Chicago Press, 1975) for a discussion of dyadic communication. K. Chukovsky, *From two to five* (Translated by M. Morton, Berkeley: University of California Press, 1963), reports many delightful examples of children's creative use of language.

References

Anglin, J. M. *The growth of word meaning.* Cambridge, Massachusetts: MIT Press, 1970.

Baratz, J. C. Teaching reading in an urban Negro school system. In J. C. Baratz & R. W. Shuy (Eds.), *Teaching Black children to read.* Washington, D.C.: Center for Applied Linguistics, 1969. Pp. 92–116.

Bartlett, F. C. *Remembering.* Cambridge, England: Cambridge University Press, 1932.

Bereiter, C., & Engelmann, S. *Teaching disadvantaged children in the pre-school.* Englewood Cliffs, New Jersey: Prentice-Hall, 1966.

Bernstein, B. Some sociological determinants of perception. *British Journal of Sociology,* 1958, **9,** 159–174.

Bernstein, B. A public language: Some sociological implications of a linguistic form. *British Journal of Sociology,* 1959, **10,** 311–326.

Bernstein, B. Language and social class (research note). *British Journal of Sociology,* 1960, **11,** 271–276.

Bernstein, B. A sociolinguistic approach to socialization: With some reference to educability. In F. Williams (Ed.), *Language and poverty.* Chicago: Markham, 1970. Pp. 25–61.

Bever, T. G. The cognitive basis for linguistic structures. In J. R. Hayes (Ed.), *Cognition and the development of language.* New York: Wiley, 1970.

Bever, T. G., Garrett, M. F., & Hurtig, R. The interaction of perceptual processes and ambiguous sentences. *Memory and Cognition,* 1973, **1,** 277–286.

Bever, T. G., Lackner, J., & Kirk, R. The underlying structures of sentences are the primary units of immediate speech processing. *Perception and Psychophysics,* 1969, **5,** 225–234.

Bever, T. G., & Langendoen, D. T. A dynamic model of the evolution of language. *Linguistic Inquiry,* 1971, **2,** 433–463.

Bierwisch, M. Some semantic universals of German adjectivals. *Foundations of Language,* 1967, **3,** 1–36.

Bierwisch, M. Semantics. In J. Lyons (Ed.), *New horizons in linguistics.* Baltimore, Maryland: Penguin, 1970. Pp. 166–184.

Bloom, L. *Language development: Form and function in emerging grammars.* Cambridge, Massachusetts: MIT Press, 1970.

Bloom, L. Why not pivot grammars? *Journal of Speech and Hearing Disorders,* 1971, **36,** 40–50.

Bloom, L. Language development review. In F. D. Horowitz (Ed.), *Review of child development research,* Vol. 4. Chicago: University of Chicago Press, 1975.

Bloom, L., Hood, L., & Lightbown, P. Imitation in language development: If, when and why. *Cognitive Psychology,* 1974, **6,** 357–420.

Blount, B. G. Acquisition of language by Luo children. Unpublished doctoral dissertation, University of California, Berkeley, 1969.

Blumenthal, A. L. Prompted recall of sentences. *Journal of Verbal Learning and Verbal Behavior,* 1967, **6,** 203–206.

Blumenthal, A. L. *Language and psychology: Historical aspects of psycholinguistics.* New York: Wiley, 1970.

Boakes, R. A., & Lodwick, B. Short term retention of sentences. *Quarterly Journal of Experimental Psychology,* 1971, **23,** 399–409.

Bolinger, D. L. The atomization of meaning. *Language,* 1965, **41,** 555–573.

Boucher, J., & Osgood, C. E. The Pollyanna hypothesis. *Journal of Verbal Learning and Verbal Behavior,* 1969, **8,** 1–8.

Bowerman, M. *Early syntactic development.* Cambridge, England: Cambridge University Press, 1973.

Braine, M. D. S. The ontogeny of English phrase structure: The first phrase. *Language,* 1963, **39,** 1–13. (a)

Braine, M. D. S. On learning the grammatical order of words. *Psychological Review,* 1963, **70,** 323–348. (b)

Bransford, J. D., Barclay, J. R., & Franks, J. J. Sentence memory: A constructive versus interpretive approach. *Cognitive Psychology,* 1972, **3,** 193–209.

Bransford, J. D., & Franks, J. J. The abstraction of linguistic ideas. *Cognitive Psychology,* 1971, **2,** 331–350.

Bransford, J. D., & Johnson, M. K. Contextual prerequisites for understanding: Some investigations of comprehension and recall. *Journal of Verbal Learning and Verbal Behavior,* 1972, **11,** 717–726.

Brian, C. R., & Goodenough, F. L. The relative potency of color and form perception at various ages. *Journal of Experimental Psychology,* 1929, **12,** 197–213.

Broca, P. Remarques sur le siège de faculté du langage articulé suivies d'une observation de'aphémie. *Bulletin de la Societé Anatomique de Paris,* 1861, **6,** 330–357.

Brown, J. Some tests of the decay theory of immediate memory. *Quarterly Journal of Experimental Psychology,* 1958, **10,** 12–21.

Brown, R. How shall a thing be called? *Psychological Review,* 1958, **65,** 14–21.

Brown, R. *Social psychology.* New York: Free Press, 1965.

Brown, R. The first sentences of child and chimpanzee. In R. Brown, *Psycholinguistics,* New York: Free Press, 1970. Pp. 208–231.

Brown, R. *A first language: The early stages.* Cambridge, Massachusetts: Harvard University Press, 1973.

Brown, R., & Bellugi, U. Three processes in the child's acquisition of syntax. *Harvard Educational Review,* 1964, **34,** 133–151.

Brown, R., Black, A. H., & Horowitz, A. E. Phonetic symbolism in natural languages. *Journal of Abnormal and Social Psychology,* 1955, **50,** 388–393.

Brown, R., & Fraser, C. The acquisition of syntax. In C. N. Cofer & B. S. Musgrave (Eds.), *Verbal behavior and learning.* New York: McGraw-Hill, 1963. Pp. 158–197.

Brown, R., & Hanlon, C. Derivational complexity and order of acquisition in child speech. In J. R. Hayes (Ed.), *Cognition and the development of language.* New York: Wiley, 1970. Pp. 11–53.

Brown, R., & Hildum, D. C. Expectancy and the perception of syllables. *Language,* 1956, **32,** 411–419.

Brown, R., & Lenneberg, E. H. A study in language and cognition. *Journal of Abnormal and Social Psychology,* 1954, **49,** 454–462.

Brown, R., & McNeill, D. The "tip of the tongue" phenomenon. *Journal of Verbal Learning and Verbal Behavior,* 1966, **5,** 325–337.

Bruner, J. S., Olver, R., & Greenfield, P. *Studies in cognitive growth.* New York: Wiley, 1966.

Carmichael, L., Hogan, H. P., & Walter, A. A. An experimental study of the effect of language on the representation of visually perceived form. *Journal of Experimental Psychology,* 1932, **15,** 73–86.

Carroll, J. B., & Casagrande, J. B. The function of language classification in behavior. In E. E. Maccoby, T. Newcomb, & E. L. Hartley (Eds.), *Readings in social psychology.* (3rd ed.) New York: Holt, Rinehart and Winston, 1958. Pp. 18–31.

Carter, A. *The infernal desire machine of Doctor Hoffman.* London: Rupert Hart-Davis, 1972.

Cazden, C. Environmental assistance to the child's acquisition of grammar. Unpublished doctoral dissertation, Graduate School of Education, Harvard University, 1965.

Chafe, W. L. *Meaning and the structure of language.* Chicago: University of Chicago Press, 1970.

Chapin, P. G., Smith, T. S., & Abrahamson, A. A. Two factors in perceptual segmentation of speech. *Journal of Verbal Learning and Verbal Behavior,* 1972, **11,** 164–173.

Chomsky, C. *The acquisition of syntax in children from 5 to 10.* Cambridge, Massachusetts: MIT Press, 1969.

Chomsky, N. *Syntactic structures.* The Hague: Mouton, 1957.

Chomsky, N. *Aspects of the theory of syntax.* Cambridge, Massachusetts: MIT Press, 1965.

Chomsky, N. *Language and mind.* New York: Harcourt, Brace and World, 1968.

Chomsky, N., & Halle, M. *The sound pattern of English.* New York: Harper & Row, 1968.

Chukovsky, K. *From two to five,* Translated by M. Morton. Berkeley: University of California Press, 1963.

Clark, H. H. Linguistic processes in deductive reasoning. *Psychological Review,* 1969, **76,** 387–404.

Clark, H. H. Word associations and linguistic theory. In J. Lyons (Ed.), *New horizons in linguistics.* Baltimore, Maryland: Penguin, 1970. Pp. 271–286.

Clark, H. H. Space, time, semantics and the child. In T. E. Moore (Ed.) *Cognitive development and the acquisition of language.* New York: Academic Press, 1973. Pp. 27–64.

Clark, H. H., & Chase, W. G. On the process of comparing sentences against pictures. *Cognitive Psychology,* 1972, **3,** 472–517.

Clifton, C. The implications of grammar for word associations. In K. Salzinger & S. Salzinger (Eds.), *Research in verbal behavior and some neurophysiological implications.* New York: Academic Press, 1967. Pp. 221–237.

Collins, A. M., & Quillian, M. R. Retrieval time from semantic memory. *Journal of Verbal Learning and Verbal Behavior,* 1969, **8,** 240–247.

Collins, A. M., & Quillian, M. R. How to make a language user. In E. Tulving & W. Donaldson (Eds.), *Organization of memory.* New York: Academic Press, 1972. Pp. 309–351.

Conrad, C. Cognitive economy in semantic memory. *Journal of Experimental Psychology,* 1972, **92,** 149–154.

Conrad, R. Acoustic confusions in immediate memory. *British Journal of Psychology,* 1964, **55,** 75–84.

Cooper, F. S. How is language conveyed by speech? In J. F. Kavanagh & I. G. Mattingly (Eds.), *Language by ear and by eye.* Cambridge, Massachusetts: MIT Press, 1972. Pp. 25–45.

Dale, P. S. *Language development: Structure and function.* Hinsdale, Illinois: Dryden, 1972.

Danks, J. H., & Glucksberg, S. Psychological scaling of adjective orders. *Journal of Verbal Learning and Verbal Behavior,* 1971, **10,** 63–67.

Danks, J. H., & Schwenk, M. A. Prenominal adjective order and communication context. *Journal of Verbal Learning and Verbal Behavior,* 1972, **11,** 183–187.

Danks, J. H., & Schwenk, M. A. Comprehension of prenominal adjective orders. *Memory and Cognition,* 1974, **2,** 34–38.

Danks, J. H., & Sorce, P. A. Imagery and deep structure in the prompted recall of passive sentences. *Journal of Verbal Learning and Verbal Behavior,* 1973, **12,** 114–117.

Deese, J. On the structure of associative meaning. *Psychological Review,* 1962, **69,** 161–175.

Deese, J. *The structure of associations in language and thought.* Baltimore, Maryland: Johns Hopkins Press, 1965.

Deese, J. *Psycholinguistics.* Boston: Allyn and Bacon, 1970.

De Soto, C., London, M., & Handel, S. Social reasoning and spatial paralogic. *Journal of Personality and Social Psychology,* 1965, **2,** 513–521.

Deutsch, C. Auditory discrimination and learning: Social factors. *Merrill-Palmer Quarterly,* 1964, **10,** 277–296.

Deutsch, M., and associates. *The disadvantaged child.* New York: Basic Books, 1967.

Dillard, J. L. *Black English.* New York: Random House, 1972.

Dooling, D. J., & Lachman, R. Effects of comprehension on retention of prose. *Journal of Experimental Psychology,* 1971, **88,** 216–222.

Dooling, D. J., & Mullet, R. L. Locus of thematic effects in retention of prose. *Journal of Experimental Psychology,* 1973, **97,** 404–406.

Duncker, K. On problem solving. *Psychological Monographs,* 1945, **58,** (Whole No. 270).

Eimas, P. D., Siqueland, E. R., Jusczyk, P., & Vigorito, J. Speech perception in infants. *Science,* 1971, **171,** 303–306.

Entwisle, D. R., Forsyth, D. F., & Muuss, R. The syntactic–paradigmatic shift in children's word associations. *Journal of Verbal Learning and Verbal Behavior,* 1964, **3,** 19–29.

Ervin, S., & Osgood, C. E. Second language learning and bilingualism. In C. E. Osgood and T. A. Sebeok (Eds.), *Psycholinguistics. Journal of Abnormal and Social Psychology* (Supplement), 1954, **49,** 139–146.

Fasold, R. W. Orthography in reading materials for Black English speaking children. In J. C. Baratz & R. W. Shuy (Eds.), *Teaching Black children to read*. Washington, D.C.: Center for Applied Linguistics, 1969. Pp. 68–91.

Ferguson, C. A., & Slobin, D. I. (Eds.), *Studies of child language development*. New York: Holt, Rinehart & Winston, 1973.

Fillenbaum, S. Words as feature complexes: False recognition of antonyms and synonyms. *Journal of Experimental Psychology*, 1969, **82**, 400–402.

Fillenbaum, S., & Rapoport, A. *Structures in the subjective lexion*. New York: Academic Press, 1971.

Fillmore, C. J. The case for case. In E. Bach & R. T. Harms (Eds.), *Universals in linguistic theory*. New York: Holt, Rinehart, & Winston, 1968. Pp. 1–88.

Fillmore, C. J. Some problems for case grammar. In C. J. Fillmore (Ed.), *Working papers in linguistics*, No. 10. Department of Linguistics, The Ohio State University, 1971.

Foss, D. J. Some effects of ambiguity upon sentence comprehension. *Journal of Verbal Learning and Verbal Behavior*, 1970, **9**, 699–706.

Foss, D. J., Bever, T. G., & Silver, M. The comprehension and verification of ambiguous sentences. *Perception and Psychophysics*, 1968, **4**, 304–306.

Franks, J. J., & Bransford, J. D. The acquisition of abstract ideas. *Journal of Verbal Learning and Verbal Behavior*, 1972, **11**, 311–315.

Friendly, M. L., & Glucksberg, S. On the description of subcultural lexicons: A multidimensional approach. *Journal of Personality and Social Psychology*, 1970, **14**, 55–65.

Fry, D. B., Abramson, A. S., Eimas, P. D., & Liberman, A. M. The identification and discrimination of synthetic vowels. *Language and Speech*, 1962, **5**, 171–189.

Furth, H. *Thinking without language*. New York: Free Press, 1966.

Gardner, R. A., & Gardner, B. T. Teaching sign language to a chimpanzee. *Science*, 1969, **165**, 664–672.

Garnica, O. K. The development of phonemic speech perception. In T. E. Moore (Ed.), *Cognitive development and the acquisition of language*. New York: Academic Press, 1973.

Garrett, M., Bever, T. G., & Fodor, J. The active use of grammar in speech perception. *Perception and Psychophysics*, 1966, **1**, 30–32.

Garrett, M., & Fodor, J. Psychological theories and linguistic constructs. In T. R. Dixon & D. L. Horton (Eds.), *Verbal behavior and general behavior theory*. Englewood Cliffs, New Jersey: Prentice-Hall, 1968. Pp. 451–477.

Garrod, S., & Trabasso, T. A dual-memory information processing interpretation of sentence comprehension. *Journal of Verbal Learning and Verbal Behavior*, 1973, **12**, 155–167.

Gazzaniga, M. A. *The bisected brain*. New York: Appleton-Century-Crofts, 1970.

Ghiselin, B. (Ed.), *The creative process*. New York: Mentor, 1955.

Gleason, H. A. *An introduction to descriptive linguistics*. (rev. ed.) New York: Holt, Rinehart & Winston, 1961.

Glucksberg, S., & Cohen, J. A. Acquisition of form-class membership by syntactic position: Paradigmatic associations to nonsense syllables. *Psychonomic Science*, 1965, **2**, 313–314.

Glucksberg, S., & Danks, J. H. Functional fixedness: Stimulus equivalence mediated by semantic-acoustic similarity. *Journal of Experimental Psychology*, 1967, **74**, 400–405.

Glucksberg, S., & Danks, J. H. Effects of discriminative labels and of nonsense labels upon availability of novel function. *Journal of Verbal Learning and Verbal Behavior*, 1968, **7**, 72–76.

Glucksberg, S., & Danks, J. H. Grammatical structure and recall: A function of the space in immediate memory or of recall delay? *Perception and Psychophysics,* 1969, **6,** 113–117.

Glucksberg, S., & Krauss, R. M. What do people say after they have learned how to talk? Studies of the development of referential communication. *Merrill-Palmer Quarterly,* 1967, **13,** 309–316.

Glucksberg, S., Krauss, R. M., & Higgins, E. T. The development of referential communication skills. In F. D. Horowitz (Ed.), *Review of child development research.* Vol. 4. Chicago: University of Chicago Press, 1975.

Glucksberg, S., Krauss, R. M., & Weisberg, R. Referential communication in nursery school children: Method and some preliminary findings. *Journal of Experimental Child Psychology,* 1966, **3,** 333–342.

Glucksberg, S., Trabasso, T., & Wald, J. Linguistic structures and mental operations. *Cognitive Psychology,* 1973, **5,** 338–370.

Goldiamond, I., & Dryud, J. E. Some applications and implications of behavioral analysis for psychotherapy. In J. M. Shlien (Ed.), *Research in psychotherapy.* Vol. III. Washington, D.C.: American Psychological Association, 1968. Pp. 54–89.

Gough, P. B. Grammatical transformations and speed of understanding. *Journal of Verbal Learning and Verbal Behavior,* 1965, **4,** 107–111.

Gough, P. B. The verification of sentences: The effects of delay of evidence and sentence length. *Journal of Verbal Learning and Verbal Behavior,* 1966, **5,** 492–496.

Greene, J. *Psycholinguistics.* Baltimore, Maryland: Penguin, 1972.

Hakes, D. T., & Cairns, H. S. Sentence comprehension and relative pronouns. *Perception and Psychophysics,* 1970, **8,** 5–8.

Hakes, D. T., & Foss, D. J. Decision processes during sentence comprehension: Effects of surface structure reconsidered. *Perception and Psychophysics,* 1970, **8,** 413–416.

Hall, E. T. *The silent language.* Garden City, New York: Doubleday, 1969.

Halle, M. Phonology in generative grammar. *Word,* 1962, **18,** 54–72. Reprinted in J. A. Fodor & J. J. Katz (Eds.), *The structure of language.* Englewood Cliffs, New Jersey: Prentice-Hall, 1964. Pp. 334–352.

Halle, M. On the bases of phonology. In J. A. Fodor & J. J. Katz (Eds.), *The structure of language.* Englewood Cliffs, New Jersey: Prentice-Hall, 1964. Pp. 324–333.

Halle, M., & Stevens, K. N. Speech recognition: A model and a program for research. In J. A. Fodor & J. J. Katz (Eds.), *The structure of language.* Englewood Cliffs, New Jersey: Prentice-Hall, 1964. Pp. 604–612.

Halliday, M. A. K. Language structure and language function. In J. Lyons (Ed.), *New horizons in linguistics.* Baltimore, Maryland: Penguin, 1970. Pp. 140–165.

Harris, R. J., & Brewer, W. F. Deixis in memory for verb tense. *Journal of Verbal Learning and Verbal Behavior,* 1973, **12,** 590–597.

Hawkins, P. R. Social class, the nominal group and reference. *Language and Speech,* 1969, **12,** 125–135.

Hayes, C. *The ape in our house.* New York: Harper & Row, 1951.

Hess, R. D., & Shipman, V. Early experience and the socialization of cognitive modes in children. *Child Development,* 1965, **36,** 869–886.

Heider, E. R., & Olivier, D. C. The structure of the color space in naming and memory for two languages. *Cognitive Psychology,* 1972, **3,** 337–354.

Hockett, C. D. The origin of speech. *Scientific American,* 1960, **203,** 88–96.

Honkavaara, S. A critical re-evaluation of the color and form reaction, and disproving of the hypotheses connected with it. *Journal of Psychology,* 1958, **45,** 25–36.

Huttenlocher, J. Constructing spatial images: A strategy in reasoning. *Psychological Review,* 1968, **75,** 550–560.

Jakobson, R. Kindersprache, Aphasie und allgemeine Lautgesetze. *Uppsala,* 1941. In R. Jakobson, *Selected writings, I.* The Hague: Mouton, 1962.

Jakobson, R., Fant, G., & Halle, M. *Preliminaries to speech analysis.* Cambridge, Massachusetts: MIT Press, 1963.

Jarvella, R. J. Syntactic processing of connected speech. *Journal of Verbal Learning and Verbal Behavior,* 1971, **10,** 409–416.

Johnson, M. K., Bransford, J. D., & Solomon, S. Memory for tacit implications of sentences. *Journal of Experimental Psychology,* 1973, **98,** 203–205.

Johnson, N. F. The psychological reality of phrase-structure rules. *Journal of Verbal Learning and Verbal Behavior,* 1965, **4,** 469–475.

Johnson, N. F. Sequential verbal behavior. In T. R. Dixon & D. L. Horton (Eds.), *Verbal behavior and general behavior theory.* Englewood Cliffs, New Jersey: Prentice-Hall, 1968. Pp. 421–450.

Johnson-Laird, P. N. Experimental psycholinguistics. *Annual Review of Psychology,* 1974, **25,** 135–160.

Just, M. A., & Clark, H. H. Drawing inferences from the presuppositions and implications of affirmative and negative sentences. *Journal of Verbal Learning and Verbal Behavior,* 1973, **12,** 21–31.

Katz, J. J. Recent issues in semantic theory. *Foundations of Language,* 1967, **3,** 124–194.

Katz, J. J. *Semantic theory.* New York: Harper & Row, 1972.

Katz, J. J., & Fodor, J. A. The structure of a semantic theory. *Language,* 1963, **39,** 170–210.

Keller, H. *The story of my life.* New York: Doubleday, Page, 1903.

Kellogg, W. N., & Kellogg, L. A. *The ape and the child.* New York: McGraw-Hill, 1933.

Kendler, H. H., & Kendler, T. S. Vertical and horizontal processes in problem solving. *Psychological Review,* 1962, **69,** 1–16.

Keppel, G., & Underwood, B. J. Proactive inhibition in short-term retention of single items. *Journal of Verbal Learning and Verbal Behavior,* 1962, **1,** 153–161.

Kernan, K. T. The acquisition of language by Samoan children. Unpublished doctoral dissertation, University of California, Berkeley, 1969.

Kimura, D. Cerebral dominance and the perception of verbal stimuli. *Canadian Journal of Psychology,* 1961, **15,** 166–171.

Kimura, D. Left-right differences in the perception of melodies. *Quarterly Journal of Experimental Psychology,* 1964, **16,** 355–358.

Kintsch, W., & Monk, D. Storage of complex information in memory: Some implications of the speed with which inferences can be made. *Journal of Experimental Psychology,* 1972, **94,** 25–32.

Klima, E. S., & Bellugi, U. The signs of language in child and chimpanzee. In T. Alloway, L. Krames, & P. Pliner (Eds.), *Communication and affect: A comparative approach.* New York: Academic Press, 1972. Pp. 67–96.

Kolers, P. A. Interlingual word associations. *Journal of Verbal Learning and Verbal Behavior,* 1963, **2,** 291–300.

Kolers, P. A. Interlingual facilitation of short-term memory. *Journal of Verbal Learning and Verbal Behavior,* 1966, **5,** 314–319. (a)

Kolers, P. A. Reading and talking bilingually. *American Journal of Psychology,* 1966, **79,** 357–376. (b)

Kolers, P. A. Bilingualism and information processing. *Scientific American,* 1968, **218**(3), 78–86.

Krasner, L. Studies of the conditioning of verbal behavior. *Psychological Bulletin,* 1958, **55,** 148–170.

Krauss, R. M., & Weinheimer, S. Changes in reference phrases as a function of frequency of usage in social interactions: A preliminary study. *Psychonomic Science,* 1964, **1,** 113–114.

Krauss, R. M., & Weinheimer, S. Concurrent feedback, confirmation, and the encoding of referents in verbal communication. *Journal of Personality and Social Psychology,* 1966, **4,** 343–346.

Labov, W. *The social stratification of speech in New York City.* Washington, D.C.: Center for Applied Linguistics, 1966.

Labov, W. The logic of nonstandard English. In F. Williams (Ed.), *Language and poverty.* Chicago: Markham, 1970. Pp. 153–189.

Labov, W. *Sociolinguistic patterns.* Philadelphia: University of Pennsylvania Press, 1972.

Lakoff, G. On generative semantics. In D. D. Steinberg & L. A. Jakobovits (Eds.), *Semantics.* Cambridge, England: Cambridge University Press, 1971. Pp. 232–296.

Lambert, W. E., Havelka, J., & Gardner, R. C. Linguistic manifestations of bilingualism. *American Journal of Psychology,* 1959, **72,** 77–82.

Lane, H. The motor theory of speech perception: A critical review. *Psychological Review,* 1965, **72,** 275–309.

Langacker, R. W. *Language and its structure.* New York: Harcourt, Brace and World, 1968.

Lantz, D., & Stefflre, V. Language and cognition revisited. *Journal of Abnormal and Social Psychology,* 1964, **69,** 472–481.

Lashley, K. S. The problem of serial order in behavior. In L. A. Jeffress (Ed.), *Cerebral mechanisms in behavior: The Hixon symposium.* New York: Hafner, 1951. Pp. 112–136.

Lenneberg, E. H. *Biological foundations of language.* New York: Wiley, 1967.

Levelt, W. J. M. *Formal grammars in linguistics and psycholinguistics,* Vols. I, II, and III. The Hague: Mouton, 1974.

Liberman, A. M. The grammars of speech and language. *Cognitive Psychology,* 1970, **1,** 301–323.

Liberman, A. M., Cooper, F. S., Shankweiler, D. P., & Studdert-Kennedy, M. Perception of the speech code. *Psychological Review,* 1967, **74,** 431–461.

Liberman, A. M., Harris, K. S., Hoffman, H. S., & Griffith, B. C. The discrimination of speech sounds within and across phoneme boundaries. *Journal of Experimental Psychology,* 1957, **54,** 358–368.

Liberman, A. M., Mattingly, I. G., & Turvey, M. T. Language codes and memory codes. In A. W. Melton & E. Martin (Eds.), *Coding processes in human memory.* Washington, D.C.: Winston, 1972. Pp. 307–334.

Lieberman, P. *The speech of primates.* The Hague: Mouton, 1972.

Lieberman, P., Crelin, E. S., & Klatt, D. H. Phonetic ability and related anatomy of the newborn, adult human, Neanderthal man and the chimpanzee. *American Anthropologist,* 1972, **74,** 287–307.

Lindsay, P. H., & Norman, D. A. *Human information processing.* New York: Academic Press, 1972.

Luria, A. R. *The role of speech in the regulation of normal and abnormal behavior.* New York: Liveright, 1961.

Lyons, J. *Introduction to theoretical linguistics.* Cambridge, England: Cambridge University Press, 1968.

Lyons, J. *Noam Chomsky.* New York: Viking, 1970.

MacKay, D. G. To end ambiguous sentences. *Perception and Psychophysics,* 1966, **1,** 426–436.

Macnamara, J. (Ed.) Problems of bilingualism. *Journal of Social Issues,* 1967, **23**(Whole No. 2).

Macnamara, J. Cognitive basis of language learning in infants. *Psychological Review,* 1972, **79,** 1–13.

Martin, J. E. Semantic determinants of preferred adjective order. *Journal of Verbal Learning and Verbal Behavior,* 1969, **8,** 697–704.

Matthews, W. A. Transformational complexity and short-term recall. *Language and Speech,* 1968, **11,** 120–128.

Mattingly, I. G., Liberman, A. M., Syrdal, A. K., & Halwes, T. Discrimination in speech and nonspeech modes. *Cognitive Psychology,* 1971, **2,** 131–157.

Mazeika, E. J. A comparison of phonological development of a monolingual and bilingual (Spanish–English) child. Paper presented at meetings of the Society for Research in Child Development, Minneapolis, 1971.

McMahon, L. E. Grammatical analysis as part of understanding a sentence. Unpublished doctoral dissertation, Harvard University, 1963.

McNeill, D. Developmental psycholinguistics. In F. Smith and G. A. Miller (Eds.), *The genesis of language.* Cambridge, Massachusetts: MIT Press, 1966. Pp. 15–84. (a)

McNeill, D. A study of word association. *Journal of Verbal Learning and Verbal Behavior,* 1966, **5,** 548–557. (b)

McNeill, D. *The acquisition of language.* New York: Harper & Row, 1970.

Mehler, J. Some effects of grammatical transformations on the recall of English sentences. *Journal of Verbal Learning and Verbal Behavior,* 1963, **2,** 346–351.

Meyer, D. E. On the representation and retrieval of stored semantic information. *Cognitive Psychology,* 1970, **1,** 242–299.

Miller, G. A. *Language and communication.* New York: McGraw-Hill, 1951.

Miller, G. A. The magical number seven plus or minus two: Some limits on our capacity for processing information. *Psychological Review,* 1956, **63,** 81–97.

Miller, G. A. Some psychological studies of grammar. *American Psychologist,* 1962, **17,** 748–762.

Miller, G. A. Project grammarama. In G. A. Miller (Ed.), *The psychology of communication.* New York: Basic Books, 1967.

Miller, G. A. English verbs of motion: A case study in semantics and lexical memory. In A. W. Melton and E. Martin (Eds.), *Coding processes in human memory.* Washington, D.C.: Winston, 1972. Pp. 335–372.

Miller, G. A., & Isard, S. Some perceptual consequences of linguistic rules. *Journal of Verbal Learning and Verbal Behavior,* 1963, **2,** 217–228.

Miller, G. A., Heise, G. A., & Lichten, W. The intelligibility of speech as a function of the context of the test materials. *Journal of Experimental Psychology,* 1951, **41,** 329–335.

Moeser, S. D., & Bregman, A. S. The role of reference in the acquisition of a miniature artificial language. *Journal of Verbal Learning and Verbal Behavior,* 1972, **11,** 759–769.

Moeser, S. D., & Bregman, A. S. Imagery and language acquisition. *Journal of Verbal Learning and Verbal Behavior,* 1973, **12,** 91–98.

Moore, T. E. (Ed.). *Cognitive development and the acquisition of language.* New York: Academic Press, 1973.

Moskowitz, A. I. The two-year-old stage in the acquisition of English phonology. *Language,* 1970, **46,** 426–441.

Neisser, U., & Kerr, N. Spatial and mnemonic properties of visual images. *Cognitive Psychology,* 1973, **5,** 138–150.

Nelson, K. Structure and strategy in learning to talk. *Monographs of the Society for Research in Child Development*, 1973, **38**(1–2, Serial No. 149).

Nelson, K. Concept, word, and sentence: Interrelations in acquisition and development. *Psychological Review*, 1974, **81**, 267–285.

Nelson, K. E., Carskaddon, G., & Bonvillian, J. D. Syntax acquisition: Impact of experimental variation in adult verbal interaction with the child. *Child Development*, 1973, **44**, 497–504.

Oller, J. W., & Sales, B. D. Conceptual restrictions on English: A psycholinguistic study. *Lingua*, 1969, **23**, 209–232.

Olson, D. Language and thought: Aspects of a cognitive theory of semantics. *Psychological Review*, 1970, **77**, 257–273.

Olson, D. R., & Filby, N. On the comprehension of active and passive sentences. *Cognitive Psychology*, 1972, **3**, 361–381.

Osgood, C. E., Suci, G. J., & Tannenbaum, P. H. *The measurement of meaning*. Urbana, Illinois: University of Illinois Press, 1957.

Paivio, A., & Csapo, K. Picture superiority in free recall: Imagery or dual coding? *Cognitive Psychology*, 1973, **5**, 176–206.

Palermo, D. S., & Eberhart, V. L. On the learning of morphological rules: An experimental analogy. *Journal of Verbal Learning and Verbal Behavior*, 1968, **7**, 337–344.

Palermo, D. S., & Molfese, D. L. Language acquisition from age five onward. *Psychological Bulletin*, 1972, **78**, 409–428.

Pavlov, I. P. Lectures on conditioned reflexes. In *Conditioned reflexes and psychiatry*, Vol. II. Translated by W. H. Gantt. New York: International, 1941.

Peterson, L. R., & Peterson, M. J. Short-term retention of individual verbal items. *Journal of Experimental Psychology*, 1959, **58**, 193–198.

Pfungst, O. *Clever Hans, the horse of Mr. Von Osten*. Translated by C. L. Rahn. New York: Holt, 1911.

Piaget, J. *The language and thought of the child*. Translated by M. Worden. New York: Harcourt, Brace, 1926.

Piaget, J. *The origins of intelligence in children*. Translated by M. Cook. New York: International Universities Press, 1952.

Piaget, J. *The construction of reality in the child*. Translated by M. Cook. New York: Basic Books, 1954.

Pietrinferno, G. The development of speaker processes in referential communication: Message choice as a function of message adequacy. Unpublished doctoral dissertation, Princeton University, 1973.

Pisoni, D. B. Auditory and phonetic memory codes in the discrimination of consonants and vowels. *Perception and Psychophysics*, 1973, **13**, 253–260.

Pollack, I., Rubenstein, H., & Decker, L. Intelligibility of known and unknown message sets. *Journal of the Acoustical Society of America*, 1959, **31**, 273–279.

Pollio, H. *The psychology of symbolic activity*. Reading, Massachusetts: Addison-Wesley, 1974.

Premack, D. Language in chimpanzee? *Science*, 1971, **172**, 808–822.

Preston, M. S., & Lambert, W. E. Interlingual interference in a bilingual version of the Stroop color-word task. *Journal of Verbal Learning and Verbal Behavior*, 1969, **8**, 295–301.

Quillian, M. R. Word concepts: A theory and simulation of some basic semantic capabilities. *Behavioral Science*, 1967, **12**, 410–430.

Quillian, M. R. The teachable language comprehender: A simulation program and theory of language. *Communications of the Association of Computing Machinery*, 1969, **12**, 459–476.

Razran, G. A quantitative study of meaning by a conditioned salivary technique (semantic conditioning). *Science*, 1939, **90**, 89–90.

Razran, G. The observable unconscious and the inferable conscious in current Soviet psychophysiology. *Psychological Review,* 1961, **68,** 81–147.

Reber, A. S., & Anderson, J. R. The perception of clicks in linguistic and nonlinguistic messages. *Perception and Psychophysics,* 1970, **8,** 81–89.

Rips, L. J., Shoben, E. J., & Smith, E. E. Semantic distance and the verification of semantic relations. *Journal of Verbal Learning and Verbal Behavior,* 1973, **12,** 1–20.

Romney, A. K., & D'Andrade, R. G. Cognitive aspects of English kin terms. *American Anthropologist,* 1964, **66,** 146–170.

Sachs, J. S. Recognition memory for syntactic and semantic aspects of connected discourse. *Perception and Psychophysics,* 1967, **2,** 437–442.

Sapir, E. Language and environment. In D. G. Mandelbaum (Ed.), *Selected writings of Edward Sapir in language, culture and personality.* Berkeley: University of California Press, 1968.

Saussure, F. de *Cours de linguistique generale.* (1st ed., 1916.) English translation by W. Baskin, *Course in general linguistics.* New York: McGraw-Hill, 1966.

Savin, H. B., & Perchonock, E. Grammatical structure and the immediate recall of English sentences. *Journal of Verbal Learning and Verbal Behavior,* 1965, **4,** 348–353.

Schaeffer, B., & Wallace, R. Semantic similarity and the comparison of word meanings. *Journal of Experimental Psychology,* 1969, **82,** 343–346.

Schaeffer, B., & Wallace, R. The comparison of word meanings. *Journal of Experimental Psychology,* 1970, **86,** 144–152.

Schank, R. C. Conceptual dependency: A theory of natural language understanding. *Cognitive Psychology,* 1972, **3,** 552–631.

Schrier, A. M., & Stollnitz, F. (Eds.) *Behavior of nonhuman primates,* Vol. 4. New York: Academic Press, 1971.

Sechenov, I. M. Refleksy golovnogo mozga. (Reflexes of the brain.) *Meditsinskiy Vestnik,* 1863, **3,** 461–464, 493–512. Cited in D. I. Slobin, *Psycholinguistics.* Glenview, Illinois: Scott Foresman, 1971.

Segal, E. M., & Halwes, T. G. Learning of letter pairs as a prototype of first language learning. *Psychonomic Science,* 1965, **3,** 451–452.

Segal, E. M., & Halwes, T. G. The influence of frequency of exposure on the learning of a phrase structural grammar. *Psychonomic Science,* 1966, **4,** 157–158.

Seymour, P. H. K. Judgments of verticality and response availability. *Bulletin of the Psychonomic Society,* 1973, **1,** 196–198.

Shafto, M. The space for case. *Journal of Verbal Learning and Verbal Behavior,* 1973, **12,** 551–562.

Shankweiler, D. An analysis of laterality effects in speech perception. In D. L. Horton & J. J. Jenkins (Eds.), *Perception of language.* Columbus, Ohio: Merrill, 1971. Pp. 185–200.

Shankweiler, D., & Studdert-Kennedy, M. Identification of consonants and vowels presented to left and right ears. *Quarterly Journal of Experimental Psychology,* 1967, **19,** 59–63.

Shatz, M., & Gelman, R. The development of communication skills: Modification in the speech of young children as a function of listener. *Monographs of the Society for Research in Child Development,* 1973, **38**(5), (Whole No. 152).

Shvachkin, N. Kh. The development of phonemic speech perception in early childhood. *Izvestiya Akademii Pedagogcheskikh Nauk RSFSR,* 1948, **13,** 101–132. Translated from Russian by E. Dernbach and edited by D. I. Slobin, in C. A. Ferguson & D. I. Slobin (Eds.), *Studies of child language development.* New York: Holt, Rinehart and Winston, 1973. Pp. 91–127.

Sinclair-de Zwart, H. Developmental psycholinguistics. In D. Elkind & J. H. Flavell (Eds.), *Studies in cognitive development.* New York and London: Oxford University Press, 1969. Pp. 315–366.

Slobin, D. I. Grammatical transformations and sentence comprehension in childhood and adulthood. *Journal of Verbal Learning and Verbal Behavior,* 1966, **5,** 219–227.

Slobin, D. I. Universals of grammatical development in children. In G. B. Flores D'Arcais & W. J. M. Levelt (Eds.), *Advances in psycholinguistics.* New York: American Elsevier, 1970. Pp. 174–186.

Slobin, D. I. Developmental psycholinguistics. In W. O. Dingwall (Ed.), *A survey of linguistic science.* College Park, Maryland: University of Maryland, 1971. Pp. 298–410.   (a)

Slobin, D. I. *Psycholinguistics.* Glenview, Illinois: Scott Foresman, 1971.   (b)

Slobin, D. I. Seven questions about language development. In P. C. Dodwell (Ed.), *New horizons in psychology,* Vol. II. Baltimore: Penguin, 1972.

Slobin, D. I., & Welsh, C. A. Elicited imitation as a research tool in developmental psycholinguistics. In C. A. Ferguson & D. I. Slobin (Eds.), *Studies of child language development.* New York: Holt, Rinehart and Winston, 1973. Pp. 485–497.

Smith, E. E., Rips, L. J., & Shoben, E. J. Semantic memory and psychological semantics. In G. H. Bower (Ed.), *The psychology of learning and motivation,* Vol. 8. New York: Academic Press, 1974. Pp. 1–45.

Smith, E. E., Shoben, E. J., & Rips, L. J. Structure and process in semantic memory: A featural model for semantic decisions. *Psychological Review,* 1974, **81,** 214–241.

Smith, K. H. Grammatical intrusions in the free recall of structured letter pairs. *Journal of Verbal Learning and Verbal Behavior,* 1966, **5,** 447–454.

Smith, N. *The acquisition of phonology.* Cambridge, England: Cambridge University Press, 1973.

Snow, C. E. Mothers' speech to children learning language. *Child Development,* 1972, **43,** 549–565.

Staats, C. K., & Staats, A. W. Meaning established by classical conditiong. *Journal of Experimental Psychology,* 1957, **54,** 74–80.

Stefflre, V., Castillo Vales, V., & Morley, L. Language and cognition in Yucatan: A cross cultural replication. *Journal of Personality and Social Psychology,* 1966, **4,** 112–115.

Stevens, K. N. Segments, features, and analysis by synthesis. In J. F. Kavanagh & I. G. Mattingly (Eds.), *Language by ear and by eye.* Cambridge, Massachusetts: MIT Press, 1972. Pp. 47–52.

Stevens, K. N., & House, A. S. Speech perception. In J. V. Tobias (Ed.), *Foundations of modern auditory theory,* Vol. 2. New York: Academic Press, 1972. Pp. 1–62.

Stewart, W. A. Foreign language teaching methods in quasi-foreign language situations. In *Nonstandard speech and the teaching of English.* Washington, D.C.: Center for Applied Linguistics, 1964.

Stewart, W. A. Toward a history of American Negro dialect. In F. Williams, (Ed.) *Language and poverty.* Chicago: Markham, 1970. Pp. 351–379.

Studdert-Kennedy, M. Speech perception. In N. J. Lass (Ed.), *Contemporary issues in experimental phonetics.* Springfield, Illinois: Charles C Thomas, 1974.

Studdert-Kennedy, M., Liberman, A. M., Harris, K. S., & Cooper, F. S. Motor theory of speech perception: A reply to Lane's critical review. *Psychological Review,* 1970, **77,** 234–249.

Studdert-Kennedy, M., & Shankweiler, D. Hemispheric specializations for speech perception. *Journal of the Acoustical Society of America,* 1970, **48,** 579–594.

Sutherland, N. S. Discussion of paper by Fodor and Garrett. In J. Lyons & R. J. Wales (Eds.), *Psycholinguistic papers: Proceedings of the 1966 Edinburgh conference,* Edinburgh: Edinburgh University Press, 1966.

Thomas, O. *Transformational grammar and the teacher of English.* New York: Holt, Rinehart and Winston, 1966.

Trabasso, T. Mental operations in language comprehension. In R. O. Freedle & J. B. Carroll (Eds.), *Language comprehension and the acquisition of knowledge.* Washington, D.C.: Winston, 1972. Pp. 113–137.

Treisman, A. M. The effects of redundancy and familiarity on translating and repeating back a foreign and a native language. *British Journal of Psychology,* 1965, **56,** 369–379.

Tulving, E. Episodic and semantic memory. In E. Tulving & W. Donaldson (Eds.), *Organization of memory.* New York: Academic Press, 1972. Pp. 381–403.

Tversky, B. Pictorial and verbal encoding in a short-term memory task. *Perception and Psychophysics,* 1969, **6,** 225–233.

van Lawick-Goodall, J. *In the shadow of man.* Boston: Houghton-Mifflin, 1971.

von Frisch, K. Dialects in the language of the bees. *Scientific American,* 1962, **207,** 79–87.

von Frisch, K. Honeybees: Do they use direction and distance information provided by their dancers? *Science,* 1967, **158,** 1072–1076.

Vygotsky, L. S. *Thought and language,* Translated by E. Hanfmann and G. Vakar. Cambridge, Massachusetts: MIT Press, 1962.

Watson, J. B. Psychology as the behaviorist views it. *Psychological Review,* 1913, **20,** 158–177.

Weinreich, U. Explorations in semantic theory. In T. A. Sebeok (Ed.), *Current trends in linguistics.* Vol. 3. The Hague: Mouton, 1966. Pp. 395–477.

Weisberg, R. W. Sentence processing assessed through intrasentence word associations. *Journal of Experimental Psychology,* 1969, **82,** 332–338.

Weisberg, R. W. On sentence storage: The influence of syntactic versus semantic factors on intrasentence word associations. *Journal of Verbal Learning and Verbal Behavior,* 1971, **10,** 631–644.

Wenner, A. M. Honeybees: Do they use the distance information contained in their dance maneuver? *Science,* 1967, **155,** 847–849.

Wenner, A. M., & Johnson, D. L. (Reply to von Frisch, "Honeybees: Do they use direction and distance information provided by their dancers?") *Science,* 1967, **158,** 1076–1077.

Whorf, B. L. Languages and logic. In J. B. Carroll (Ed.), *Language, thought and reality: Selected writings of Benjamin Lee Whorf.* Cambridge, Massachusetts: MIT Press, 1956. Pp. 233–245.

Wickens, D. D. Encoding categories of words: An empirical approach to meaning. *Psychological Review,* 1970, **77,** 1–15.

Wickens, D. D. Characteristics of word encoding. In A. W. Melton & E. Martin (Eds.), *Coding processes in human memory.* Washington, D.C.: Winston, 1972. Pp. 191–215.

Wickens, D. D. Some characteristics of word encoding. *Memory and Cognition,* 1973, **1,** 485–490.

Wickens, D. D., Born, D. G., & Allen, C. K. Proactive inhibition and item similarity in short-term memory. *Journal of Verbal Learning and Verbal Behavior,* 1963, **2,** 440–445.

Wiener, M., Devoe, S., Rubinow, S., & Geller, J. Nonverbal behavior and nonverbal communication. *Psychological Review,* 1972, **79,** 185–214.

Williams, F. (Ed.) *Language and poverty*. Chicago: Markham, 1970.

Winograd, T. Understanding natural language. *Cognitive Psychology*, 1972, **3**, 1–191.

Wright, P. Transformations and the understanding of sentences. *Language and Speech*, 1969, **12**, 156–166.

Wright, P. Some observations on how people answer questions about sentences. *Journal of Verbal Learning and Verbal Behavior*, 1972, **11**, 188–195.

Yngve, V. H. A model and an hypothesis for language structure. *Proceedings of the American Philosophical Society*, 1960, **104**, 444–466.

Ziff, P. Some comments on Mr. Harman's confabulations. *Foundations of Language*, 1967, **3**, 403–408.

Zipf, G. K. *The Psycho-biology of language*. Boston: Houghton-Mifflin, 1935. (Paperbound edition published in 1965 by MIT Press).

Author Index

223

Subject Index